RED BLUES

MIGRATION ACROSS TIME AND NATION
Population Mobility in Historical Context
by Ira Glazier and Luigi de Rosa

VOICES FROM SOUTHEAST ASIA
The Refugee Experience in the United States
by John Tenhula

DISTANT MAGNETS
Expectations and Realities in the Immigrant Experience,
1840–1930
edited by Dirk Hoerder and Horst Rössler

BRANCHING OUT
German-Jewish Immigration to the United States, 1820–1914
by Avraham Barkai

FAITH AND FAMILY
Dutch Immigration and Settlement in the United States,
1820–1920
by Robert P. Sweirenga

TIES THAT BIND, TIES THAT DIVIDE
One Hundred Years of Hungarian Experience in the United States
by Julianna Puskás

**Ira Glazier and Luigi de Rosa,
series editors**

RED BLUES

VOICES FROM THE LAST WAVE OF RUSSIAN IMMIGRANTS

Dennis Shasha and Marina Shron

with a Foreword by Steven J. Gold

HOLMES & MEIER
New York / London

Published in the United States of America 2002
by Holmes & Meier Publishers, Inc.
160 Broadway • New York, NY 10038

Copyright © 2002 Dennis Shasha and Marina Shron

All rights reserved. No part of this book may be reproduced or transmitted in any form or by any electronic or mechanical means now known or to be invented, including photocopying, recording and information retrieval systems, without permission in writing from the publisher, except by a reviewer who may quote brief passages in a review.

This book has been printed on acid-free paper.

designed by Brigid McCarthy
typesetting by JoAnne Todtfeld

Library of Congress Cataloging-in-Publication Data

Shasha, Dennis Elliott.
   Red blues: voices from the last wave of Russian immigrants/
  Dennis E. Shasha and Marina Shron; with a foreword by Steven Gold.
   p. cm.—(Ellis Island series)
   ISBN 0-8419-1417-6 (acid-free paper)
   1. Russian Americans—Interviews. 2. Immigrants—United States—Interviews. 3. Russian Americans—Social conditions. 4. Immigrants—United States—Social conditions. 5. United States—Emigration and immigration. 6. Russia (Federation)—Emigration and immigration. I. Shron, Marina. II. Series.

E184.R9 S53 2002
305.891'71073—dc21

2001051952

Manufactured in the United States of America

Table of Contents

Foreword   VII
Preface   XI
Acknowledgments   XIII

PRIVILEGE LOST

Georges Nakhitchevansky: Aristocrat by Birth	3
Vadim Shron: An Enemy of the People	13
Semyon Slutsky: Communist and Patriot	36
Alexander Bolonkin: Missle Designer and Political Prisoner	42
Lidia Sechkina: Lights Out	48

GOD AND RELIGIOUS DISSENT

Father Michael: Russian Orthodox Priest	55
Yelena Mandel: From the Jewish Underground to Bankruptcy Law	62

ARTISTS

Mela Tannenbaum: A Musician's Journey	71
Vladimir Kanevsky: "Parasite" and Sculptor	78
Eteri Shkodua: Painter with an Attitude	88
Mark Kopelev: The Tailor	93
Aaron Kanevsky: A Documentary Filmmaker	105
Yevgeny and Larisa Ryzhik: Freedoms Lost and Found	110

SCIENTISTS AND DOCTORS

- Boris and Tatyana Girshovich: Astrophysics and Politics — 117
- Konstantin Likharev: The Decline of "Big Science" — 128
- Anatoly and Olga Borisov: Science Pure and Impure — 136
- Alex and Masha Feoktistov: Starting Over — 140

ENTREPRENEURS

- Tatiana Alexa: Winners Don't Cry — 151
- Ella Kozhevnikova: The Twelve Chairs — 162
- Sergey Tchavretov: Business in the New Russia — 176
- Roman Kaplan: Art and Food — 181

SURVIVAL

- Boris Kardimun: Itinerant Spirit — 191
- Matvey Kanengiser: In His Own Style — 200
- Sergey Artushkov: What's Missing? — 205

THE GRAY ZONE

- Yelena: New York Madam — 211
- Lana: Topless Dancer — 217
- Julia: Dominatrix — 224

IT'S A NEW OLD WORLD

- Nikolai Stepanov: Night Driver — 233
- Alexander Sinitsin: Dreaming of Past Glories — 237
- Alexander Obraztsov: Fighting Oblivion — 244

Snapshots 249

Epilogue: The Open Question 253

Chronology 255

Foreword

According to the 1990 census, nearly three million people in the United States claim Russian ancestry. Russians have a long and unique history of migration to the United States, having come here for many different reasons. They come with distinct skills and dreams, and adapt to life in America in strikingly different ways.

The first Russians came to the West Coast as colonists rather than immigrants, exploring Alaska, the Pacific Northwest and California. Starting in the 1880s, political and economic turmoil, coupled with the government-sanctioned persecution of Jews (called *pogroms)*, caused millions of Russian Jews to come to the big eastern cities of the United States. Non-Jewish immigrants of the time, mostly farmers, found work as laborers in mills, meatpacking, construction, and mining. The Russian Revolution of 1917 led to the creation of the Soviet Union and the emigration of most of the Russian aristocracy (the first wave). Joseph Stalin's brutal dictatorship (1926–1953) led to the escape of several hundred thousand people after World War II (the second wave).

From the late 1950s to the early 1980s, Soviet society went through a series of changes in both leadership and political climate, during which time opportunities for open expression of ideas, contact with the West, and emigration expanded and contracted. Finally, the partial opening of emigration policy in the late 1970s coupled with easy U.S. immigration for Soviet Jews, Ukrainian Catholics, and Evangelical Christians formed the beginning of the third wave that extends through today.

The life stories of this third wave illustrate the high levels of education, ambition, and independence of Russian migrants—they also characterize their broad ethnic mix. In fact, of the millions of people who have come to the United States from Russia in the past 120 years, less than 20 percent have actually been ethnically Russian; about half were Jews, others were Catholics, Protestants, Latvians,

Poles, and Armenians. Although deeply immersed in Russian culture and language, members of these groups suffered discrimination at the hands of the Russian Orthodox majority.

As is evident in many of the interviews, Soviet citizens have been proud of their ability to "make do" and have enjoyed a high standard of living despite the discrimination, war, shortages, and purges that they have had to endure. Often, they became skillful manipulators of the system. As Erving Goffman pointed out in *Asylums*, his classic study of totalitarian institutions, the sense of accomplishment a person derives from obtaining scarce privileges or goods through unconventional means is often more valuable than the actual possession of the privilege or good. In maintaining a decent standard of living, a Soviet citizen could prove the strength of his or her character and an ability to triumph over adversity. This "culture of savvy" is retained by many former Soviets in the United States. It provides motivation in times of difficulty and contributes to positive feelings about their Russian identity.

Russians' ability to cope with their environment is rooted in their families. Due to the widespread shortage of housing in the former Soviet Union, it was common for families consisting of three or four generations to live together in very close quarters. Further, because of the low birth rate among urban, middle-class Russians, Soviet youth maintained close relationships with their parents and kin. Relatives provided young Soviets with political/bureaucratic influence (useful for securing school and career opportunities) as well as emotional support.

The former USSR adhered to socialist-inspired egalitarian ideology that called for women's involvement in the paid labor force. Further, because many men served in the military or died in war, women's labor was in very high demand. Before entering the United States, Soviet women were accustomed to working outside the home as well as taking care of their households. Having already adopted a pragmatic approach to their lives and careers prior to migration, Russian women have been better equipped to adapt to life in the United States than Russian men. As some of these stories illustrate, men often mourn the careers they lost by emigrating, and may spend months or even years in an effort to secure an equivalent position. In contrast, women usually resolve to do what is necessary to support and care for their families. Russian women also master English and achieve acculturation earlier and more easily than their male counterparts. Russian women's survival techniques appear to work well in the United States, and they acquire a greater degree of security and optimism about their own and their children's future.

The interviews in *Red Blues* present a diverse, inclusive, and highly compelling personal overview of the most recent wave of Russians to enter the United States. In their own voices, these immigrants tell the complex, fascinating stories that encompass the major events of Russian history during the twentieth century: the Revolution, Stalinism and the secret police, World War II, dissent against the Soviet regime, Gorbachev's perestroika and glasnost, the collapse of Communism and the Soviet empire, and the emergence of a free-market economy. Relying on narratives of personal experiences, these stories reveal the forces spurring emigration, the challenges involved in resettlement and adapting to a different society, and the immigrants' close connection to Russian culture as well as their insightful and often humorous perceptions of American attitudes and values.

STEVEN J. GOLD
Professor and Associate Chair
Department of Sociology
Michigan State University

Preface

WE HAVE WRITTEN this book about leaving a family. The Soviet Union was much like a big family. That was what Soviet propaganda used to say, and there is often truth at the core of propaganda. But it was a dysfunctional family. Most of its citizens had spiritually left the Soviet system long before it collapsed. And when it finally did collapse, there was a brief period of hope, and then a great despair. Suddenly there arose the very real danger of being buried alive under the wreckage.

The people who tell their stories here have dodged this wreckage either by emigrating or by avoiding the falling pieces. We have focused on artists, scientists, entrepreneurs, and sex professionals, because they are the most mobile, the most like world citizens. While they articulate a loss of connection, they mostly talk about the creative ways in which they have formed new lives. In this they tell a universal story.

Still, leaving Russia for the United States offers particular twists to this story. After all, the United States was the country of the enemy, the country of capitalism. We wanted to find out why people would undertake such a move.

One reason we heard was the simple desire to live an adult life as a real adult. As Marina Shron explains, "Russia represents my childhood despite the fact that I lived there for over twenty years, was formed as a writer, got married, got divorced. I never really had a chance to grow up there because it was not necessary. There were some advantages in that particular state of being: You were allowed to dream endlessly. What I didn't realize then was that I was limited in my dreams, too. The Soviet regime not only deprived us of material things, but also deprived us of many basic human desires, replacing them with monstrous dwarf-desires, like the desire to live in your own private room, rather than share a room with your parents, and sometimes with the parents of your parents. Along with the dwarf-desires were the walls, half-hidden but impossible to get over, because behind each wall there was always another, bigger one. The idea of freedom was on everyone's mind. And it seemed merely a word, an abstract concept that had no relevance to our lives. But maybe it was, after all, a genie bottled deep within us—and once the magic word *perestroika* was pronounced, it materialized, taking, to our big surprise, most unexpected forms."

The Soviet Union promised material security and stability, but was totalitarian to the very end. What does this totalitarian label really mean, ignoring what the Cold War propaganda said? How does this affect everyday life? Most of the people we interviewed came to maturity under the Soviet regime. Their motivations and experiences tell us not only about life in the former Soviet Union, but also offer Americans a new way of looking at our own lives, at what is special, good, bad, colorful, and mysterious about our own country.

The interviews (compiled between 1997 and 2000) explore the fundamental experiences of emigration: life in Russia, external reasons for emigration such as religious oppression or political dissent, internal reasons for leaving such as the desire for adventure, as well as initial and later impressions of the new home. Marina Shron puts it this way: "You die in one life, and you emerge in the other. And each person has his or her own process of going through it, dealing with it. Some do it superficially, some don't do it at all, some throw themselves into it: not a few drown." We have written about those who are still swimming.

DENNIS SHASHA
MARINA SHRON

Acknowledgments

OUR FIRST DEBT is to Studs Terkel. His books showed how pivotal moments in history could be captured through the life stories of its unsung protagonists. He chose the American perspective on the Great Depression and World War II. We have chosen the tales of passage of a group of fascinating immigrants. Next, we thank the Holmes & Meier publishing group led by Publisher Miriam Holmes, Editor Maggie Kennedy, Series Editor Ira Glazier, Editor Sheila Friedling, and Designer Brigid McCarthy. Amanda Brauman, Karen Shasha, and Angela Shashoua offered many helpful comments on the manuscript. Most of all, we would like to thank those who gave their time and their stories to us. Courage, imagination, lust, and art—these stories come from full lives.

To my parents and grandparents,
who also crossed an ocean.

—Dennis Shasha

To my friends,
those who dared to leave and those who dared to stay.

—Marina Shron

PRIVILEGE LOST

Georges Nakhitchevansky
Aristocrat by Birth

GEORGES *is a New York lawyer in his late thirties. Speaking English with a slight French accent, he explains that he is the great-grandson of an aristocratic landowner who was both the head of the Imperial Cavalry Guard and an officer who fought the Reds in the civil war following the rise of the Bolsheviks. His grandfather left Russia as part of the "first wave," primarily aristocrats, who emigrated in the early years of Soviet power. The last several generations of his family have seen more than their share of war and conquest.*

My family happened to be on the wrong side at the time of the revolution. My great-grandfather had been an aide-de-camp of the czar and head of the Imperial Cavalry Guard. It was an elite unit that sometimes would be mobilized in battle, or sometimes used to protect the czar. It would be dispatched to different areas. For example, before the czar abdicated, my great-grandfather was with the Imperial Cavalry Guard outside of St. Petersburg, waiting for word on whether he should march to stop the riots or just hold his position. Eventually he received the order to hold his position. So he never marched on St. Petersburg. Then the czar abdicated.

So, he was bound up with certain elements that the Bolsheviks were not too pleased with. After the revolution, my great-grandfather and other members of the family joined the White Russians to fight against the Reds in the civil war. My great-grandfather was captured by the Reds, shot, and killed. After their offensives fell apart, the Whites began to surrender, and many of them ended up getting shot or murdered in other ways. In the meantime, other members of the family started to leave the country, mostly the women and children. My grandfather eventually left for France with his wife and one of his children.

My family descends from a conquered people. The Russians had always wanted to obtain warm-water ports. So, part of their policy had always been to encroach on Turkey. This meant that they had to pass through the Caucasus and through Armenia and all of the adjoining areas. Right below Armenia there is a region area called Nakhitchevan, which has been linked with Azerbaijan since the fall of the Soviet Union. But at that time, in 1827, back when the Russians advanced, it was a separate khanate allied with Persia. My great-great-great-grandfather, at the time when the Russians invaded, was ruler of the khanate. After the fall of Nakhitchevan, he couldn't bear to look at the Russian troops advancing to take over the region, so he had his eyes burned out.

According to the 1828 treaty that resolved the war with Russia, two khanates were ceded to Russia. One was Erevan, which was the Armenian component, and the other Nakhitchevan. What the Russians would do was take the eldest son of the ruler and "Russify" him. They would bring him up to St. Petersburg and raise him as a Russian. That was the Russian way of annexing any territory that they conquered; they wanted to Russify the people. They viewed it as a way in which they could build loyal allies. My great-great-grandfather was the one who was taken and Russified, along with other members of the family. Some, however, escaped to Persia.

My relatives in Persia also went into the military. They were involved in the coup that brought the Shah to power. The last male in that line was a general under the Shah. His name has a different spelling: Nakchevan. When he died, he had only one daughter. So that line basically has ceased to exist.

As for the Russification process, it involved many interesting "rules." For example, if you were a Russified Muslim, you were not entitled to marry a Russian Orthodox woman. But you could marry Russians who were Protestant, or Catholic, or Jewish, whatever, as long at she was not a "believer," Russian Orthodox. So eventually, what happened was that a couple would try to raise their sons as Russian Orthodox because they could then marry Russian Orthodox women. My great-grandfather, however, remained a Muslim. But his son, my grandfather, was raised as Russian

Orthodox. And he raised his children as Russian Orthodox, too. And my father did the same with us.

Like many families, after the revolution our family lost everything, and they had to go to France and rebuild their lives as well as they could. Some of them came over with the expectation that they would return to Russia in a week or in a month, and they kept their suitcases packed, ready to go, but it never happened. And others were completely destroyed by having lost everything. They weren't trained to make a living on their own. They had been living a sort of idyllic existence. They had land holdings and servants. Also my family had the title to Nakhitchevan, which is a huge province. They remained the rulers of that region.

Some of my relatives were able to take jewelry and other items of monetary worth with them from Russia. They could rebuild their lives in terms of finding a new place in society, maintaining a certain standard of living. But others left with nothing. They ended up working as cab drivers. There was a running joke in Paris that most of the cab drivers were former Russian counts and princes. They'd take jobs that were the antithetical to everything they were raised to be. Some former Russian aristocrats even became domestics and housekeepers because that was the only kind of work available.

A lucky thing for many of these people was the fact that they already knew French, which had been the aristocratic language in Russia. My grandfather saw opportunities in the French colonies. So he moved the family to Lebanon, which at the time was known as French Syria, and he did very well there. He became the regional representative of the Ford Motor Company in all of the Middle East; he built a market there and spent many years developing it. He was doing quite well until World War II.

Many of my family's friends who fled Russia after the revolution, however, never figured out how to get out of that mess, and basically they lived in poverty. But, over time, those Russians who managed to get ahead would help out those people who didn't. It happened in both Europe and in the United States. When a lot of children arrived having lost their parents, a charitable society was created to help those needy children. In a way, this created a "tradition of charity" that continues to this day in the Russian community.

The immigrant generation also maintained "a tradition of the aristocracy." The aristocracy had a certain sense of itself, its purpose, and its role in society. And these aristocrats viewed their role as important in society; they "knew it was proper," a kind of birthright. They had grown up in a system where they had possessed everything, controlled everything.

They did a tremendous disservice to their children, because many of them instilled these beliefs in their children who now lived in societies with different values. For instance, even though titles are meaningless in the United States, and you have to renounce your titles to become a citizen, Russians used their titles here. Many Americans were impressed: "Yes, maybe it's an interesting thing, and maybe I'd like to invite this person, socially, because he has a title." But, of course, in terms of actual advancement in society, the title was useless. Yet I know people in my own family, and lots of other families of an earlier generation, who were completely messed up by this notion of the title. They got carried away with it, making sure that everybody knew, to the point that it was ludicrous.

A lot of people who came to the United States became politically involved. Many people of the older generation wanted to see the demise of the Bolsheviks, so their politics were very strongly anti-Bolshevik. Certain family members, for example, were affiliated with the Intelligence services in the United States, doing espionage against the Soviet Union. Afterwards, even when that came to an end, they tried to do things in Russia to kind of bring back some of the traditions and make people aware of their history. Indeed, a tremendous disaster had happened there, putting aside whether the aristocracy had been right or wrong. It was a disaster for the Russian people. Suddenly a group had decided that they wanted to make a clean break with the past, starting almost from ground zero, and they systematically went across the country destroying, for example, churches, synagogues, everything, because religion was considered to be poison for the people. There was a museum in the former Leningrad, a museum of atheism that showed all the terrible things that religion had done to people. A lot of churches were closed down, some were even turned into prisons, into warehouses, and some were destroyed altogether. There was one in Moscow, for example, a beautiful cathedral that was destroyed to build a swimming pool.

Even basic manners in dealing with other people were viewed as a holdover from the aristocratic tradition. One of the things I noticed during my trips to Russia—maybe it's changed in recent years, but it was present in the 1970s and '80s—was that people seemed to just smash into one another, rushing back and forth without the slightest apology. Here, if you knock somebody down or bump into them, it's considered rude, and you automatically say "excuse me." But in Russia, nobody would say a word; it wasn't part of their upbringing.

It was the destruction of their past that made Russians in the West maintain Russian traditions and record their links to that past. In the 1980s and '90s, Russians became very interested in their history. The Russian community here became very excited because they suddenly felt that there was a role they could play. And a number of people from the "first wave" started traveling to Russia. Some of them were driven by economic motives, but others just wanted to go and transmit their sense of history.

One historian, now in his eighties, has recorded much information about the traditions of the "aristocracy," including genealogy, who is who, who belonged to what family. He also has opinions on the role of the aristocracy. Most Americans find these views uninteresting, but they are interesting to Russians; they have this incredible curiosity, because it's a part of their past that has been chopped off. So they're willing to listen to this guy. And he talks about the importance of having an aristocracy, how it can guide the nation as its "moral light." He talks about traditions and how they should be maintained. He gives interviews and writes articles which get printed over there: people there want to hear it; they want to read this stuff.

A large number of first-wave emigrants refused to go back to Russia, even when it was possible. My father, who was deeply entrenched in the first-wave tradition, with its notions of aristocracy and so on, never visited Russia. And I tried to get him to go on a number of occasions. But he wouldn't go. I never could quite understand it totally, but I can only assume that he and others of his generation had a vision that was given to them of what life was like there; it was given to them by parents who had been granted certain privileges and led a certain type of life. Their whole childhood was based on this vision, and then somehow it was taken away. I went to Russia for a visit twenty years ago. I went to one of the family apartments, which was in a palace near the Hermitage. It used to be my great-grandfather's spacious palace. And when I went there, I saw that it was chopped up into zillions of little apartments. And the building was run down and looked terrible. When I started telling my father about it, he didn't let me talk. "I don't want to hear about this! They destroyed it," he said. "They destroyed everything."

Others were just so utterly anti-Soviet that they couldn't bring themselves to go back while the Soviets were in power. After the Soviets fell from power, some immigrants returned to Russia, and some even got notions of getting back their lands. In fact, some of them got back pieces of land, but there always were strings attached. In some cases, you would get back the property, but you'd have to pay for it by renovating the building within a short period of time. And there were many properties that were now occupied. So once you got the property, you had to take care of the people who lived there. It soon became apparent that land ownership wasn't a very attractive proposition. Some people did receive certain lots of land or houses and then tried to find ways to renovate these places. But it was very difficult to get anybody to put up the financing. In Russia today, there are still disagreements over land ownership. The state used to own everything. And then this agency says that you can have this parcel of land, and you start putting in money, and then you could be told, "That agency had no right to give it to you."

Some went as far as to believe that some sort of reparations should be made. I think there was a similar movement in Poland and Hungary. But in those countries, the loss of property had been a more recent phenomenon, so there was more cachet to it, and more possibilities. In Russia, things were so chaotic at the time that it was virtually impossible for the Russian government to do anything to help the immigrants. There was even talk, at a certain time, of the possibility of getting Russian citizenship, the notion being that a Russian passport would enable you to do certain things, business-wise, in Russia. Some people were seriously looking at that angle. There may be some interesting aspects to it, but I would never want to become a Russian citizen.

My father left the Middle East when his father died soon after the war. He was essentially bankrupt. My father decided to come to the United States to do business. That's when he met my mother, who was French; eventually they got married, and I was born. They lived in the States initially and later moved to France. After many years in France, we came back here. So I ended up having contact with the Russian community both in France and the United States. And because we moved around here—living first in Chicago, then in

New York—I made contact with different kinds of Russian communities. In Chicago there was no first-wave community.

It was a second-wave Russian community. A lot of Russians immigrated during or around World War II. Some people had fled after the collectivization by Stalin in the 1930s. Many Ukrainians had fled, and also some Russians. There were also Russians who came after the war. Some had fought against the Soviet Union during the war. When Hitler first attacked Russia, a lot of Russians believed that joining the Germans was a way to get rid of Stalin. A group known as the Vlasov Army* was formed. These Russians started to fight alongside the Germans to defeat Stalin.

But it soon became apparent to at least some of them that Hitler was psychotic, more so even than Stalin. But now they were trapped, because Stalin would never let them return to Russia. And if he did, they knew their lives would probably be hell. So you had large numbers of people who suddenly found themselves completely isolated. The Germans had stopped trusting them and had imprisoned some of these people. And when the Americans were advancing into Germany at the end of the war, a number of them tried to surrender to the Americans: Some were even liberated by the Americans. A group of these people didn't want to go back; they preferred to come to America. So there was a large influx of people from Russia at that time. I often heard first-wave immigrants who had just met second-wave people at a function like an Easter celebration refer to these people in the second wave as *muzhiks*—peasants.

The second-wavers started their own churches, which were ultimately grouped in an organization called the Orthodox Church of America. Those churches were generally not attended by the first-wavers, who had formed their own churches, particularly in New York. In fact, New York ended up in a very bizarre situation: first-wave people came over and decided to form their own Russian Orthodox church. They obtained a building up in the nineties, a townhouse, which they converted into a church. There had been another church up on 97th street, run by the Moscow Patriarch,

---

* Vlasov was a Soviet general who helped the Germans organize Soviet prisoners to fight the Soviet regime.

which had been started under the czar. But after the revolution it was thought to be cooperating with the Bolsheviks, particularly at one time when the Metropolitan of the Russian Orthodox Church was believed to be a KGB person.

Up until recently, a lot of first-wavers had never entered this 97th Street church, which was viewed as a "communist devil" church. And this view, I believe, was true to some extent, given the persecution of the Russian Orthodox Church and all religions in Russia and the Soviet Union's efforts to co-opt religious leaders. For example, in the pantheon of Russian saints, there is a patron saint called Archbishop Tikhon. Tikhon had come to the United States and consecrated a church up in Yonkers. When he went back to Russia, he was executed by the Soviets because he would not bend to the wishes of the Soviet government. So he became a martyr of the church.

The third wave is a very curious wave of immigration. It started in the 1970s, more or less, when people in Russia were not permitted to leave the country. The only way you could leave was if you married a foreigner who then petitioned to get you out. Or somehow you could be expelled from the country, or you defected. And another way, because there was a huge lobbying effort here to help the Russian Jewish people, was to demonstrate that you were Jewish. The third wave was largely composed of Russian Jews.

At one point, I got involved with one of the groups that helped some of these people get relocated in Chicago. They were settled in different neighborhoods and given a basic apartment and furniture to help to get them going with their lives. When they heard me talk, they would ask, "You seem to know something about Russia, why?" And I would start talking about my background, and they'd get very curious about the past, and we'd get all nostalgic about Russia.

That wave has grown, and now Russians are immigrating from very different backgrounds, but for a long time, this third wave was largely ignored by the first wave. One can only hypothesize why that is. I believe that the first-wavers really had nothing in common with these people. Russians of the first wave were raised under certain notions of aristocracy, certain notions of ethics concerning what was proper in society. And on top of that, they were now essentially American. The third-wave people were Soviets, and they seemed to have a rougher character, not as polished. Some of these people were very colorful and interesting, but they certainly weren't up to the first-wavers' "station" in the world.

I also believe that the religious aspect played some part in separation of the two immigration waves. That the third-wavers weren't "believers," weren't Orthodox, probably had an impact. And one can add that there was a history of anti-Semitism that has existed in Russia for a long time, perhaps continuing to this day. I think that was possibly a reason for the dislike at times. Yet a lot of Russian Orthodox also came over, and many in the first wave didn't want anything to do with them either. But there were some who got in with the first-wavers. Usually, those people were more educated and could speak many languages, maybe artists, scientists and the like. There have been some contacts between the first and third waves—a sort of mutual symbiotic relationship—when both groups can benefit from each other.

One such contact occurred when some first-wavers wanted to go to Russia in the late 1980s and early '90s to avail themselves of the black market. A number of third-wavers who immigrated brought along organizational ties with the very strong Russian Mafia. There were deals that you could make. You could arrange to pay someone in the United States in dollars and then go to Russia to get rubles in exchange. Somebody would meet you in Russia, party with you, go drinking with you, and then give you your rubles. The offered exchange rate was $1.50 for a ruble, but you could get, even before hyperinflation, 20 rubles to one dollar.

A lot of young people also wanted to do business in Russia, for example, dealing in art items. They needed connections, and the third-wavers had these connections and really knew what was going on there day-to-day. But beyond that, socially, it was very rare to find people from the third emigration mixing with the first-wavers. It's really sad in a way, because I think they could have learned a lot from each other. But maybe they were just being realistic to think that, for these third-wavers, "we are Americans, they don't care about us, about our past, our relation to Russia—they probably don't want to have anything to do with us."

People of my generation look at the revolution differently than did the generation of our parents. They viewed the Bolsheviks as evil opportunists who wanted to profit from the revolution and ended up destroying the country. A lot of people in the older generation never thought, or didn't want to think, that their forefathers actually had done something wrong, or that the system was so inequitable that it created a dangerous underlying tension. And yet there are others who openly admit that was the cause of it. I don't think they see the cause of the revolution in terms of religion or conspiracy. Of course, some people still look at it as a sort of Free Mason conspiracy responsible for all kinds of revolutions. But that is not the norm. Even though the first wave may have had unreal notions about the aristocracy, in a larger sense they were rather realistic about the system. It's usually true of people who have lived in a society that has been uprooted that they tend to be realistic about the system because they have lived it firsthand. People from the outside, who haven't lived in that system, tend to resort to scapegoats much more easily.

My uncle used to tell me a story about the time when he was a young man in St. Petersburg. He could see the hatred in the face of people who were in rags, impoverished, starving. He recalled how once he was caught in the middle of a crowd of ordinary people, the type of people he had little or no contact with, and he realized at that moment that there was this anger in the country, waiting to be unleashed. On the other hand, there are some people who blame the whole Bolshevik thing on just one event: World War I. The war certainly precipitated events. Maybe if the war had not occurred, Russia, which was the fastest growing nation at the time, would have eventually become a constitutional monarchy. Who knows what could have happened?

Vadim Shron
An Enemy of the People

VADIM'S father was a Party boss until Stalin decided to purge him in 1937. But Vadim, still a child, preserved his idealism about a system he believed in up until Stalin's death. Only later did he learn the truth about his father's arrest, imprisonment, and torture. Vadim's story spans the entire history of the Soviet Union, from the dream of world revolution to dictatorship, war, stagnation and then perestroika. In 1997, Vadim and his family emigrated to the United States. He now lives in Washington Heights in New York City, with his wife and twenty-year-old daughter.

I have never talked much about my life. That's been a tradition in my family. My father never told even his children much about his life—partly because he wanted to protect us. We grew up as very well-to-do kids. We were Pioneers, an organization of children who aspired to be in the Communist Party, and later, we were committed members of the Komsomol, the League of Young Communists. The period in which we came of age was an extremely difficult, controversial time for our country and its people, as we came to realize much later. I'm talking now about the 1930s and '40s. Our father didn't want us to live under the burden of a double life. What happened to him contradicted everything that we had been taught at school or heard around us, everything we knew about the Soviet regime and the country we lived in.

My father was born in a small town near Warsaw called Viskov, into an Orthodox Jewish family. His father, my grandfather, was a

Hasid, who devoted all his whole life to studying Torah. That was all he knew from a very early age, and he was a quite intelligent, scholarly person, although at the time that I met him I didn't give a damn about his knowledge. I considered him almost an ignorant man because he believed in God. That seemed very stupid to me, a young Pioneer and an atheist, who knew for sure, already in the first grade, that God didn't exist.

While my grandfather was studying Torah and Talmud, his wife kept a small store that supported the family. They had six sons and two daughters. A couple of other children died in infancy.

Even though they were born into such an Orthodox, deeply religious Jewish family, three out of six sons became Communists. For a religious Jew, communism was the biggest insult. For my grandfather, the fact that his three oldest sons joined the Communist Party was like spitting in his face. He condemned all three of them. After the revolution in Poland had failed shortly following the end of the First World War, the eldest son ended up in Argentina. Another son, a Communist, emigrated to Chile. My father, youngest of the three, left Warsaw with the Red Army in 1920 when it was chased out of Poland by Pilsudski; he was only sixteen when he crossed the border to Russia. He didn't really speak Russian—only Yiddish and Polish. Right away he went to study at the Communist University in Moscow. With its two branches—one for Peoples of the West and the other for Peoples of the East—the Communist University was, in fact, preparing Soviet agents to infiltrate their native countries. But my father had health problems, which saved him from being sent back to Poland.

Instead, after graduation he stayed in the Soviet Union and started working for the party. His first position was in Kirovograd, in the Ukraine. He was twenty-two when he was sent there. In a small town called Bobrinets, near Kirovograd, he worked as the director of an orphanage. There he met my mother, the daughter of a local tailor, and they got married. Both were very young: my father twenty-two, my mother sixteen. Soon they had me: I was born in Bobrinets. The next year, my father was transferred to Kirovograd—Zinovievsk at that time, named after the popular party leader, Zinoviev, soon to be executed. My father first worked as director of the Workers' University, an institution of higher education for workers, where my mother studied and received her degree in chemistry. But soon my father was promoted to director of a big local plant called Red Star, a major manufacturer of agricultural equipment in the Soviet Union. And along with that, he served as a member of the City Soviet, the local governing body, so he was quite a prominent figure in town. A very committed Communist, nearly a fanatic, he was good at what he did. People respected him. I remember as a very small boy calling him at work. All I had to say was "Father, please," and, right away, he was on the line. I was very proud of him as a kid.

I had a very happy childhood, "bright and radiant as the sun," as one of the Soviet songs of that period put it. The people surrounding me, whether at home, at school, or at the summer camps I was sent to, were all good, kind, and very reliable. Because of my father's position, we lived very well. We rented a spacious apartment with a huge living room, four other rooms, and a kitchen. (The kitchen by itself was much bigger than my entire apartment in Leningrad many years later.) I remember the ham hanging from a ceiling in that kitchen, emanating the most delicious smells. We had a housekeeper. We were very wealthy. I was a very happy kid.

All that lasted until 1937, when my father suddenly was arrested. That was his first arrest, and I have only a vague recollection of it: I was nine at the time. I remember some people came to search the apartment one night. I wasn't frightened because I had no idea about what was going on. Even after my father was taken away, our life, at least from my perspective, didn't change much. I went to school, every day, as before. The main change was that now my mother would visit the Internal Affairs Office every day to make inquiries about my father. A little while later, a new girl came to live with us; both her parents had been arrested. We continued to live in the same apartment.

My mother was laid off from her job shortly after father was arrested, but she went to see the Internal Affairs officer. "If my husband is an enemy of the people," she said, "then you should arrest me as well. But if you don't arrest me, give me a chance to work and support my children." She was soon reinstated in her job.

I found out about all that much later. At that time I didn't understand a thing. I remember the so-called heights near the city, hills on which the prison stood. We'd go every day—me, my mother, and my younger brother—and stand there for hours, along with thousands of others, waving to prisoners behind bars and trying to catch a glimpse of them waving back. My father had a red handkerchief, and I tried desperately to see it, but I couldn't. But mother swore she could see it, which meant he was still alive. I believed that my father would be released in a couple of days, and when, after a couple of weeks he was still in prison, I wrote a letter to Ezhov, the Commissar of Internal Affairs and chair of the KGB. "My father has been arrested," I wrote. "It must be a mistake. Oh, I understand: it is a test. You're testing his commitment to the party and to the people. But I'm sure that once you realize what a devoted Communist he is, you'll let him go." I truly believed everything I wrote. I believed my father was simply undergoing a "test." What else could it be?

What I later found out about my father's arrest, which was one of many that took place at that time,* was that he was accused of being a Polish spy. To support this ridiculous accusation, some kind of testimony was needed, "facts" to illustrate exactly what it was that he did. Interrogations obtained two such "testimonies": one from a mechanic-in-chief of the plant where my father was a director, who claimed that my father had planted a bomb in the basement of the new plant's energy station. Of course, a bomb was never recovered; nobody had even looked for it. The second testimony came from someone in the family.

My uncle, the husband of my mother's younger sister, wrote a letter to the KGB accusing my father of being "an enemy of the people." He did it out of envy for my father, who was an important figure in town and probably got a lot more respect within the family, too. My uncle was a hairdresser. Somehow, this difference in their positions humiliated him and made him hostile toward my father. Who can know the human heart? In his letter to the KGB, this uncle accused my father of spending so much money that he must have been paid by some foreign intelligence agency for anti-Soviet activities. That was enough to get anybody locked up at the time. No further proof was needed.

We found out about the letter during the interrogation in prison, when my father was put face-to-face with my uncle, who, at that point, felt very uncomfortable. It was one thing to write the accusation, another to face the man he accused, a relative. My father was

---

* The year 1937 was the start of a huge wave of arrests of party officials.

also incriminated because of his connection to Pyatakov, a former Minister of Industry executed in 1936. As director of a big plant my father regularly reported to Pyatakov in Moscow; and he knew his family, although they weren't close friends. I should probably explain something about that period.

Beginning in 1933, Stalin began to methodically exterminate all the top Communist figures, people who participated with Lenin in the revolution and later occupied key positions in government, industry, and the army. They were all accused of being enemies of the people. In fact, their only fault was that they knew the past too well. They knew the real—and not exaggerated—role that Stalin played before and after the revolution, "that little Georgian man," as Lenin used to refer to him. That made them dangerous to Stalin, who at the time was beginning to revise and rewrite history. They were dangerous for other reasons, too: as competitors, as political figures with power and influence. They had to be replaced by people loyal and committed to Stalin personally, because that was the only commitment he could trust.

He first got rid of all the top figures in the Politburo. Zinoviev, Kamenev, Bukharin—all close associates of Lenin—were executed one after another following their tumultuous public trials. But that wasn't enough. People who were working under their leadership— Communists at the so-called second level—had to be eliminated, too. The situation in Russia turned out to be handy for Stalin: the hunger of the 1930s, poverty and devastation in the cities and villages, and often, really poor management. Stalin's policy served two purposes at once: he was both eliminating people for his own reasons and using them as scapegoats. There were several layers to that process of elimination: first Stalin would remove his enemies, and then he would remove the people at whose hands they had been eliminated. Ezhov, for example, was placed by Stalin in charge of the KGB, and was directly responsible for all the 1930s massacres. People called him an "angry dwarf" because of his short stature. For a while, he was the most powerful person next to Stalin. But at the end of 1937, when most of the "cleaning" was done, Ezhov suddenly disappeared. His name was simply never mentioned again. Ezhov's replacement was Beria, who was transferred from Georgia to Moscow.

People expected liberalization when Beria first became head the KGB. He began by reviewing a couple of cases and releasing people who hadn't yet been sent to the Gulag, because nobody returned from the Gulag.* My father was one of the fortunate ones to be released. Maybe my mother's persistence had played a certain role: she never stopped traveling to Moscow, making calls to people, appealing. My father was on his way to the Gulag when suddenly an order came for his release. He was sent back home. I remember the day when he returned in the winter of 1938. He came back in the evening. We were all sitting in the living room, near the fireplace, when I heard a sudden noise in the hallway and saw my father standing in the doorway. He had on his old military coat, with its peculiar smell, a scent of prison—strong disinfectant mixed with something else. My father seemed an old man to me at that moment. Now I realize that he was only thirty-five back then. We hadn't expected his arrival. Nobody told us he was released. The next day, he shaved himself, dressed up, and went out with me and my brother. We walked around the city, first stopping at his plant.

Everywhere people congratulated him. Everything seemed to be again as in the old days. The only thing was that he had not been reinstated in the Communist party. At first we didn't worry about it, convinced it was just a matter of time. But days passed and he never got back his party membership card. And without it he could not return to his old job. He couldn't even hope to hold a position of leadership.

He found a job as an office worker in a small building in Kirovograd. He never told us much about what he went through in prison. He told things to mother, but not me or my younger brother. He protected us, maybe himself, too. He didn't want us to feel hatred for the regime, because he himself didn't have any hatred. Even after his arrest, he remained a devoted Communist, believing that what happened to him was the doing of enemies who had infiltrated the KGB.

In 1939, at the start of World War II, my father's family in Poland spent forty days in Warsaw during its seizure by the Germans. They had escaped to Warsaw from Viskov when the Germans invaded Poland. They experienced all kinds of terror: bombing of the city and artillery shelling. During one such shelling,

---

* The Gulag was the vast prison system described in Alexander Solzhenitsyn's book *The Gulag Archipelago*. The word "gulag" is an acronym for Chief Administration for Corrective Labor Camps.

my grandmother was killed by a shell. Finally, the Germans took hold of the city. They began to hunt out the Jewish population and confine them to the ghetto. What saved my father's family from almost inevitable death was the pact between Hitler and Stalin that divided Poland into two zones of influence—German and Soviet. The people in both zones were allowed to cross to the other side if they wished. My grandfather, his two young sons, and a daughter crossed to the Soviet side.

There was one more son in the family, the only one to become a capitalist, not a Communist. A rich man, he didn't want to leave his property behind, so he remained in Poland. He was killed by the Germans. But the rest of the family immigrated to Soviet territory. One day, our father gathered all of us at the table and announced that his family from Poland was coming to join us. And a couple of days later, my grandfather himself appeared in our luxurious apartment, dressed like a typical Hasid in black, with a long beard. Well, his beard was actually cut short by the Germans, a humiliating procedure they made old Jewish men undergo; a beard is a great treasure to a religious Jew. My first impression of my *dzyant*—that was what we called grandfather—was one of wonder. He seemed to come from another world. For one thing, we were raised in atheism, and suddenly, there was my grandfather praying to God, referring to God on every occasion. The day they arrived, after the big family dinner, my grandfather took my father aside and whispered in his ear. Then he went with my father into the living room.

The door of the living room was closed, and father warned us not to enter. Of course, that warning only increased my curiosity. I approached the living room quietly, opened the door slightly, glanced inside, and almost screamed in fear: what I saw looked like God himself. I had never seen a Jewish prayer ritual before. Dzyant was dressed in a tallis, or prayer shawl, with red on its fringes. I saw a black leather cube on his forehead, and a leather strap twisted around his left arm.* I was terrified. I ran to my father, asking him to stop whatever it was that was going on. With difficulty, he managed to calm me down. Later he told us about Jewish prayers. He explained that my grandfather believed in God.

---

 * *Tefillin* or phylacteries, small black leather cubes containing parchment with verses from Deuteronomy and Exodus, attached with straps to the forehead and left arm of Orthodox Jewish men during morning prayers.

I couldn't comprehend how an adult could believe in such nonsense. I tried to convey the scientific truth to him. Once I went so far in my desire to demystify the religion that I decided to cut his beard short in his sleep. My logic was simple: if the beard was supposed to bear some mystical power, once he saw that my act of blasphemy didn't make the Earth split open and swallow me or him, he would realize that God didn't exist. That was the kind of atheistic logic I learned at school. So I took the scissors, and under the cover of the night, I tiptoed to dzyant's bed. Fortunately, my mother caught me before I could do any serious damage to the beard, although I did manage to nip one or two strands. Soon after this incident, dzyant and his family moved out to their own apartment. That was the year 1940. Only one year remained before the war broke out.

In 1941 the Germans invaded Russia. I remember that day very well, June 22, 1941. I was playing with some other boys in the courtyard. Our first reaction to the news about the war was a boy's kind of excitement and also surprise.

It seemed strange to us that Hitler would challenge our country; it was obvious that it wouldn't take more than a couple of hours for our army to destroy the enemy. We had no doubt about a quick and triumphant end to the war—as all the Soviet songs proclaimed. That night, I learned for the first time what an air raid was, and an artillery attack. We lived very close to a military airport. When the shooting started, we all went down to the first floor. There was no basement in our building, so people hid on the first floor, under the staircase. I heard the bullets smacking the pavement outside. Suddenly I threw up because the sound was so scary. We expected our father to go to the front as a volunteer. Instead, three days after the start of the war, he was arrested again. That second arrest I remember very well. The KGB came in the middle of the night, and they searched the apartment.

They checked out the room that I shared with my brother. We had a huge map of Europe on the wall, and on that map we would mark with little flags the movements of Soviet and German troops. After the search was over, they told my father to say goodbye to his family. One of the men laid his hand on my father's shoulder. I remember father turned to him and said, "Don't worry, I won't run away." Then they took him down the stairs to the car waiting on the street. We watched from the window as father waved to us from the car. And again, we'd go to the prison on the hill every day and wave. Soon a trial was held, a tribunal. We weren't present. We stood outside the courthouse. We saw father led from the car into the building. Then, a little while later, he was taken by convoy back to the car. He made a sign to us with ten fingers, meaning a ten-year sentence. He was put in the car and taken away. Meanwhile, the city was preparing to evacuate. A couple of days after the trial, my mother asked a public prosecutor to find out where father was sent. He told her that she could forget about him. He had been executed by a firing squad.

That is what we believed for quite some time. But in fact, father had not been executed. For the second time, a twist of fate saved him. When the Germans were about to enter Kirovograd, all prisoners were marched under convoy to the closest train station. It was a long distance to walk under the burning sun. Some of the prisoners were old and sick. When they became exhausted and stopped, not being able to walk any further, they were shot by the convoy right on the spot.

Dr. Dashevsky, our former family doctor, walked in line with my father. He used to treat us as kids. By the time he was arrested, he was already an old man. He was shot right in front of my father. When the prisoners reached the nearest train station, they were crammed into one compartment and sent further east. That ride was a complete horror: the prisoners went without or almost without food. And the worst thing was that there was no toilet, and they weren't allow to go out. Soon dysentery spread, and people were dying, one after the other. Corpses were taken out of the convoy once every few days.

The dead lay next to the living, the sick infecting the healthy. They traveled like this for about a month all the way to Aldan, in Siberia. My father survived the trip. In Aldan, he was supposed to work in the gold mines. But it happened that in 1942 a Polish Liberation Army was being formed in the Soviet Union with a division composed of former Polish citizens who were incarcerated in camps or in Siberia on the grounds of being Polish spies. These people were suddenly released to join this newly formed Polish legion, and among them was my father. One day, he found himself outside the gates of the camp wearing only a prison robe and trousers in the freezing cold. He had no money to buy clothes, but once again he was lucky. Standing on that street in Aldan, not knowing what to do, he was discovered by a former student from Kirovograd, who was working in the mines as an engineer. He recognized my father, and he gave him shelter and money. My father started searching for us.

He was not reinstated in the Communist Party until 1956. After the Twentieth Communist Party Conference, my father was invited to Moscow where, ceremoniously, he was given back his party membership card. Right away, he became one of the oldest and most esteemed members of the party with a record dating back to 1920. In 1956, he was only fifty-two and still full of energy, although he had had two heart attacks by then. Only then did he finally tell us the complete story of what he had experienced during his first and second arrests. He told us how, during the interrogation, he was put in the same cell as criminals who had beaten him almost to death, and how, in order to make him sign a confession, his interrogator had shown him a copy of a local newspaper with the text of my mother's public denunciation.

The copy was fabricated, but for a while my father believed in my mother's betrayal and even refused to accept the food packages she was sending to him in prison. Maybe the only thing that saved his life after that first arrest was that, despite the torture, he had never signed a confession. And he never stopped being a Communist, faithful to the party and to Stalin. He still believed that what had happened to him, and was happening to other people, was the doing of enemies who had infiltrated the KGB. After he was released for the first time, he sent letters to Moscow trying to expose those "enemies" and demanding that they be tried. Those letters may have played a certain role in his second arrest. During his second trial they were referred to by a prosecutor as "lies meant to discredit our security organs." That led him to demand a death penalty for my father. It was the same prosecutor who later told my mother that father had been executed.

While my father was suffering his ordeal, our family experienced the ordeal of evacuation. The Germans were advancing toward Kirovograd at great speed. The city authorities had not issued an order to evacuate, although they were evacuating their own families. The population of the town was starting to panic. One day, hundreds of people streamed into a train station looking to escape the city. The station was packed, and trains that were leaving overflowed with people. Then the authorities issued an order: whoever attempted to leave town without special authorization would be shot. So the people returned from the station.

It seemed as if nobody was defending the city. The German bombers made their appearance every three hours with frightening punctuality; you could almost set your watch by their arrival. We had to leave our apartment since it was dangerously close to a military airport. One day, mother sent my brother and me to pick up some things we had left in the apartment. As we approached the building, there was an air raid: The house was hit by a bomb and destroyed before our eyes.

We kids watched the bombing with fascination. The war was still pretty much a game for us. I remember when the Red Star plant was struck by a firebomb and went up in flames: the view was so amazingly beautiful that we stood there watching; we couldn't take our eyes away from the blaze. One day the city was left unsupervised: the authorities seemed to have fled the town. The last traces of order were gone. I remember a militia soldier on the corner firing at a German plane with his pistol, trying to shoot it down. That was when mother decided it was time to leave, no matter what.

We found a wheelbarrow, loaded it with our stuff, and rode to the train station. When we arrived, we found that no trains were running; the station was getting bombed every three hours. And because of its location, it was open to artillery shooting. There was no place to escape. People would hide behind some thin cardboard sheets on the platform, which, of course, provided no protection against bullets. Then my mother did something I will never forget: she took my brother and me by the hand, and holding one of us on each side, stood in the middle of the platform till the shooting was over. If we were killed, at least we'd all be together. We couldn't survive without her, and she didn't want to live without us—she knew that. I was crying through the whole thing, trying to break away, but she held my hand tight. We spent three days at the station, waiting. Not a single train left the station; there was nobody to give an order for them to move. Finally, when the Germans were entering the opposite side of the city, a rumor spread that one of the trains was about to move. Thousands of people rushed to that train, our family among them. "Our family" included twelve people. Besides my mother and us, there were my mother's parents, along with dzyant and his family.

So we got to the train and climbed on the platform. Still, nobody gave any orders. People were throwing their last possessions onto the train—bicycles, sacks with food. Finally, the train moved. We were on a bare flatcar that had been used for transporting coal. We were open to the winds, unprotected. As soon as the train left the station, a German fighter appeared out of nowhere, circling above us. We sat quietly, waiting for it to shoot. But the plane simply accompanied us all the way to the next station, waved with his wings, and turned back. It was a spy-plane.

For nine days we rode on that train, on the same flatcar, bearing the heat and rain and hunger. We had no food, except for a bag of zwieback, dried bread that my grandmother had kept since the civil war. She had kept this stale bread, spotted with dung, in a barn with her chickens for twenty years; it saved our lives. For two weeks we were on wheels. Finally, we arrived at a small station called "The Pit," near Rostov-on-Don, where we got off the train. We were put on an *arba,* a wheelbarrow dragged by two bulls, and driven off somewhere. The road seemed endless; we didn't know where we were heading. The sun was unbearable, and the bulls walked slowly. We reached our destination in the evening. It was a small *stanitsa* [Cossack village].

We went to the administration building, where my mother introduced us to the chair of the collective farm, who looked somewhat puzzled. "Who are you?" he asked, when my mother finished her introduction. "We are evacuated persons," my mother replied. She was doing all the talking. Her answer only increased the man's confusion; he had no idea what the word evacuated meant. But because he didn't know its meaning, it sounded impressive to him; it created respect. And when my mother produced a letter given to us by local authorities at the station, it confirmed his assumption that we were "important" people sent to his care. So we were accommodated in grand style: put up in a big farmhouse and fed with lamb, milk, and honey. After days of starvation, it was too much. The next day we were laid flat, sick to our stomachs. So we began to live in the stanitsa. At first, it seemed we'd stay there for good. My mother was thinking of getting a job at the farm. The chair of the collective farm was nice to us; he particularly fancied my mother: "You've got spirit, Faina," I remember him saying. But a couple of days later we again saw a German spy-plane in the sky. That meant the Germans were getting closer. "Let's not take any chances," my mother said. And the next day we left.

My mother's instinct was really quite extraordinary. A few days later that entire area came under German control. So we boarded the train again and once more headed east. We arrived in Stalingrad, where we stayed with a German family. A lot of descendants of seventeenth-century German settlers lived in that area around the Volga river. Known as Volga Germans, they were very hospitable people. We lived in their big wooden house with a terrace overlooking the Volga. But after a while, the German planes got there, too. We left Stalingrad. That was in September of 1941.

This time, my mother decided to move further east. Somebody mentioned a city called Chelyabinsk, a major industrial center in the Urals. She decided to go there, hoping that not only would we be safe there, but that she could also find a job for herself. So we went to Chelyabinsk by boat, down the Volga River. We traveled for ten days, surrounded by the most beautiful scenery. It would have been a gorgeous trip if not for the hunger: we had no food. I was used to hunger by that time and took it stoically; after all, I was twelve and the only man in the family. But my younger brother cried all the time.

When we arrived at Chelyabinsk, my mother laid out blankets and pillows right there on the street, and as she had done many times before, made beds for us. We woke up in the morning surrounded by a crowd of staring people. We must have looked like a gypsy camp to them. We had no idea where to go, but again, we were helped by a coincidence: in that crowd of strangers happened to be a few people who had known my grandfather back in Bobrinets. They took us to their place and gave us refuge for a couple of days. From Chelyabinsk we were directed to a small village called Malushevka. A couple of months later, we moved to the district center, called Yesaulka, thanks to my grandfather who was a tailor—a rare and valuable profession, particularly in the country. We stayed in Yesaulka for a couple of years.

There I went to school, to seventh grade, and afterward, I started on my first job—rolling felt boots in a local shop. In Yesaulka, I heard the word *Yid* for the first time and learned about anti-Semitism. The first day in town, I overheard a conversation outside the house where we were staying: "Have you any evacuated persons in your place?" "Yes, we've got some Jews, too." "Jews, really? And what do they look like?" That was how I discovered I was a Jew, which together with my being a city boy, made me the target of hostile jokes at the village school. Despite that, I have fond memories of Yesaulka, the place where I came of age.

Being an urban boy gave me certain advantages in village life. I was a bookish boy, I had always read a lot, and we had owned an excellent library at home back in Kirovograd. I remembered a lot of what I'd read and was good at retelling the stories. When I started working at the boot shop, that provided me with a certain status, that of a storyteller. While people were working, I was entertaining them by telling stories from the books I'd read. Sometimes I felt guilty about not doing enough work, but my supervisor—the shop manager, an old villager—would say, "Don't worry, you'll catch up with the work. Now it's time to tell stories." So I told the stories, and my coworkers listened.

In 1944, we received a letter from my aunt Raeesa: she and her family had been evacuated to a small town near Alma-Ata, in Kazakhstan. She invited us to come there: "It's warm here, and we've got a lot of food. You'll be much better off here," she wrote. "Semyon's got a job, we'll be able to help you." Semyon, her husband, was the man who had falsely reported my father to the KGB back in 1937. But during the war the families had made up; the past was forgotten. Our family council decided to go. We all went, except for my father. He had gotten a job in Chelyabinsk, but couldn't bring us over because there was no place for us to live. So instead, we went to Kazakhstan to stay with my aunt and Uncle Semyon, who was particularly nice to us.

I was fourteen, and my family wanted me to continue my studies. A school of technology was opening up in Alma-Ata, and it seemed like the right place for me. So I was sent to check it out. My grandfather accompanied me: together we walked all the way to Alma-Ata, about 30 kilometers; there was no transport. I was accepted into the school with no difficulty and placed in a dormitory with the other students. In Alma-Ata, I got to know real desperate hunger. The daily ration for students consisted of 200 grams of bread and a broth. It was hard to survive on such a ration, let alone to study. All we could think of was food. In search of something to fill our stomachs, students wandered the city, taking odd jobs here and there, like unloading beets, hoping to snatch a bit of food that would fall to the side. In the evening, we'd come back to the dormitory, which was unheated, like most of the buildings in Alma-Ata. We lived with a constant feeling of cold and hunger, which was hard to overcome. The few parcels of food I received from home never lasted for long; I shared them with roommates who had no relatives at all.

With all that, there were some pleasures in my life in Alma-Ata. This was the first time that I had lived entirely on my own. And unlike other places I lived in, Alma-Ata was a big city, a capital, with all the attractions of a big city. It had an opera house, where we could go for free. The parents of a fellow student worked in the theater; his father was a fire inspector and his mother a cleaning woman. Their positions gave us unlimited access to all the shows. We didn't miss a single show, and it was a bit warmer in the theater than in the dormitory.

While in Alma-Ata, I was admitted into Komsomol, the League of Young Communists. I was fifteen. Of course, I wanted to be admitted very badly. When I applied I hadn't concealed any facts in my biography, including my father's arrest. I held on to the interpretation of events I had made up as a child: that my father's arrest was merely a test. Surprisingly, I received a recommendation to join Komsomol. To complete the procedure, a general meeting was held, and I stood in front of the committee. Once again, I had to repeat my biography. "I was born in the city of Zinovievsk." But I wasn't given a chance to continue. "What city?" the chair of the committee asked. "How dare you to even pronounce this name. Don't you know who Zinoviev was?" I knew, of course. He was an enemy of the people. But what could I do? That was, in fact, the name of the city at the time when I was born.

After a year of preparatory study, I was accepted into the newly formed Technological Institute. I was a first-year student, except that I was two or three years younger than most of the other students. In my first year, I was expelled from the institute for smoking in the auditorium. Maybe it was a bit of bad luck. Because, believe me, I was not the first person to smoke in school.

Our first year was marked by an air of complete, unlimited freedom, which none of us had experienced before. We could attend lectures or not attend as we pleased. There were jazz concerts and parties every night. And that was true for the entire country during that one year, at the end of the war. Foreign movies brought from Germany were shown everywhere. They would have been considered obscene, ideologically unacceptable, just a couple of years ago, but now they were okay. The country was loosening up. The general mood in that year of 1944–45 was one of relief and hope. Everyone expected the future to be different, glorious. Soldiers were returning from the front. After what they had been through—facing death and coming out of it alive—they were not afraid of anything. They brought with them a special sense of freedom. The atmosphere in the country was intensely political: the Komsomol meetings in our school would last until four in the morning, in hot debates. And often we would come up with resolutions not at all agreeable to the first secretary of the City Komsomol Organization. But that freedom didn't last long. By the end of 1945, order was being restored everywhere, including in my school. Coming back from winter vacation one day, we discovered a new director's order posted on the wall prohibiting smoking in the auditorium. Well, we didn't pay much attention to it: such orders were issued each day and completely forgotten the next day.

So during the following lecture, I stretched out on the auditorium bench and puffed a cigarette. When the director walked in, I didn't even look at him. It was one of those student traditions: don't show any respect to authorities. I wasn't the one to invent that tradition, but I was one of its most fervent followers. "Have you read my new order?" the director asked. "Do you know what it says?" "Yes," I replied, "so what?" "Come with me," he said, and I followed him, smiling. When we got to the dean's office, the director told a secretary to prepare a letter expelling me from school. He dictated the letter very calmly. I stayed calm, too. I wasn't worried: orders expelling students from school were not at all uncommon. Posted on the wall in great numbers, they were usually replaced the next day by orders reinstating the expelled students. I was sure that would happen. But this time things turned out differently. The administration decided to make my case a warning to the other students. When, after a couple of days, I was still not reinstated, I became frightened. Despite all my bravado, I was still just a kid. The possibility of being kicked out of school frightened me terribly. The director proposed a deal: he would reinstate me but on the condition that the departmental Komsomol give me an official warning. I accepted the deal gladly. I couldn't care less about a "warning." But the school Komsomol branch showed more moral integrity: they refused to give me a warning. I can't say I was grateful to them for that: my last chance to be back in school was vanishing. I was ready to cry. I almost begged our Komsomol secretary to "warn me," but he wouldn't, out of principle. Finally though, I was given the warning and reinstated in school.

I graduated from the Technological Institute at age twenty, with a degree in tank manufacturing. I was then assigned to a famous tank manufacturing plant in Nizhniy Tagil, in the Urals, as an engineer responsible for testing new tank models. It was an interesting job, and I was quite good at it. I developed procedures for testing the tanks, and then took the tanks on a test run myself. It was an exciting job, particularly for a young man. I worked closely with many famous designers, like Morozov, who had designed the T-34 tank used during the war. Of course, my position was highly classified. Clearance usually took some time—a couple of months, at least.

After I had worked at the plant for a while, I was suddenly invited to the administrative office and told, "We like the way you work. We want to offer you a promotion. How about if we make you a senior engineer?" "Sure," I replied. It turned out they were offering me a Senior Engineer position in a different division, in the Office of Mechanic-in-Chief. The plant had two production branches. The official branch was involved in manufacturing trains and known as UralVagonZavod, or Ural Car Plant. Tank building was the classified branch. Being transferred to the Office of Mechanic-in-Chief meant being removed completely from tank productions. Of course, I resented it. But there was nothing I could do. My special work pass was taken away from me at once. Now, I couldn't even walk into the building where I used to work. My documents hadn't made it through clearance. I never found out the reason: maybe it was my father's arrest, or perhaps, the fact that my father's two eldest brothers had immigrated to South America many years ago. He had never heard from them, didn't even know their whereabouts, but the KGB may have known more about it than he did. I felt humiliated, even though I wasn't fired but instead offered a promotion. I wanted to work with tanks, not trains. I was a tank builder, as my diploma stated. Restless, I sent off a couple of letters to Moscow, directly to the ministry. After that I was fired.

So I returned to Chelyabinsk, feeling that I was a failure. I started looking for a job and soon found a position as a design engineer in the Institute of Metallurgy. This was not strictly my occupation, but I came to like my new job; it expanded my horizons as an engineer. My life went along peacefully for a while. But peace didn't last for long. In the winter of 1951, the country learned about what came to be known as the Doctors' Plot.*

First, vague information appeared in the press about a few Jewish doctors in Moscow caught in terrorist attempts to poison our party leaders. This "information" initiated a huge anti-Semitic campaign. The propaganda was so severe that in many health clinics and hospitals in the country, patients refused to be treated by Jewish doctors. And there were a number of Jews in the medical profession. Many doctors were fired right away. From physicians, the Stalinist campaign spread to other professions, including engineers. The campaign's slogan was the "struggle against Zionism."

The press never actually used the word Jew, only Zionist, or "agent of the Joint." But most of the population had no doubt about what that word in fact implied. In my institute, I worked next to highly qualified engineers, because the nature of our work required people with high qualifications. Many of them were my friends. Yet, when the whole thing started, they changed. The institute facilities were located outside of town. A special bus brought employees to work in the morning and drove them back to the city at the end of the day. One cold winter day, I stepped inside the bus, and the other people—who had been talking animatedly—fell silent immediately. I could read in their eyes that they had been talking about me. Nobody said hello. I walked between rows of seats in heavy silence. Even the intelligentsia were not immune to the anti-Semitic virus.

As a kid, I always came up with seemingly rational reasons for my father's arrest, for example, that he was put to a test. I was pretty good at making up these rational explanations for things my mind refused to comprehend. I would do anything to avoid seeing the truth. My imagination refused to go beyond a certain point. To force it to do so would make me step on myself. But the time came when rational explanations no longer worked. The anti-Semitic campaign was handled so shamelessly and brutally that I could no

---

* At the time that the Soviet Union supported the establishment of the State of Israel in 1948, Stalin also mounted a campaign against Jews and Jewish culture, accompanied by mass arrests and purges, and culminating in the libel that Jewish physicians plotted to murder Stalin. After Stalin's death in 1953, the doctors were rehabilitated and their accusers denounced.

longer believe in any "righteous" logic behind it. One of the first victims of the campaign was my friend's father, a doctor. A professor of medicine, a renowned pediatrician, he was arrested and accused of poisoning his little patients. I knew him: he was the loveliest, kindest person I had ever seen, a great lover of jokes. It was impossible to imagine him doing any of the horrible things he was accused of.

Then, in 1953, Stalin died. I remember that day very well. People were overwhelmed with grief, a genuine grief. I was too. When my father announced that "the tyrant is dead," my brother and I confronted him furiously. Well, my father knew what he was talking about, but even he felt lost. Life without Stalin was simply inconceivable to us. We didn't know what would happen. In the last years of his life, Stalin was not even perceived as a human being anymore. He was God, an omnipotent creature soaring above us. And suddenly he was gone. It was a shock. We couldn't imagine any figure capable of taking his place. In addition, the anti-Semitic campaign was at its peak. All the while that it was unfolding, we saw Stalin, ironically, as the only one who could protect us and prevent worse things from happening.

Before Stalin's death, rumors had spread that all the Jews would be deported to Siberia or to Birobidzhan, a desolate region that had been established for Jews after the revolution as the Jewish Autonomous Republic. My memories were fresh of a Communist Party conference, held some months earlier at the metallurgical plant in Chelyabinsk, one of the biggest in the country. The conference had come up with a resolution: to recommend to the Central Party Committee in Moscow that all Jews be sequestered in a ghetto as "untrustworthy elements." Stalin seemed to us to be the only person capable of making sure that wouldn't take place. Even my father believed that Stalin was the last hope for Jews in the country. So when Stalin died, in addition to the general grief that we shared with the rest of the Soviet population, we had the feeling that we were now defenseless.

Two weeks after Stalin's funeral came the news of the complete rehabilitation of the doctors accused in the Doctors' Plot. All the accusations were denounced as lies, the accusers given severe punishments. The press covered all of this. You should have seen the day after the publication. The entire Jewish population of Chelyabinsk poured out on the streets. It was a bright sunny day in

April, and people were laughing, embracing each other, kissing. I had seen such joy only once before—on the day when the war ended. Then the entire Russian population was celebrating—now, only a small part of it.

There was one city I had always dreamed of living in—Leningrad. I had been there once before on a short visit, and I immediately fell in love with the city. In 1956, I moved to Leningrad. It took some time for me to find a job, but finally I found a position at the Institute of Fire Resistant Materials. My life went on pretty smoothly after that. The Leningrad period in my life—the late 1950s, '60s, '70s—was for me, as well as for the entire country, relatively free of turbulence. It was a period of stabilization, both in politics and in social life. I worked, wrote my dissertation, and received my Ph.D. degree. I got married and had kids. Of course, there were some unpleasant factors: I always knew that possibilities for my professional and career growth were limited by the fact that I was Jewish.

The employment policy in Russia made it very hard for a Jew to reach top positions in science, or any other field. I had very little chance of ever becoming head of a laboratory, for instance, and that was the only way to conduct independent research. But I accepted those limitations, as all of us did. I learned to live with them. Then came perestroika. The first years of perestroika, approximately from 1986 to 1989, were actually quite promising. We had never been paid big money for our work; the range and quantity of work had been determined by five-year plans. But after perestroika, it became possible for the first time to solicit projects on our own, make contracts with clients independently, and negotiate deadlines, budget, and pay. We finally began to make some money. At the same time, official anti-Semitism was also decreasing. For the first time, work results became the most important criteria for promotion. Suddenly, the administration made me an offer to head the laboratory where I had worked for many years.

I had been performing the head's duties for years, simply due to my influence and dominant position in the lab, but I was never acknowledged. Now I was offered the top position officially, with all the rights it implied. In 1992, a major economic reform law was finally adopted. We anticipated it with great hopes. During the previous years, from 1989 to 1992, the economy was in limbo: the state was still very much in control of finances, but government funding had significantly decreased. In 1992, the decisive step was taken. We were now on our own—seeking clients, negotiating contracts; we were supporting ourselves.

Yet new problems made business difficult. Our clients were mostly metallurgical or machinery enterprises. Reform made the prosperity of an enterprise depend directly on product quality, and that quality often was not too good. Take the machine production industry: most products in the Soviet Union could not compete in the world market. When Russia opened its gates widely to foreign cars and machinery, the demand for domestic machinery and cars dropped. And that meant that somewhere down the chain, the demand for metallurgical production, such as steel, also dropped. And further down the same line, that caused demand for fire resistant materials to drop, too. So, the freedom of the free market turned into failure for many. Most enterprises weren't prepared for it. We couldn't find clients. Many people were laid off. Some started their own businesses.

I actually tried my own business, too, and turned out to be pretty good at it. Creating joint ventures with foreign investors became the style of the day, and I formed a joint venture of my own in our lab. All the work done in our lab now passed through this company, which meant we had to pay much higher taxes to the state; but our earnings were significantly higher, too. We did some work, on contract, for Chinese, British, and Egyptian companies. Here's a typical scenario: I would receive a memo from the director of my institute giving the technical specifications of a fire-resistant press being produced for one of the metallurgy plants our country was building in Nigeria; the specs would be sent by a German firm producing the machine. I was supposed to provide an evaluation and report back to the ministry. Suddenly it occurred to me: why do we need to buy this machine from Germany when we've been designing a similar machine in our lab? Why couldn't we offer our own machine to the ministry of metallurgy? It seemed like a good thought, a simple solution. I went to Moscow and called on the ministry for metallurgy. I gave them my idea. I explained that the German machine needed some technical adjustment to fit the specifications of work with fire-resistant materials, and it was also twice as expensive as our own. I suggested that we supply Nigeria with the domestic machine developed in my lab. To that the ministry responded: "We don't want our machine. We don't trust our machines. Nigeria is a developing and wealthy country; it deserves a better machine."

Nigeria fell apart shortly after that, but then it was still considered wealthy. Anyway, I figured out right away what stood behind the refusal: the ministry bureaucrats had their own special interest in purchasing a machine from a German firm; the firm had promised to pay big bribes for the contract. Still, I didn't want to give up.

I came up with another idea: "All right," I said. "You don't trust Russian machines. What if I offered you a machine manufactured by another foreign firm, for instance, Norwegian?" "If it's a foreign firm," they told me, "why not give it a try?" I knew a Norwegian businessman, who was doing business with Russia, whom I had met earlier on some business occasion. So I went back to Leningrad and arranged to meet the guy right away. I offered him a deal: we would produce the machine, but it would be sold to the ministry by his Norwegian company. The terms I suggested to him were very attractive. At first he hesitated, but he finally agreed. We went to the ministry in Moscow together. To my big surprise, the deal went through. Nobody even objected to the price of $400,000 that seemed astronomically high to me. Still, it was half the price Germans were asking for their machine.

The ministry even raised the price a bit, proposing that the final seller of the machine would be the original German company, which would contract with the Norwegians who would then contract with us. The additional intermediary was needed so that people in the ministry weren't left without a payoff. And taking a bribe from the Norwegian was too risky, because they didn't know him. Anyway, we made the machine in time, and everyone was pleased: the Nigerians, my lab, the ministry, and the Norwegian who received almost $100,000 practically for nothing. Yet, despite this and other successes, things were changing for the worse. The entire institute was on the brink of closing down. Of its 1,500 employees, only 300 were left by the end of 1995. And the number kept decreasing. So I knew I was running out of time, and I had to think of my family more than of myself. I was sixty-eight, but my family, my wife and daughter, are much younger; this is my second marriage. I had to think about their future. It was time to move on.

I left Russia with a heavy heart, not knowing what to expect in a new country. I realized that I wouldn't be able to continue working in my profession, and I had always liked my work. I was preparing for the worst. So when I got to New York and saw the apartment that was waiting for me—nice and clean and twice as big as the apartment I left behind in St. Petersburg—I calmed down. I like my new country. I like New York, even though I felt overwhelmed by it at the beginning, overwhelmed by its bigness. I wouldn't call this city beautiful in the sense that you call St. Petersburg, or other cities in Europe, beautiful. But I am fascinated by it. It has everything, and it has the best library collections, philharmonic concerts, even fireworks. I like the people here, the feeling of calm they emanate, particularly in a crowd. There is none of the nervousness that marked any mass gathering in Russia. People seem to be good-natured. They may not care too much about each other, but at least, on the surface, they come across as nice and friendly. People smile at each other, and that smile alone fills me with gratitude. It's mere civility, of course, but I wasn't used to it in Russia.

Semyon Slutsky
Communist and Patriot

S<small>EMYON</small> starts speaking right away—no introductions, no long expositions; he is a military man. It doesn't take much effort for him to recall the past: it seems to be always with him. He fought as an officer in World War II, and liberated the Reichstag. Later, he shared a cell in a KGB prison with the soon-to-be executed Jewish writer, Peretz Markish. He has always been a loyal Communist and a patriot. His children emigrated from Russia in 1970s. In 1991, he came to America to join them. He and his wife now live in Brooklyn. "If not for my age," he says seriously, "I would take a pledge of loyalty to America, would fight for it if needed. But I'm too old."

I happen to be the same age as the October Socialist Revolution of 1917. Recently I turned eighty. I was born in the Bryanskaya region, near Moscow. After high school, I went to study at the Military Engineering School in Tombov. After graduating with honors at the end of 1940, I was sent to the Finnish front, because the war with Finland had just begun. When the Finnish campaign came to an end, on March 12, 1940, I was sent to western Byelorussia.

Between 1941 and 1945, I fought against the Germans in the Great Patriotic War. Our small town was attacked from the air by the Germans at four o'clock in the morning of June 22, 1941, the day the Germans first attacked the Soviet Union. From that town, our regiment fought all the way to the east, to the town of Brest. We were saved, as was most of the Byelorussian population, by the

Byelorussian woods. On June 29, I was wounded, and with the first echelon, I was sent to the east. We were bombed twice along the way. Only on July 1st did we arrive in the city of Mogilev, where our unit was greeted by Kalinin, former chair of the Presidium of the Supreme Soviet.

We were the first soldiers wounded in the war, and we received a most honorable welcome, being lifted on people's shoulders. But on the road we experienced all kinds of difficulties: the poor food we received from White Russian peasants, and bandages that weren't changed for days. Many died along the way, left to the local people for burial. I remained in a hospital in Voronezh until July 31, 1941. From there I was sent to the Moscow area, to the First Tank Army under the command of General Katukov. With this troop I marched all the way from Moscow to the west, through Europe to Berlin, where on May 9, 1945, I put my signature on the wall of the Reichstag. "Semyon Slutsky, Moscow," I wrote on that wall. I remained in military service in Germany until 1947, when I was sent to Leningrad. There I studied at a military academy.

In January of 1951, my nephew, Boris Slutsky visited me in Leningrad. His father had been killed in the war. Boris was a talented young man, and he had visited me earlier in Germany, staying with me through the difficult year of 1946. He had applied to Moscow University, but was not accepted because he was a Jew. Instead, he attended the Teacher's College. Later I found out that at college, he had organized and headed a group of students to protest Stalin's regime. When Boris visited me in Leningrad, the group was already under surveillance by the KGB. But I had no idea about any of that at the time because Boris lived in Moscow. I remember that he brought over a friend; we sat at the table, talked, and then the friend left. They had come to Leningrad with a particular goal. Their organization had branches in many cities, made up of students who gathered together to express their opinions freely and talk about things that were wrong in society. But they didn't take any anti-Soviet or anti-government actions; they didn't have arms.

It was an awfully difficult period, 1951—the whole business with the Jewish doctors.* In Leningrad, most of the top Communist officials were arrested around that time. This was the time of mass

---

* See footnote on page 30.

arrests, not only of civilians, but of the military as well. Of course, I was assimilated like most of the Jews in the Soviet Union. I never experienced any persecution on a national or religious basis, neither before nor after the war. I even felt it was an advantage to be a Jew and an officer when I served in western Byelorussia, where the Jewish population revered me greatly. I was a Communist and, of course, a patriot. From my cradle I was taught patriotism and love for my motherland and the Communist party. I joined the party in 1942, the most strenuous year of the war. I fought for my country; I risked my life for it. That visit of my nephew turned my life around. You see, these students, they had done everything on their own. They didn't talk to any adults. Their connections in the big cities throughout the country were students like themselves. But the KGB was looking for a leader, an adult who, they assumed, was directing their work.

On February 23, I was invited to the office of the director of the military academy. There I was arrested by a KGB officer, who immediately went for my epaulets. He managed to tear off the first one, but before he could get to the second, I grabbed his hand and shook it off my shoulder: I was a good boxer, and had a strong blow. I couldn't understand what was going on. They all knew, knew who I was, the kind of patriot that I was. From the director's office I was led down the stairs of the building—with all the officers, the academy students, standing around and watching—and taken to the street, where a German Mercedes waited. In this Mercedes, accompanied by the three KGB officers who came to arrest me, I was driven to the so-called Big House—KGB headquarters on Tschaikovsky street. My mother was visiting me at the time: my first child, a daughter, had been born just six months earlier.

They searched my apartment but couldn't find anything. I was sent to Moscow anyway, to KGB headquarters. The day after I was taken, my mother also took a train to Moscow. In Moscow I was placed in Lefortovskaya prison, in solitary. I had seen this before only in the movies. Then came the endless interrogations. I was questioned for almost twenty hours a day: they wanted to know who was the head of the student underground organization. I was interrogated by two officers, and until the end of my days, I will remember their names: Lieutenant Colonels Sidorov and Pankratov. I knew nothing about what they asked me. I didn't sign anything. I was charged with Article 58:10, part 1, "Anti-Soviet propaganda."

I was never involved in any propaganda against my country. I was a patriot, like many who were prosecuted and later killed in Stalin's camps. For six months, I was held in the Lefortovskaya prison. After about four months, they returned the buttons of my military jacket: they had been torn off in prison. Suddenly they were sewn back on the jacket. I was put in a car and brought to the fourth floor of Petrovka 38, an infamous Internal Affairs building. It turned out that it was Abakumov, the Minister of National Security, who had sent for me. After six months in prison, sleepless nights, endless interrogations, I had lost my composure: I was a live corpse, so to speak.

"Tell me how you conducted the group's activity?" Abakumov went. "Which group?" I asked. They were convinced that, since I had access to arms, I was supplying the group with pistols and ammunition. During the search of my apartment they had found one small 6-caliber pistol, a present from a general that I held as a memory. That pistol was considered evidence.

"We are waiting for your confession," Abakumov said. And there, for the first time, I lost my temper. "I have nothing to confess to," I replied. "What do you want? You executed the best generals and officers before the war. You killed Blucher and Tukhachevsky." I was shouting.

I knew all this, of course. Everybody knew. Marshal Tukhachevsky was one of the greatest commanders in the army, a legendary figure. Never for even a second did I believe he was guilty of what he was accused of. I knew that, before the war, many generals, heads of divisions and regiments, were arrested and killed. The Soviet Army was literally beheaded. But that hadn't undermined my faith in the regime: the war came and swept away every feeling but the desire to crush the enemy and free our country. It was not only my greatest desire, but our entire people's. And before the war, well, we all knew what was going on. Deep in our soul we never believed the accusations. We never talked about our doubts out loud. That would mean following in the footsteps of those others, but deep inside we knew. Anyway, that was the first time that I actually got a chance to spell this all out. My arrest gave me the freedom to do that.

I didn't confess to anything, I didn't sign any of the protocols. The only thing I asked for was an appointment to see my nephew who was held in the same Lefortovskaya prison. I never got that appointment. In 1952 he and other members of his group were shot in prison, three young men. I remember when he was taken away.

He had been arrested in my apartment in Leningrad. He hugged me and said, "Forgive me, uncle. I shouldn't have stayed in your apartment." A month later I was arrested; his sister, a nineteen-year-old student, his mother, and his other uncle, who was an actor, were arrested, too. The whole family was arrested. I was kept in prison for six months and then sent to a camp in Ukhta, far to the north. I got a five-year sentence. In the camp only two people out of ten thousand had a five-year sentence: the rest got fifteen, twenty, or more years. So, mine was almost a nominal sentence.

They couldn't dig up anything on me. I remember Sidorov, one of my interrogators, telling me in the end: "You understand, Semyon, you can't just walk out of here. If you do, I'd have to go in your place." That was their position: he couldn't have just let me go. He was a lieutenant colonel. I was a major at the time. He could allow himself to be frank with me.

Almost immediately after Stalin died, I was released. Stalin's death saved the lives of hundreds of thousands of people wrongly accused. I remember those people I met in the camp—brilliant people, professors, artists, officers. While still in Lefortovskaya prison in Moscow, I was in the same cell as a well-known Jewish writer, Peretz Markish, who had been arrested in 1949. After spending so much time in solitary, we were so happy to see another human being that we embraced each other. We talked all night. Being in prison much longer than I, he knew about wire-tapping devices in the walls so he made me a sign to be careful. Nevertheless we talked, not about politics but about our lives. He was arrested, also for nothing, as a member of the Jewish Anti-Fascist Committee. He told me the story of his life, talked about his sons. We spent only one night together; the next morning he was interrogated and then transferred to another cell. I never saw him again. Soon after that, he and other members of the Anti-Fascist Committee* were shot.

---

* From November 1948 until Stalin's death, the Soviet authorities started a deliberate campaign to liquidate what was left of Jewish culture. The Jewish Anti-Fascist Committee was dissolved, its members arrested. Jewish literature was removed from bookshops and libraries, and the last two Jewish schools were closed. Hundreds of Jewish authors, artists, actors and journalists were arrested. Twenty-five of the leading Jewish writers arrested in 1948 were secretly executed in Lubianka prison in August 1952.

The camp was a good school for me. You had to learn to stand up for yourself and for others. I remember that we formed a team of officers—young and still strong people like myself—to protect the elderly prisoners from the criminals who were constantly terrorizing political inmates with the support of the camp administration. There were ten people on our team, and we gave a kind of ultimatum to the criminals: if you touch one of ours, we'll touch one of yours. Once we almost killed one of those guys—beat him almost to death. But after that we were left in peace. In camp you have to be able to protect yourself, fight for your life. I was always hot-tempered.

In 1953, after Stalin's death, I went back to Leningrad. I was offered a military position, but I refused. I felt that they had not been able to protect me when this thing happened. So I went into civilian service. Because I had a background in engineering, I had no trouble finding work. I took a position at the Transportation Administration in Leningrad. I started as a foreman and wound up a director. My life went along pretty peacefully.

In 1980, my daughter emigrated to the United States. I had some trouble at work because of that. But, thank God, that was in the 1980s, not in the 1950s; things were much easier. In 1977 my wife died, and in 1980 I got married again. In 1991 my wife and I decided to move, too: both my son and daughter were here, working as engineers. They were living on Long Island; both were well off. They invited us over, paid for the airplane tickets for me and my wife. We left our apartments in Moscow to the state and came only with what we had on us.

Things have gotten really bad lately in Russia. I feel great shame for my country, seeing old women fighting for a trashcan so that they can pick up discarded food. It was never that bad, even during the war. And there is no real democracy in Russia. It's all about power, all these democratic leaders trying to get a fatter slice while they can. Nothing connects us to Russia. Here we have children, grandchildren. I'm proud of them: they are decent people, educated, competent professionals. That's what I gave to my new country: my children. They are all I have . . . there's nothing else to give. If not for my age, I would take a pledge of loyalty to America, would fight for it if needed. But I'm too old.

Alexander Bolonkin
Missile Designer and Political Prisoner

It's early afternoon, but the heavy drapes on the window are drawn, and the room is dark. In Russia he was an engineer, first designing airplanes, then missiles, all in top-secret laboratories. Later he became a dissident, spending years as a prisoner in Soviet camps—because he had invented a handmade portable copier. His punishment was extended many times, partly for quoting Lenin.

Upon graduation, I was sent to Kiev, to the airplane design laboratory led by Antonov, a leading Soviet aircraft designer. There I prepared my graduate thesis project, a hydro-airplane with underwater wings. They liked my ideas, and they hired me after I completed my degree. I participated in the development of many new airplanes, from the AN-8 to the AN-225. Two years later, I left Antonov's lab to attend the postgraduate program at the Moscow Institute of Aviation, Department of Dynamics of Flight and Aircraft Control Systems. My scientific adviser, Ivan Vasilievich Ostoslavsky, was a famous scientist and the author of many scientific works and textbooks. I wrote my Ph.D. dissertation on "The Optimization of Trajectories for Multistage Step Rockets." After receiving my Ph.D., I worked with Glushko, a member of the Russian Academy of Sciences, in his Laboratory of Aviation Design. It was the major Soviet lab designing missiles. Although I liked my job, I wasn't happy with the practical nature of the work. Soon I left Glushko's lab and began teaching, first at the Moscow Institute of Aviation and Technology and, in 1970, at the Moscow Institute of Technology.

It was around the same time that I met some dissidents. It happened accidentally. My wife and I were moving to a new apartment. One of the movers helping us to load and unload the truck looked somehow different from his pals: he was too intelligent and didn't ask for a tip. I was curious enough to ask who he was, and he told me that he was a former university student who had been expelled from the university because of his interest in dissident literature. He gave me some books to read. Later on, he asked me if I could hold some of his literature, since his apartment was about to be searched by the KGB. He brought a suitcase filled with all kinds of dissident literature, and I read all of it in the two months it was stored in my apartment.

I soon formed a group with other dissidents. I invented a simple printing device that allowed our new dissident group to print and make multiple copies of all kinds of materials. It was a very simple, portable handmade device, easy to hide from the KGB in the event of a search. We made eight such devices. Just one of them allowed us to reproduce about 150,000 pages of printed texts, including texts by Sakharov and Robert Conquest, along with some underground magazines. Our group even published its own underground magazine, which we called *Free Opinion*. I wrote a number of articles for this publication, analyzing and comparing the quality of life in the Soviet Union and Western countries. We also printed other Soviet dissident publications, such as *Democrat, Light of Freedom*, and *Veche* (Parliament).

We also printed flyers, about 3,500 during the period our group was active. In 1972, we made and distributed flyers on the issue of price increases. Prices were raised back in 1962, and at that time the Communists claimed this action was a temporary measure that would last no more than two years. As soon as the situation in agriculture improved, they promised prices would go down. It didn't happen. Prices continued to rise for the following ten years. So we printed and distributed thousands of flyers, telling people the truth.

Of course, our action was noticed by the authorities. The KGB grew alarmed: they were confiscating thousands of printed copies, instead of a few typed pages as in the past. Yakir, one of the dissidents, showed our flyer to some foreign journalists in Moscow. Soon Western mass media and newspapers spread the news that flyers demanding social, political, and economic reforms were being distributed in the Soviet Union.

The Central Communist Party Committee immediately ordered the KGB to find and smash the culprits. Our flyers were distributed in June 1972, and we were arrested that September. I believe that Yakir betrayed us. The facts of his case prove it. He was arrested in July of 1972. And he was an alcoholic by that time; he couldn't live a day without vodka. Of course, you're not served vodka in jail. The KGB promised him tons of vodka if he agreed to cooperate. He started talking and couldn't stop—volumes of confessions. We were among the people he turned in to the KGB. So, in September, everyone in our group was arrested. I was already under suspicion by then. I had given some literature to a relative in Leningrad, a book called *A Daughter of the Despot,* about Stalin's daughter. He showed it to his wife, and she brought it to her office. But she soon realized that one of her coworkers had an uncle working for the KGB. Before long, my relative was called to the KGB for interrogation, and he gave them my name. He didn't have to do that. His wife had burned the book by that time, so nobody could prove anything. But people were too scared.

My own transformation from ordinary citizen to dissident activist was not sudden. My mother used to tell me about the 1930s, about the infamous black cars, the "ravens," which took people away at night. But I had no idea of the scope of events. We had no information. So when I started to get some critical information, I began to question things. For example, I read that our famous five-year economic plans had never been fulfilled. It was 1971, and the 1965–70 Five-Year Plan had just come to an end. Everywhere our officials praised its success, telling us that we accomplished, even over-accomplished. But I looked at newspapers from 1965, which projected results for 1970, and compared them with the reports published in 1970 by the Central Bureau of Statistics. I was horrified by what I found: of the 67 economic classifications, we succeeded only in three, and those were the least significant categories, like furniture sales, for instance. The plan was to earn 50 million rubles in furniture sales, and in fact 60 million rubles worth of furniture was sold. But that was "accomplished" only because furniture prices had risen significantly during those five years.

As for other industries, only about 10 percent of the plan was realized in some of them, 20 percent in others, the average being 50 percent. So, half of what was planned was actually achieved. It wasn't just a lie, but a shameless lie, to dare call a failure of that magnitude an "overaccomplishment." When I explored the subject, I found that exactly the same could be said of the previous five-year plans. I was surprised that nobody had really noticed it before—not those wise old men sitting in academic institutions, doing their economic analyses, summarizing and praising our achievements. How could they not see? But of course they did see. After that, I grew more and more interested in the data relating to past party conferences, meetings, and so on. I compared what was promised to what was in fact achieved. And the gap between the two was tremendous. It was especially ludicrous in light of the plans' strict deadlines, which were all a sham. For instance, in 1960 the Communist Party Conference had adopted a program to bring about "pure" communism in Russia by 1980. We were supposed to reach the economic level of the United States by 1970, then exceed that level, so that by 1980, we'd be living in a Communist paradise. Of course, it was evident by 1971 that the program was a complete failure.

In September of 1972, I was arrested. I spent fifteen years in concentration camps and in exile in Siberia. The investigator on my case, Anatoly Trofimov of the KGB, was promoted after my trial. Initially, I was given four years in camps plus two years in exile. But after I had served my term, another case was fabricated against me, just to keep me in exile. They accused me of receiving excessive wages; I had worked in a factory while serving my term. So they gave me another four years for that "crime." "If you paid me more, take the difference out of my salary," I told them. "It's not my fault, it is the fault of the person who did the payroll." They told me, "It's you who we need to keep locked up, not him." It was a madhouse. Earlier, during the trial, they had used my notes citing the Party Conference's resolutions against me. They used words like "anti-Soviet rubbish and lies." When I asked my investigator why he called the Communist party's resolutions "anti-Soviet rubbish and lies," he replied: "Bolonkin, you're not stupid. Why did you have to dig into the old promises? We've got new conferences and new promises."

So I spent nearly fifteen years in the camps. I was harassed constantly by the KGB officers on duty. They wanted to rehabilitate me. For three years I was held in prison inside the camp, where conditions were particularly harsh. For 400 days—more than a year—I lived in a cold cell with walls that were frozen. I was kept on bread and water for days. It's hard to survive all that: hunger and cold, constant terror, being attacked by criminal inmates. And the psychological torture was even harder. I wasn't allowed any correspondence. My letters were held back for six months. They confiscated the letters I wrote to my family and friends, labeling them anti-Soviet.

I conducted an experiment. I spent a lot of time in the camp's library. I was supposed to read books by Lenin, Marx, and the other founders of communism. So I wrote down some paragraphs from Lenin's letters to his wife, Krupskaya, and to his friend, Armand. Then I presented those letters to the camp censor as my letters to friends. I never added a word of my own; I kept them true to the original text. None of those letters ever got through. They were confiscated as slanderous, cynical, anti-Soviet. Finally, they took me to the psychiatrist, convinced that only a mentally ill person could come up with letters like that.

I was released from the camp in 1987. I immediately applied for a visa, but they turned me down. I wrote a very harsh letter to the authorities. "Don't try to keep me here," I wrote. "I hate you, all of you, I'm your enemy forever." Perestroika had already begun. They let me out.

At that time, you could leave Russia only with an Israeli visa, which was possible for me because my wife is Jewish. The authorities took away my Soviet citizenship and our apartments, and we had to leave all our property behind. Not only did they take away our citizens' rights, but they made us pay compensation—700 rubles each, 1,400 rubles for both of us—a ten-month salary for an average Soviet citizen at that time. The tickets to Vienna were also quite expensive. So basically, they threw us out of the country without a penny.*

In the United States, I worked in the Courant Mathematical Institute at New York University for a while. Then, for two years, I worked in the Central Research Laboratory of the Air Force in Dayton, Ohio. I also worked as a senior researcher for NASA, at

---

* Until 1989 Vienna and Rome were the transit centers for all emigrants. In Rome they had to choose Israel or America as their final destination. After 1989, emigrants had to obtain visas for a particular destination before leaving Russia or the Soviet Union.

the Dryden Flight Research Center in Edwards, California, for two years. I published about eight articles in scientific magazines, participated in three congresses on astronautics, and in national conferences on aviation and spaceship design. The work I've done here, as well as in Russia, was top-secret work, involving the military. Currently, I'm teaching at the New Jersey Institute of Technology.

Soon after I arrived in the States, my friends and I founded the International Association of Former Soviet Political Prisoners and Victims of Communism. We currently have about 31,000 members. One of the things we're demanding from the Russian Government is compensation for former political prisoners. The dissidents who left Russia up until the late 1980s, unlike the current refugees, had to give up their citizens' rights and property. We demand that all this be returned to them now. I don't see that any real democratic changes have taken place in Russia. The former Communists still have the power; only now they call themselves democrats. But they are the same people. The investigator on my case, for instance, Anatoly Trofimov, was recently promoted to the rank of General Colonel, which is the second highest military rank in Russia, just below Marshal. He's a deputy director of the new Russian KGB, which is called the FSB (Federal Security Service).

After perestroika, I was officially "rehabilitated" by Soviet officials and cleared of all charges. But when I wrote to Yeltsin to ask for the return to my family of at least one of the apartments confiscated when we left Russia, I received no response. I believe they should restore the rights of all dissidents, as well as our apartments and pensions. I say this not because I want to live in Russia. I like America, but I'd like to go back for a look and then decide where to live. I want the right to return; I'm entitled to it. A new regime arose in Russia because of the efforts of people like me; it was nourished by our blood. The least they can do is to return to us our rights, to apologize for all that was done to us—and to invite us back. That would be fair. What I want is justice.

Lidia Sechkina
Lights Out

LIDIA *now lives in Boston. She emigrated from Dushanbe, the capital of Tajikistan. A historian specializing in Oriental Studies, she found herself in the middle of violent anarchy, when, with the collapse of the Soviet empire, nationalities turned against each other and riots erupted in Central Asia. It did not take long before Lidia became a refugee.*

In October 1990, the bloodshed started in Dushanbe. It began with the arrival of Armenian refugees, victims of the earthquake.* They settled in the outskirts of the city, where the authorities gave them a few buildings that had just been put up.

When rumor spread that the Armenians were taking over the city, a huge crowd of Tajiks gathered and marched toward the new Armenian settlement. That's how the whole thing began—with anti-Armenian riots. The Armenians quickly packed up and rushed to the airport. Planes were waiting for them; the Armenian government had sent the aircraft from Yerevan. Immediately, they were put on the planes, boarding without tickets, and taken away. But the Tajiks, once they realized they were feared, could not stop. The dark times had begun.

They soon turned their national rage against the Russian population of the city. When we first moved to Dushanbe, the Tajik pop-

---

* On December 7, 1988, a pair of devastating earthquakes struck Armenia. Up to 100,000 people died, mostly children in poorly built school buildings. Five percent of the population lost homes.

ulation seemed to be adopting Russian culture and language without resistance, willingly even. The official language of the republic was Russian, even in the schools. All textbooks were written in Russian. Nobody really had any objections at the time. But that riot started a real war throughout the republic. Historically, Tajikistan was subdivided into large provinces—kind of like states—with a so-called *Bey*, the leader in charge of each province. Each Bey was responsible for paying dues to the Emir of Bukhara.

The provinces differed in language and custom. The differences were small, but still, when this war began, different ethnic groups turned against each other. Tajiks from Pamir came to Dushanbe. They put up their tents in the central square and simply lived there: made a fire for cooking their meals, ate, and defecated on the same spot. They had no intention to leave. Forty tanks were sent into the city by the centralized government to scare away these unwelcome guests. Transport no longer functioned, buses and trolleys stopped running. Walking on the streets was dangerous.

Soon the natural gas supply ran out. Cylinders containing gas used to be kept on the streets. Each building had a container in which the gas was stored, and each container was locked with a padlock. Once every twenty or thirty days, when you ran out of gas, you'd call the gas service for a new supply. This was how it used to be.

A couple of days after the riots started, all the gas containers were gone—simply stolen. Since the gas supply was gone, there was no hot water available, and no way to heat a stove. Most districts had no electricity. We were better off than others, because we lived on Central Street where the city authorities lived. That meant that the electricity could not be turned off in our building, because the city leaders would be left without light.

The most terrible things began when the city's bread supply was exhausted. Then bread was sold right at the bakeries at night. A big crowd would form a line near the bread truck. You'd have to grab your five loaves and run. There were a few instances when the trucks were robbed and bread stolen. After that, soldiers with machine guns guarded the trucks. People fled the city. Entire families, with all their possessions, were just taking off. Selling an apartment was difficult.

Then the railroad tracks were blown up. Trains filled with refugees were stranded in the train station, each compartment occupied by a family or two. These people had to live on the trains. They had lost their apartments; they had been sold, the furniture packed up, so there was no place to go. So they lived in train compartments, and not just for a day or two, but for more than a month until the track was fixed. And it was very cold, already January when they finally left the city. Traveling by train was dangerous, too. We heard stories of trains being stopped, the passengers killed and robbed. The railroad tracks in that region ran through a desert, empty of human beings for miles around. The train traveled for two days through that barren land.

Anything could have happened during those two days: the train could have been attacked, the conductor shot, and every passenger robbed. So people were afraid to travel by train, afraid to leave the city. But some left anyway, because staying was even more terrifying. That was to commit yourself to death. Planes weren't flying because there was no gasoline. The airport authorities expected fuel to arrive by air. We waited. My husband spent nights at the airport, waiting in line. Every night he would join a shift there. Finally, on December 15, they started selling plane tickets. Ticket prices rose rapidly; before they cost 300 rubles, and now the price jumped to 800 rubles. We weren't able to sell anything. The apartment, our furniture, it all stayed where it was. There was nobody in the city to buy it. Everyone was leaving. We hardly managed to get on the plane: a huge crowd was gathered in the airport; the passengers boarded ten at a time.

Later I found out that the same day we left Dushanbe, December 15, 1992, nationalist troops entered the city. At the very moment our plane took off in the south of the city, the rebels entered the city from the north. The war went on for a long time, with power continually shifting from one side to the other. I have no friends left in Dushanbe. Everyone who could leave left.

My husband's brother, sister-in-law, and daughter had immigrated to America. They lived in Boston. My brother-in-law invited us to come, so we went directly to Boston. We couldn't have stayed in Russia, even if we had wanted to. There was no place to stay. My daughter lived in Leningrad, and we stayed with her for a couple of days. But she had one room in a communal apartment, and we couldn't live with her much longer. We also had no money. We had left our property in Dushanbe and weren't able to sell anything. And even if there had been a place for us to stay in Russia, we couldn't remain. The situation was too frightening.

Recently a Tajik woman came for a visit to Boston. We used to work together back in Dushanbe. She was wealthy and had a beautiful apartment in the center of the city. Strong and ambitious, she had been a member of a Communist party. She had always wanted to get married, and finally she did. "Aren't you happy?" I asked her. She said: "Yes, but, you know, I'm a second wife." So, her husband, a merchant, has two wives, and she's the second wife. The first wife is above her. My friend is assistant director of a research institute in the Republic of Tajikistan. But she's a second wife. And her husband can get himself a third, and a fourth wife, if he so desires. Polygamy was officially restored in Tajikistan.

And I don't want to go back there, even for a day. Even if I was given a free ticket to fly to Dushanbe, take a peek, and come back the same day, I would say "no." I don't want to see the ruins of what I once loved. I'd rather never go back.

GOD and RELIGIOUS DISSENT

Father Michael
Russian Orthodox Priest

FATHER MICHAEL is in his late fifties and has been a priest for twenty years. Half-Russian, half-Jewish by birth, raised as an atheist and educated as a historian, he turned to Russian Orthodoxy as an adult, while still in the Soviet Union. He left Russia in 1972 because of his participation in the religious dissident movement. An articulate, soft-spoken intellectual who holds a doctorate in history, he serves a Russian Orthodox parish on East Seventy-first Street in New York City. He has seen many sides of the curious interplay between religion, government, and freedom of thought.

I left Russia in 1972, among the first dissidents to emigrate. The year 1971 was a time of crisis in the dissident movement. A few activists were arrested, and they provided information to the KGB.

I left the country a few months before a fellow dissident mentioned my name in an interrogation. Had I not left, I would have been arrested. The situation in Russia was not very favorable for me. I had wanted to become a priest, but I could not hope to be accepted at the Orthodox seminary in Russia for two reasons. First, I had attended university; and second, I had taken part in the dissident movement.

I turned to religion in my adult years. Although I was baptized as a child, my upbringing was utterly atheistic, much like everyone in Russia. But, I am also half-Jewish: my mother is Russian, my father Jewish. I was always searching for God, first on my own.

Later I met Father Alexander Men, a prominent figure in the Russian Orthodox Church, a priest and a philosopher. He was an extremely magnetic personality who played an important part in my conversion. For many years before I left the country, I worked closely with him in publishing underground *(samizdat)* books, an activity that was considered illegal and severely punished. We published Men's own manuscripts, as well as works by Solzhenitsyn, and by Russian philosophers and theologians of the early twentieth century. These authors are all published openly in Russia today, but back then it was a dangerous venture. I had to choose between arrest and emigration.

My religious faith always put me in the position of an outsider, a minority in the Soviet Union. At the university I had to conceal my faith, particularly because I was trained as a historian, a profession closely linked to ideology. On the other hand, the movement toward or, rather, back to religious tradition was already gaining ground among the intelligentsia. It came to complete fruition after perestroika, when the authorities saw it as a convenient substitute for the departing Communist ideology. But what's happening with Orthodox religion in Russia today can hardly be called a renaissance; it rather reminds me of the dark ages. But in my time, this emerging Orthodox movement brought a sense of enlightenment and discovery. I was always interested in Christianity. After I joined the Orthodox church, I studied other Christian denominations as well—Catholicism, Protestantism. I had ample curiosity about all religious traditions, and my interest was greatly stimulated by the pervading atmosphere of spiritual search in the intellectual circles to which I belonged. People were searching for, and finding, new religions and new beliefs. The walls between religions seemed very thin—in fact, almost nonexistent. Later, people became divided by religious faith and ideological trends—so much so that members of different groups stopped talking to each other. But, in my time, we all shared a great interest in one another.

So when I chose to emigrate, I had no idea where I was going. It was like a trip to the moon for me. In the early 1970s, we had no information about the West, or very little, often not quite accurate. I left Russia with an Israeli visa. I first went to Vienna, and from there to France. I had connections with some of the Russian émigré publishing houses abroad. Only a few were left in the West by that time: the generation of Russian émigrés writing in Russian was dying out. That first generation of people who had emigrated after the revolution was already gone; the people with whom I was dealing belonged to the second and the third generations. They didn't have any serious contact with Russia. My idea was to make connections between these Russian-language publications abroad and the new political and intellectual movement forming in the Soviet Union. I served as a liaison between the two groups. I stayed in France for a year, but came to feel quite lonely. The life of the Orthodox church in France was not exactly exciting. So I moved to America.

Leaving Russia was very difficult. I can describe that experience as an "interior death." It was hard to leave my friends. Many of them eventually moved to the West, but at that time, it seemed that I was leaving them forever. I had no idea that we were at the very beginning of a vast emigration process that can only be compared in its magnitude to the emigration of intellectuals from Germany in the 1930s. Of course, there were other waves of mass immigration in history, but only two countries—Russia and Germany—allowed themselves to throw overboard such large numbers of intellectuals. Immigration may be hardest for an intellectual, because he lives off his mind and his language. I mean language in the broadest sense of the word—language as culture. It is the air the intellectual breathes. Without it he melts down like a snow-maiden in a fairy tale. And that has become a catastrophe for an entire social group. Only a few of the Russian intelligentsia managed to stay true to their professions, and even fewer to continue growing in them. I am a priest, so it's a different story. I can't say that I'm functioning here intellectually, even though I have received my Ph.D. and write articles in English. Still, it's not a full, intensive intellectual existence. I can't compare it to the intensity of my intellectual life back in Russia, or to that of my friends who remained there. I envy them in a way.

The situation in the Orthodox church in Russia is quite conservative now. The Church is not free; it's rather narrow-minded; there aren't many active theological debates. But outside, in related areas of philosophy and psychology, one can see some really exciting developments. So, if I had stayed in Russia and survived the most difficult years, survived prison and the psychiatric wards—many of my friends and allies in the dissident movement did not survive—I might have become a distinctive part of this new intellectual force in Russia.

Russia is strongly connected to the European culture, with which it is in constant dialogue. The Russian tradition of religious and theological thought is rooted in Orthodox tradition, as well as in poetry and history. America perceived its goal from the beginning as a departure from European culture. It has its own system of values, its points of departure. Although science and philosophy do exist here as well, they are professional fields of study rather than domains of culture. In Russia, philosophy was never an academic field of study. Philosophy embraced everything. It was the comprehensive contemplation of issues of life and spirit. There is an element of dilettantism, of course, which has its bad and good sides. But America doesn't accept dilettantism, refuses to see any value in it.

America is also a Protestant country. Protestant religious thought is centered around the Bible, its content and interpretation. It's not that much interested in religious traditions, in the Church as a tradition, in the Orthodox church and its roots in Byzantium. These traditions are so important for Russian religious thought.

So, a lot of what constitutes the Russian mentality, the Russian spirit, remains unrequited here. It's one of these things that doesn't translate into other languages. The same holds for the experiences of recent Soviet immigrants, whose lives cannot be understood adequately, not only by Americans but even by Russians who have not lived in the Soviet Union. That explains why there is such a wall between Russian immigrants of different generations. Even though we came from the same country, we belong to different worlds.

When I came to New York, I was put in a cheap immigrant hotel on Twenty-ninth Street and Park Avenue. I was astonished by the number of cockroaches I discovered. I described them in one of my letters to friends in Moscow. I was writing regularly, and my letters became quite popular, read widely not only by friends but by many people preparing to leave or simply contemplating emigration. Later I was told that my "information about cockroaches in New York had put the issue of emigration into a whole new perspective." Well, even if this information had some impact on people, that didn't last for long. A new rising wave of emigration from Russia in the late 1970s far outweighed the first one. Even cockroaches in New York didn't stop anyone.

I missed Russia, particularly my friends. But with time, a new circle was formed around me. Some of my friends also moved to

New York. So eventually, a small oasis of Russian life was created in New York. In a way, this New York Russian circle is more authentic than what you can find in Russia today. Here it was preserved intact.

Russia has undergone a huge transformation. When I first went back, in August of 1991, my trip coincided with the Communist attempt to overthrow Gorbachev. I saw tanks on the streets and couldn't help feeling terrified. I was sweating cold sweat. But the others on the street, the ordinary Soviet people, didn't show any signs of fright at all. They talked back to soldiers, swore at them, spat at them. The population that I saw on the streets of Moscow in those days in August was not the same population I had left behind in the seventies. But I had remained the same. I hadn't gone through the same process as they had. I had lived in a free country all this time, of course, and taken advantage of its freedom; but certain psychological mechanisms remained inside me—my fears and anxieties—and when I returned to Russia, they all came back.

I have been an Orthodox priest for twenty years now. As a priest I feel part of American life, part of its religious process. I don't feel inferiority in this regard at all, none of the inferiority of the immigrant. In fact, I am grateful for the opportunities I received here that I could not have gotten in Russia. Still, I am not sure to what extent an immigrant can be a part of his new country's life, its historical process. I came to America in 1973, and I know that from 1973 to 1997 the country has changed. When Americans say, "The country has changed so much," I agree with them, but I don't know how and in what ways. I would not be able to tell you what precisely has changed in the past ten or twenty years, even though I've been here all that time. But any American would be able to tell you right away, to name those changes because they are real for him. He notices the slightest shift in society. My case is a special one, of course. As a priest in a predominantly Russian parish, I live within the American society, yet also outside of it. New York is a special city, too. Nobody is at home here.

I entered the Orthodox seminary right after I moved to New York from Paris. It was an American Orthodox seminary. There was nothing Russian about it whatsoever. The only student to whom I could speak Russian was a black man who was interested in languages. His interest in Russian went so far that he eventually married a Russian princess of Russian-American heritage—who actually didn't speak a word of Russian. After I graduated from the seminary, I was given this Russian parish on Seventy-first Street and Third Avenue.

Serving in a church takes a lot of time and energy. People come to me with their confessions. They come to me for all kinds of advice. Many members of my parish are recent emigrants from Russia. Some of them are converted Jews; some are "converted" Russians—people who turned to Christianity at a certain moment in their lives. When I came to this parish in the late 1970s, there were still some Russian immigrants of the first wave, or their descendants, left in the church—I mean Russians who had fled the country after the Bolshevik revolution. Kerensky, the first minister of democratic Russia in 1917, was singing in our church chorus until his death in the late seventies. Balanchine attended our parish, too. Those were the last of the first generation of Russian immigrants in New York. Now they are gone, for the most part. The Soviet or post-Soviet immigrants came in their place: they constitute the majority of members of the parish. Because of this circumstance, even though the purpose of our parish is fundamentally religious, it also has to perform certain social functions—like bringing people together. People come here to practice their faith. The relationships formed in the community are like those in a family. Here people can find the warmth that they need so badly.

I view my experience of immigration as a positive one. It allowed me to begin life all over again. Early Christianity gave great importance to breaking all ties with one's family and environment. This was one of the first principles of Christian asceticism. But that's what also happens naturally to every immigrant: he leaves familiar ground to step into an unknown territory. It's a great spiritual challenge. Not everybody can survive it intact. It's particularly hard for a Soviet person: we all were raised to be conformists. But it's easier for a religious person: God is one and only, everywhere, in every language.

I am glad that I became a priest here, and not in Russia. I could not have served my church in Russia with the same commitment and freedom as I do here, just because the church there is not as free. For instance, last summer, in Russia, Father Kochetkov—a very prominent Orthodox priest and a missionary—was dismissed by the Patriarch. He was not allowed to conduct services in his parish, the parish that he himself had created. The reason for this severe punishment was that he had tried to slightly modernize the service, make it more comprehensible to the ordinary people. He would read parts of the New Testament during the service in Russian, rather than in ancient Slavic. As a friend in Russia put it years ago, "We have defeated the State, the Party, even the KGB. Now only the Church is left." And it's true. The Orthodox church is now one of the most rigid bureaucratic institutions left in Russia. Its structure hasn't changed since Stalin's time. It's a true relic of the old regime. So I appreciate being able to serve my church here, in a free country.

Yelena Mandel
From the Jewish Underground to Bankruptcy Law

WHEN she was six years old, Yelena's mother told her: "You should keep in mind that you are Jewish, so all the other kids will hate you." Brought up an atheist in Russia, Yelena became a Jewish activist in Moscow during the seventies. With her former husband, she studied Hebrew, then Jewish religion and history. They came to America in 1979, and both received degrees from the Jewish Theological Seminary, "mostly to learn how to be Jews," as she put it. An energetic woman, she became a social worker, then a lawyer. She now practices bankruptcy law in a high-profile law firm. She enjoys law for the challenge and the game. She feels she is well equipped to meet the challenge. As for the game, it is as if her life has prepared her for that. "I enjoy the feeling of estrangement. It allows me to experience reality on two levels at once."

I left Russia when I was twenty-four. I had graduated from the Teachers College in Moscow, where I studied in the Department of English. I lived all my life in Moscow. In 1975, I married my ex-husband. When he proposed, he told me: "You should know that I am not going to live here, I will definitely leave this country sometime soon. So, if you are not ready to come with me, you had better say 'no.'" I said "yes." But we didn't leave until 1979. Between 1975 and 1979 we led the very active life of underground Jewish radicals.

It happened accidentally: we had a friend in Moscow, a linguist who knew many languages and had decided to add Hebrew to his collection. He came to us one day and said, "Would you like to take Hebrew lessons together?" It seemed like an interesting idea, so we started to study Hebrew together, without thinking too much about it. Through those classes, however, we became involved in Jewish social and political life.

My ex-husband started to teach Hebrew himself. For about four years, we hosted a Jewish club in our apartment. Every Friday my husband and I would go to a synagogue and pick up some English-speaking Jewish foreigner who had come there just to meet Russian Jews. We would invite him to spend an evening at our apartment, where a crowd of twenty or thirty people would be waiting for us.

People came each Friday without an invitation. We would discuss Jewish themes with the guest in English. Many rabbis visited our home during that period, rabbis from America, England, South America. Our Fridays became more popular over time, and more and more people would come to the club. Most of these people planned to leave Russia. In addition to the club, I gave private English lessons. I had been doing it for many years. A synagogue sent me all the prospective emigrants who wanted to learn English. My family had never been traditional. On the contrary, my parents were extremely assimilated.

My Jewish education at home came down to one incident. When I was six and about to go to my first day in kindergarten, my mother told me: "You should keep in mind that you are Jewish, so all the other kids will hate you." That was all the warning I got. "And you must hate them, too," she added. She did not explain why or for what reason. She simply sent me out into the great world with this warning. I can't say that I always strictly followed her advice. But it made a big impression on me. I was always very well aware of the fact that I am Jewish.

Both my husband and I experienced anti-Semitism in Russia. We weren't accepted to university. I was warned against ever trying to get into university, but I told myself, "I should at least try, I would never forgive myself if I don't." I was eighteen then and silly enough to apply to the Department of History at Moscow University. The examination commission was clearly and explicitly trying to knock me down. They had to work hard, because I did know a lot; I had been an A student all my life. They asked me question after question, until finally they asked me something I couldn't answer; then, triumphantly, they gave me a grade of B. I was not accepted to the university. This was the kind of thing that happened to all the Jews. And I was prepared for it.

Much of my childhood was spent having physical fights with the other kids, mostly boys much larger than myself, who insulted me with pejorative words about Jews. Once I even got a concussion in a fight with a guy at a pioneer camp. This physical assault, along with my not being accepted to the university, were perhaps the only traumas I had suffered because of anti-Semitism. Of course, it felt bad not to be accepted—especially because the Department of History that year had accepted one of the worst students in my high school class.

But I did not know what Judaism meant until my early twenties, when my husband and I began to learn Hebrew, and then Jewish religion and history. Even though we felt very Jewish, we had never considered emigrating to Israel—maybe because our motivation for leaving was more political than ethnic. We had lived long enough in one socialist state—why move to another one.

So we did not want to go to Israel, but we did want to come to America and get a real Jewish education. That was the script. And we pretty much followed it. As soon as we arrived in America, we went to study at the Jewish Theological Seminary, the educational center of conservative Judaism in the country. Both of us graduated with the degree of Master of Jewish Theology. The year I received my master's degree in Theology was the first year that they admitted women to rabbinical school at the Seminary. I seriously considered attending rabbinical school, but then I changed my mind. We were the first Russians to study at the Seminary; plenty of Russian students came after us, but we were the first. And they wanted very much to ordain a Russian rabbi. They didn't consider me seriously for this "part," but they were very interested in my husband. They introduced him to other rabbis who kept talking to him about the wonderful life of a rabbi. But my husband did not attend the rabbinical school. Neither of us did. Still, they soon got their first Russian rabbi.

My husband started his classes at the seminary in our second week in New York. I began the following semester; somebody had to earn the money. My third week in America, I went to work as a secretary. I could speak English perfectly but it was about the only thing I could do. I didn't have any marketable skills. My husband had his degree in engineering, but he hated engineering with all his heart and was never going back to it.

We were studying at the Seminary mostly to feed our souls. The idea was to get a systematic Jewish education—to learn how to be Jews, so to speak. We didn't think of making it our profession, although my husband, while still a student, taught in various Hebrew Schools throughout New York and New Jersey. He was teaching Hebrew and Jewish History to American kids. How he did it remains a mystery to me: his English was almost nonexistent at that time.

I was working as a secretary at a small architectural firm. I had found this job through the *New York Times*. I studied the job listing thoroughly from my first day in America. I remember taking five interviews a week. The problem was that I couldn't type, couldn't do anything. The company that finally hired me was tempted not by my skills, but by the opportunity to pay me a very low salary. I received the minimum wage, which at that time was about $3.50 an hour. I worked there for six months, and then left to study at the Seminary. But I found a part-time position as a librarian in a big legal firm on Wall Street. I worked there for almost four years, all the while earning two graduate degrees.

While still at the Seminary, I realized I also needed to acquire a practical profession, one that would allow me to survive. The Seminary offered a joint program with the Department of Social Work at Columbia University. So I decided to enter this program. It seemed like a good idea. As a child I had loved to read Freud, so I'd be happy as a psychotherapist. So, after I received my degree in Theology, I went back to school for a master's degree in Clinical Social Work. Then I did in fact work as a psychotherapist at the Jewish Board of Family and Children's Services—in one of their clinics in Washington Heights, not far from where we lived; I could actually walk to work. Only one-third of my patients were Russian immigrants. The other two-thirds were immigrants from the Dominican Republic, elderly Orthodox German Jews, professors and students at Columbia University, the Irish who lived in Inwood—the diverse population that inhabited Washington Heights. The caseload was quite interesting.

But after four years, I was fed up with my job. I guess I am not a very compassionate person. Listening to complaints, other people's problems, was annoying after a while. My specialty was marriage counseling. The problems most couples have are pretty much the same. "If I hear about this problem one more time," I thought after a while, "I will beat my head against the wall." It became clear to me that I had to change my occupation. I went to law school. I must say, the credit for this ingenious idea—and it was truly an ingenious idea—belonged not to me, but, again, to my former husband.

By that time, he himself had graduated from law school and was working as a lawyer. He was convinced I was made to be a lawyer, and he almost forced me into law school. To me it was all a game—a game and a challenge. The idea was to figure out the rules of the game and to play by these rules. That was a lot of fun for me—figuring out the rules. I now work in a fancy law firm. Some people would kill for the job. It's the best. I fit into this world quite organically; I feel fluent and free in it. At the same time, I can't get rid of a feeling of estrangement, as if I were watching myself from the outside. I play the game so well that nobody but me can even tell it's a game. But I know it is, and I like that. I enjoy this feeling of estrangement. It allows me to experience reality on two levels at once.

When we first came to America, like most of the Russian immigrants—especially those who came here in the seventies—we held extremely conservative political views. For a while I used to write on Jewish topics for the *New American,* a Russian-language newspaper that was very popular in the Russian community. One article that I wrote was about Jewish conversion to Christianity. I wrote that most of the converted Jews are baptized out of ignorance: they don't know anything about Judaism and won't make an effort to learn, preferring the much less demanding and more clearly defined path to Christianity. This article caused a big scandal: half of the Russian immigrant population of New York stopped talking to me after it was published, and some of them still shun me.

But this is only half of the story. The other half was a person named Moishe Haim Levin, a Jew from Riga and a Lubavitch rabbi, who read the article and took a great interest in me. He offered me a job on a newspaper for Russian Jews that he was about to publish. He invited me to meet him at his home in Brooklyn. I went with my husband. During the first five minutes, we had a civilized conversation. But then he asked me, "How come you know so much about Judaism?" And I replied, "I am studying at the Jewish Theological Seminary." Well, what happened after that is hard to describe. For an ultra-Orthodox Jew, a Hasid, the conservative Jew is the worst. The rabbi accused us of being worse than other Russian Jews, who, he said, "are simply ignorant, and don't know any better." "But you," he went on, "you should know better." Then his wife appeared out of nowhere with an infant in her arms and started cursing at us, too. We left.

During my first six years in America, I was very religious, observing the Sabbath, keeping kosher. Now I eat pork again. After my divorce, I held a grudge against God and started eating pork. My approach to religion is now very American. I participate in many panels and commissions as a representative of Russian Jews; I've become a token Russian. In other words, my Jewishness is becoming a social responsibility, rather than a spiritual one.

I don't agree with many complaints of Russian immigrants that it's impossible to be close friends with Americans. I have some very close American friends—no less close than my Russian friends. My general impression is—and it could be an unfair judgment on my part—that Americans are, overall, more decent than Russians. They are more honest in their friendships—a quality that Russians, whom I dearly love, often lack. It's true of both business and personal relationships.

American women, for instance, would never steal your husband, but Russians could do it. Americans would never talk bad about you behind your back. I know for sure that my American girlfriends would never do that. As for my Russian girlfriends, I don't have the same certainty. If the occasion arises, they would gossip and with pleasure. On the other hand, I also lack this purity and idealism characteristic of Americans. I don't have it at all. I am more like the rest of the Russians.

I specialize in bankruptcy law. The subject is quite dry. But what I like about law, what attracts me the most, is, first of all, the intellectual thrill. It's like solving riddles in math. Law reminds me the most of algebra, which I used to love as a child. I've always liked logical paradoxes. Of course, there is a boring part to every job; but, for the most part, my job requires a lot of thinking. The other thing I like about it is that it pays very well. This combination of intellectual interest and good money, I think, is absolutely unbeatable.

Now there is a big demand for lawyers with knowledge of Russian. But unfortunately, not in my field, not in bankruptcy law. The greatest need is for corporate lawyers. Of course, I could change my profile, but that kind of job would require constant trips to Russia and dealing with the new class of Russian businessmen, which I really don't want to do. I've had some Russian clients during my eight years with the firm. And every time that I had to take a Russian client, I thought to myself, "Why am I doing this? I left Russia so that I'd never have to see these people again. Why do I need all this!"

A couple of years ago, I represented a Nikolaev aluminum plant sued by some companies in New York. The case had nothing to do with bankruptcy, but was assigned to me because the clients didn't speak English. It was a very unpleasant experience, having to communicate with the general director of the plant. At some point, I told him directly that he was an anti-Semite and that I hated to talk to him. I remember us shouting at each other for about an hour. Oddly enough, after this incident he seemed to develop some respect for me. But I'm trying to avoid these kinds of experiences as much as I can.

When I first came to America, I remember, it felt like being on Mars. America was not just another country, it was another planet. Everything was new and mysterious. I often miss this feeling, when perception was so keen. But, then, I like my present life. What I like the most is that I'm independent and self-sufficient. And I like that. I like it a lot.

ARTISTS

Mela Tannenbaum
A Musician's Journey

MELA decided to leave Kiev, where she was a soloist with the Kiev Philharmonic, following the devastating nuclear reactor explosion in Chernobyl. She recounts a Russian folktale about two frogs that fell into a milk jar: "One of them gave up immediately, saying 'there is nothing I can do,' and drowned. The other started moving around, trying to get out until she whipped the milk into butter. I wanted to be like this frog. I couldn't whip the butter yet, and I may never do it, but at least I'm trying." A virtuoso performer on three string instruments, Mela is once again a soloist, giving concerts throughout the world with a renowned chamber orchestra, the Philharmonia Virtuosi.

I was born in a small town called Chernovtsy. It belongs to the Ukraine now, but earlier it was part of Romania. In another time, as Czernowitz, it belonged to Poland and later to the Austro-Hungarian Empire. So it had a very special culture. Most of the people in this town could speak three languages and were highly educated. Aside from that, Chernovtsy was one of those Jewish towns that had its own Jewish professor, Jewish shoemaker, Jewish doctor, and even Jewish alcoholic. So I was raised in this very special environment, where I spent my childhood and part of my adult life. I studied at a music school in Chernovtsy. It was a very good school.

All of my former schoolmates now work as professional musicians in different parts of the world—some in Russia, some in Tel Aviv, and some in New York. The cultural differences between my native town and the rest of the Soviet Union were so immense that when I moved to Kiev to study in the conservatory in 1964, it was no less dramatic than my immigration to America. For instance, going to a concert was always a big event at Chernovtsy. People would prepare way in advance, thinking of what they would wear, how they would look. In Kiev, you could easily attend a concert wearing slippers, or a T shirt; it was a much more casual event.

It's not easy to explain why I decided to leave Kiev. We used to say it was because we were Jews. In truth, it was the Chernobyl disaster that completely turned our lives upside down. My children became sick after the explosion of the nuclear reactor in 1986. I thought we'd lose them. My eldest son was twenty-seven at the time, my daughter twenty-five, and my youngest son was ten. After the catastrophe in Chernobyl,* the general mood in Kiev was one of doom. People really felt hopeless. At first we expected measures to be taken to improve our living conditions, such as new apartments or raises in salary. But nothing happened. The authorities didn't spend a cent on social benefits. So we lost all hope of better living conditions. My family lived in a tiny apartment, and I had no room to practice. I wanted very much to leave, but that wasn't so easy.

I was a soloist with the Kiev Philharmonic. I went on wonderful tours and played with the best orchestras in the country. At a certain point, I made a deal with myself: that I'd never regret anything, even if I happened never again to play the violin. In the Soviet Union, musicians were always a privileged caste. The belief was that if you're an engineer, you were trained to become an engineer; but if you're a musician, you were born to be one.

Yet, after Chernobyl, we decided to leave the country. I left with my husband and children. Four days before our departure, I gave my last performance with the Kiev Philharmonic. So I had these fresh memories of the audience's applause. They all knew me and loved me. From the time I was a child, I remember being always

---

* On April 26, 1986, Chernobyl's number four reactor exploded, spewing a cloud of radioactive material across a swath of Europe in the world's worst civilian nuclear reactor disaster. Officials estimate that about 30 people were killed immediately and more than 15,000 people died in the emergency cleanup afterwards. Experts reckon that radiation equivalent to 500 times that released by the atom bomb dropped on Hiroshima was measured in the atmosphere around Chernobyl after the 1986 explosion.

surrounded by people, wherever I'd go. Part of it was language: I knew and loved my language, the Russian language, I could express myself with precision, express the slightest shade of meaning in this language. And now I was going to a country whose language I didn't know at all. I couldn't ask for a piece of bread in English. I knew German very well. I could have gone to Germany, like a lot of our friends from Chernovtsy. In Germany we would receive passports right away. They don't call Jewish immigrants "Jews" in Germany, they call them "German citizens who practice Judaism." I loathed those words the first time I heard them. Anyway, I couldn't seriously think of going to Germany.

We took a train from Kiev to Vienna. It was a peculiar experience. Imagine it: you throw your luggage, your suitcases, through the window into the train, and next to you in the compartment is a family of ten people, only three of whom are men. Two women are pregnant, and one of the men, the youngest, drinks nonstop. The oldest tries to carry the suitcases, but he's ninety-two years old so everybody shouts at him to leave the suitcases alone. But there is nobody else to carry those suitcases because the third man has no legs. So, all this: tossing the suitcases, children who are always ill on the road, overcrowded trains, kids looking for their parents. When we finally arrived in Vienna, we stood in this long line on the platform with the other immigrants, absolutely faceless, because what matters to a Soviet person is his passport, not himself. So, we were waiting on this platform, with my son lying ill on the trunks, and suddenly we saw a crowd coming out from the nearby opera house. The show had just ended. We saw all these dressed-up people, talking, and not laughing—Austrians don't laugh, they cackle, they roar. And I began to cry: it was actually the first time that I cried in my adult life. I had this piercing feeling that I'd never again play the violin, never again be on stage. But I knew I had made my choice.

We went to Italy. It happened that we spent five-and-a-half months in Italy. We had wanted to go to New York, but New York was overcrowded with immigrants at the time, so we had to wait in Italy. We spoke Italian relatively well. We lived in a house in the mountains, near Florence, with nine other immigrant families. There were all kinds of people: a shoemaker, musicians, engineers. There is one observation I made about Russian emigrants. When they had to write their résumés, describing the positions they held back in Russia, somehow they all turned into "supervisors." If someone was a shoemaker, he was a "supervisor-shoemaker." If he was a doctor, he was a supervisor-doctor. I remember my first English teacher in America once asking her students, "Why have things turned out so badly in Russia?" And I replied, using whatever bad English I had at the time: "Because all the supervisors have left."

Our Italian friends tried to talk us into staying in Italy. One of them owned a photo shop. He often visited us and heard me play. There was a man who belonged to Italian high society. The man owned an enormous estate, as well as coffee plantations in Brazil. He had graduated from the conservatory in Rome and considered himself an artist. He was a painter and a hunter. Anyway, he invited us to his home for dinner one evening. I'll never forget his mansion—all that land, a huge lake with white swans. He greeted us wearing tall leather boots and a hunter's hat with a feather—an artistic look. Two tables were set up: one was for his wife, the woman who had introduced us, some other couple, and my husband; the second table was for himself and me. There were two servants to take care of us. The women were all wrapped in white sheets, like tunics. After dinner, he took a brush and began to paint these sheets, their dresses. I felt as if I were in a Fellini movie, only this was much more ridiculous. After he finished painting the dresses, he told me, "Well, now, we can play some music." He sat at the piano. I took my violin. I thought I'd choke with laughter, but I had to accompany him. The women in painted dresses were sitting at his feet.

Eventually, we arrived in New York and settled in Brooklyn. We had friends living in Brooklyn, and they found us an apartment. Compared to our tiny apartment in Kiev, it seemed like paradise. Two of my cousins were born here, both doctors. Their father was the only one in the family who had emigrated to America before the Revolution. After he had immigrated, one of his sisters wrote him about how hard life in Russia was at the time. What she really meant, but couldn't spell out, was the threat of pogroms that was spreading. Her letter may have been a cry for help. But he hadn't understood and wrote back, "Don't think that life in America is easy, it's not." Five months later she was killed, buried alive with her five small sons. And he bore a burden of guilt throughout his entire life. "If at any time someone from Russia tells you that life in Russia is hard," he told his sons, "don't respond that it's hard here, too. Because what they mean by 'hard' is an entirely different thing."

My cousins are wonderful people, and they did their best to help us. I don't think they understood precisely what we were going through. Many Soviet people, when they come to America, are very needy. So I think they were scared a bit. But now, they're the ones who keep calling us, inviting us over, asking why we don't call them. Now they eagerly follow my tours with the orchestra.

From the beginning, I decided that I'd never be on welfare. I realized that if I said to myself, even just once, "Come on, relax, there's nothing bad about it," there would be no way out. I often recalled this Russian folktale about two frogs who fell into a milk jar. One of them gave up immediately, saying, "There is nothing I can do," and she drowned. The other started moving around, trying to get out, until she whipped the milk into butter. I wanted to be like this other frog. I couldn't whip the butter yet, and I may never do it, but at least I'm trying.

I remember my first job in America. I was supposed to hand out flyers on the bridge, above the Battery Tunnel. My English wasn't great at the time. I was supposed to pass out flyers to truck drivers. But I had never driven a car in my life. I couldn't tell a truck from a cab. My supervisor, an Indian guy, obviously didn't trust me very much. He stood next to me on this bridge, watching what I did. One time, a small car stopped next to me. It was so small that even I was able to notice it wasn't a truck. The driver asked me, "Can I have this paper?" And I said, "No, this is only for the truck drivers." He reached into his pocket. During the training session, we had all been warned that if somebody didn't want a flyer, we should never insist, because he could draw a pistol and shoot. So, when I saw that driver reaching for something in his pocket, I felt funny. But what he took out was a quarter. He handed it to me and said, "Lady, I'm giving you a good-citizen price. Take it and give me the paper." So I took the twenty-five cents and gave him the flyer. When I turned around, I saw the Indian guy laughing so hard he had to hold his stomach. Then he asked me, in this quiet, almost intimate voice: "Are you Jewish?" "How do you know?" I answered. "Only a Jewish person can sell something that nobody wants to take for free," he said, adding: "If you could sell this piece of paper, you will never be without a job."

That's another thing I came to realize: if you do something professionally, you've got to be paid for it. Otherwise, people don't take you seriously. In my first year here, I didn't understand it. I remember one day walking down the street in Brooklyn, carrying my instrument. A man approached and introduced himself as the director of a school orchestra. He asked me to play for the school but said he couldn't pay me: the school had no money and was trying to raise funds for its music program. I agreed. My husband and I gave a concert. The principal of the school was there, along with some people from the Board of Education. After the concert, they kept thanking and hugging me. A year later, an old friend told me that he had gotten a call from that school. They were looking for professional musicians who lived in Brooklyn. About a year earlier, they told him, two people had come to play in their school, and the concert helped them to raise money for the music program. But now that they could pay, they wanted professionals, not people from the street.

That taught us a good lesson. In Russia we had gotten used to barter: you don't pay the doctor for treating you and he doesn't pay you for playing the violin. Or a neighbor asks you to give music lessons to her son, and you refuse the money; so she brings you a box of chocolates instead. But here it's different: if you don't accept money, then people think you're not a professional musician. The more money you take, the better they think that you play.

I never stopped practicing. And then I met a woman, an organist. She suggested that we ask the Chamber Music Society to arrange a concert for us. They asked us for a tape, a professional recording. The recording was very expensive, fifty dollars for an hour of work. For me, at the time, it was a lot of money. But we agreed and decided to share the cost. We found a sound engineer who had a studio, a Russian who had lived here for seventeen years. I'll be grateful to him for the rest of my life—and my future life, too. Everything good that happened to me in the next five years, I owe to him. We had arranged to make the recording in a small church in Queens. My friend was playing the organ; I was playing viola d'amore. We had hoped to finish recording in an hour, playing nonstop, so that it wouldn't cost more than fifty dollars. As soon as we began to play, he stopped us and asked for my name. "You don't have to pay me anything, Mela," he said. "I'll pay you, just to hear you play." So we made the recording and sent it to the manager of the Chamber Music Society. Of course, he never even listened to the tape.

But I was lucky. It happened that this sound engineer, Misha Liberman, was listening to the tape in his studio when he had a visit from the orchestra conductor that I'm working with now. The conductor heard the tape and asked who it was. Misha told him about me. The conductor said, "I would like to meet this woman." And we met. Because I played the viola d'amore on the tape, he was convinced I was a violist. "I'm very impressed with your playing," he said. "Would you play just a few notes for me?'" And I did. After I had finished, he asked me to play with his orchestra in two weeks. It was the Philharmonia Virtuosi, one of the finest chamber orchestras in New York. I hadn't told him I could play the violin.

I gave solo concerts, playing both viola and viola d'amore. But one day—the way it happens in Hollywood—the concertmaster became sick, and there was nobody to play first violin. "It's too bad you don't play the violin," the conductor said. And I replied, "Of course I play the violin." He was so surprised that I'd kept it a secret for two years. But I couldn't tell him any sooner. Competition was so intense among the musicians, and I felt I was, well, too strong for them. I couldn't just say, "Here I am, and I can play violin and viola and viola d'amore." They would have killed me. You have to respect the rules, especially if you're in another country. Anyway, it has worked out well. I've been playing with the Philharmonia Virtuosi for five years now.

What I learned in this country is that one has to work hard in order to achieve something. Another thing I learned is that so much is left to chance—as Americans put it, "being in the right place at the right time." Because the competition is so tough, being good at something is not always good enough.

I travel a lot now, touring with the orchestra. We've been to the most remote parts of the world. What we've seen in these past five years is enough to last a couple of lives. So I don't have any regrets. Still, I miss Russia terribly. I miss the snow especially. But I have a house in Canada now. I went to Canada two years ago and found this house on an island. Suddenly, there was everything I remembered so well from my childhood—only here it wasn't scary. I decided it was time to stop being frightened. There is always a place for snow in your life. It doesn't have to be in Russia.

Vladimir Kanevsky
"Parasite" and Sculptor

WE *sit in his loft in Jersey City, which serves both as Vladimir's apartment and studio. The studio takes up most of the space. He's in his late forties, but looks much younger. Vladimir talks about his career, in which he has reinvented himself time and again—first as an architect, then makeshift archaeologist, painter, ceramicist, and cultural bureaucrat in Leningrad, and eventually—a sculptor. Arrested while attending an underground lecture on Jewish culture, he was registered as a parasite. Then he rose to become the director of a prominent art cooperative, though the KGB was still inquiring about him. He came to the United States in 1989. "I believe that only pressure—be it moral, physical, or intellectual—can move a person forward," he says. "Immigration involves all three."*

I can't say why I left Russia. For a long time, I tried to convince myself that the only reason I did not leave was that the Soviet authorities wouldn't let me go. In fact, that was just an excuse. The fact is that I had a pretty good life for myself: a beautiful apartment, a car, and I was doing what I liked to do. Mostly, I was doing sculpture—very bad sculptures, I realize now. But life was good then, it was wonderful.

I had the opportunity to participate in new business enterprises, so during the first years of perestroika, I had the chance to become rich, too. But there was something in the air—the smell of gunpowder, anti-Semitic gunpowder. Suddenly, it was all right to say out loud things that earlier you could only hear whispered behind your back, somewhere on a tram, or waiting in line for watermelons. Suddenly, I was reading it in the newspapers.

And it made me feel funny. I remember one of my close friends, Vova Shaposhnikov, an excellent architect, telling me then: "Anti-Semitism in Russia will never take over, because the Communists will never allow it to happen. As long as the Soviet Union exists, nationalists have no chance to win." And then my wise, clairvoyant friend added, "And the Soviet Union will last forever, because the Communists will never let it be destroyed." Well, he was wise, my friend Shaposhnikov, but in this case his prophecy proved to be wrong.

Finally, I decided that it was time to leave, and I began doing a lot of talking. But, my wife preferred action to talking; actually, I never *would* have emigrated. I recall the morning when we left our apartment holding the visa applications we had filled out the previous night. We were heading for OVIR, the Visa and Immigration Department. It was a moment of truth. Once you submit an application to OVIR, there is no way back. So, it was quite hard for me to leave my luxurious apartment that day, turn the key in the expensive lock on the door, then press the button to summon the elevator, the absolutely noiseless, new elevator in our new luxury apartment building.

It arrived. My wife and I stepped inside and saw two enormous men with enormous bellies. They were probably the movers who had just carried a piano to the apartment upstairs. So we stood there, our heads at the level of their stomachs. And suddenly I heard one of them telling the other, "So he was a *Yid*, you said?" And he burst out laughing. That happened at the same moment that I was hesitating about taking the documents to OVIR. I think it was God, Himself, trying to tell me something. In a moment, my hesitation was gone.

Leaving Russia at that time, in 1989, wasn't difficult. In fact, it was a pleasure. The paperwork went so smoothly. I remember I had to get a letter from the Military Commandant's office giving me permission to leave the country. I had served in the army. I was a senior lieutenant in the reserves. Naturally, on the way to the commandant's office, I was shaking a bit. I didn't expect them to be happy with the fact that I was emigrating. When I got there and approached the receptionist, she looked at me, and said rudely, "Sit down and wait." I tried again, and then she asked, without even listening, "What do you want?" I said, "Well, you know I'm leaving for Israel, and I need this letter." At which point she suddenly smiled and said, "Oh, yes, of course. Come here, it'll be ready in a second." And it was ready in a second. Handing me the papers, she smiled again, saying, "Have a nice trip."

Then I had to inform my bosses at work. How I came to get that job is a story in itself. I had gotten that job through the police department. I had been working as an architect. It was my first occupation, and I'm still very fond of it. At that time, I loved it. I lived in the Ukraine, in Kharkov. I was an active young architect, a member of the Union of Architects. I won awards. I was so good that I was accepted at the Lenproject Institute in Leningrad. In one day, I went from being a promising young talent to a white-collar worker in a room with some ladies who spent their working hours knitting. I was bored to death. I tried to entertain myself by making drawings; there was no real work for me. I designed the blueprints for the Ship Station Building in Leningrad, but nobody consulted them. The construction people never even unfolded the plans.

I decided to find a new job. It was a third-rate institute, not at all prestigious like Lenproject, but it was the only institute in Leningrad posting an ad at the gates that said "Architects Needed." They couldn't believe that a person with my credentials would go to work for them; they thought something was wrong with me. But they took me. On my first day at work, however, my boss gave me a kind of embarrassed look, and told me: "You know, we don't need architects anymore." When the personnel department reviewed my questionnaire, they discovered I was Jewish. I went to a lawyer and asked, "Can I sue them?" "Of course you can, but you'll lose," he replied. I couldn't go back to my old job.

It was summertime. I was recruited for an archaeological expedition that a friend was putting together at the time. I was hired as a ditch digger, painter, and architect—all three in one. We were digging out a seventeenth-century ironworks. We lived in the monastery, in what had been the monks' cells. The diggers and restoration people were heavy drinkers who drank raw alcohol that was intended for restoration. The air in the cells was so stuffy from alcohol and tobacco that I slept with my head sticking out the window. Every day, going to bed at night and waking up in the morning,

I confronted the same terrifying image: a blue-faced restoration worker with a container of the diabolic mixture in his hands, who leaned over me, whispering, "Have a few drops with me, brother."

We finished the excavation pretty fast and began to look for something else to do. There were plenty of old monasteries around, and almost all of them had been turned into mental hospitals. We started to visit these facilities, one after another, offering our services as artists. Most of the work assignments were to paint entrance signs. I made the signs, and my friends handled the negotiations. We were doing well. It was an incredible journey. I remember the director of a mental hospital, who pointed to huge barrels of pickles stored in the basement. They were for the patients. "Well, you're artists, can you make barrels like that?" he asked. "No, we can't," we said. He became very upset, repeating: "What am I to do? There are more and more fools, and fewer and fewer barrels." In preparing to emigrate, I often recalled these words.

I came back to Leningrad, still without a job. One day, soon after I returned, a friend called to tell me about a gathering: "A group of people who study Jewish culture are giving this lecture, an underground lecture on the Jews in Spain. You want to come?" The apartment was somewhere on the outskirts of the city. Three minutes after the start of the lecture, the doorbell rang. Forty men, some dressed in uniform, others in civilian clothes, stormed into the room. First they occupied the balcony to block any escape route.

They began to photograph the people in the room. People reacted in different ways: some stuck their tongues out, some posed in front of the cameras, and others hid under the sofas. Then the most experienced people, mature dissidents, told us, "Join hands, form a circle, men in the outer circle, women and children inside. Don't let them provoke you." And they began to sing soulful Jewish songs. It looked like a scene from a heroic old Soviet movie: Bolsheviks arrested by the police. The policemen shouted, "Shut up! Quit singing!" But the singing grew louder and louder. One girl in the room was provoked, and she slapped a policeman in the face. They grabbed her, gladly, by the arms, put her in a car, and took her away.

We were all taken outside. By that time, a large crowd of Russians, mostly neighbors, had gathered. And as Russians always feel compassion for victims of authority, the crowd was shouting: "Don't give up, friends! Keep up your courage!" Then someone in the crowd asked, "Why are they taking you, guys?" And someone replied, "Because we are Jews."

At once, the crowd changed its opinion. "You got what you deserved!" we heard. "Should have gotten it long ago!" One old woman was particularly eloquent: "Go to your Israel and we will stay here and eat bread, drink water, and dance," I remember her saying. We were taken to the police station. One of the questions I was asked was "Your place of work?" "Won't tell you," I replied. "Okay," they said. "That means nowhere." I was registered as a parasite. I was given a month to find a job; otherwise, I was told, I'd get a year in prison, followed by permanent exile. I was young and foolish. I made no attempt to find a job.

The last day of the month, sitting in a friend's apartment, I heard the telephone ring. It was my father. "A new design enterprise is opening up," he told me. "Do you know how to draw?" "Yes, I do," I lied. The next day, I went to an interview. I was waiting in line with many artists.

They asked for our portfolios. I didn't have one. But I had a badge from the Union of Architects pinned to my chest. And the man who interviewed me noticed it: "OK, you're fine." The next day I went to work, and the other employees-painters-alcoholics gave me a lesson on how to mix paint. That was how I began working at the Art Design Enterprise.

It was an absolute catastrophe, because none of my work was accepted by the enterprise's artistic board. The general rule was that you made a sketch of whatever you were working on, you presented it to the artistic board, and you got their approval. But I couldn't make a sketch on my own because I couldn't draw. So, mostly I did errands for the other painters, shopping for them, buying vodka and cigarettes. One day, I came to my boss in a state of complete despair and asked if there was any work for me. I needed money and we worked on a contract basis, from project to project. She told me that she had an assignment to design 36-foot-high windows for a popular bar. "You can have it if you want," she said.

I had to come up with an idea for the design. I thought to myself: why not do the windows in ceramics? Now that I have some experience with ceramics, I would never attempt a thing like that, because I know how much work it takes. But at that time, I was absolutely ignorant, and therefore audacious. I was ready to do it, but I lacked two things: first, space with equipment, materials, and a hearth; and, second, any idea about how to do it. So I put together a team consisting of two friends, one who had a studio and another who could mold. But the team fell apart. I couldn't bring us all together at the same time. While I was chasing them around the city, the months passed by. I began to panic.

One day, in a state of complete despair, I took a piece of clay and began to mold something. I made a figure of a man. I had done some sculpture in college, but I had always failed. But this time I molded this little figure, and suddenly I liked it. Then I began to create more compositions, some quite abstract. My mother, who had come to visit me, once looked over my shoulder at what I was doing and said, "Well, this looks pretty good." I was encouraged. I finished a few more compositions. Now I had to present them to the artistic board.

When I brought my work to the board, I felt quite ashamed. It seemed so infantile. But a miracle happened: I was standing in a corner of the room with my work, hiding from people's sight, and suddenly the director of the artistic board noticed my ceramics: "And what is this? Looks beautiful," he said. He was the one who had kept on rejecting my work, and I was convinced then that he hated me. He looked at it from afar, then came closer, and began to praise my work. "Approved," I soon heard. I was shocked. But I finished the project, got paid, and suddenly I had lots of money in my hands. But that was only the beginning.

One day, I came home and found my mother waiting. I had gotten a call to come to a meeting of the artistic board. "You're a member of the board now," she said. I didn't believe her, but I went, just in case. "Here you are," they told me. "Well, sit down and make yourself comfortable." In a few days, I had moved from the least of the artists to the first in the enterprise. I felt weird and a little embarrassed in front of the other painters whose errands I'd been running: now I had to approve or reject their works.

Two weeks later, the director of the board quit, and I was offered his position. I tried to decline, since I had never done anything like that before. I went for advice to my uncle, a prominent Soviet architect: he had designed most of Lenin's monuments in Russia and abroad. A member of every artistic board and panel in the country, he told me, "Of course you should accept. It's a big honor." I accepted. The next three years were very productive: I worked a lot, made my first sculptures—and it was great fun.

I had a great deal of responsibility. Our company was the major design enterprise in Leningrad, affiliated with the city's Department of Cultural Affairs. We designed all the big political events, including anniversary parades. For instance, the draft of the design of the Palace Square for the November parade had two signatures: that of Romanov, mayor of the city at the time, and mine.

One day, I held a board meeting in the conference room: we had to make a decision about an important project. It's quiet in the room. People are afraid to talk too loud. It's such a charged moment. I'm making my directorial speech, and in the next room, the telephone rings: it's from the police department.

They called to find out if the parasite Kanevsky worked here. And then they began to ask questions from their questionnaire: Is he a good worker? Does he behave well? Does he drink? Does he come to work on time? Does he miss any days? Does he have contacts with foreigners? In our country the right hand is not always aware of what the left is doing. Parasite Kanevsky and big boss Kanevsky were the same person, but nobody knew that.

Then came perestroika. I suggested that the artistic board be elected, not appointed. We held the first elections. I can say, with pride, that I was elected director of the board. I should also say, and without any pride, that it probably happened because I was a very malleable director.

I decided we should escape from under the wing of the Department of Culture. So, two of my deputy directors and I called on the director of the Department of Cultural Affairs. I had never come across this type of person before. It took me some time to realize that I was in a wolf's den. At the meeting, I began to speak about our rights as a collective: I was quoting a new law on workers' collectives that had recently been adopted. And the director looked at me like I was a fool and said, "Yes, the law was adopted. But it's not enforced yet. It has no power." And I began to blush, mumbling, "Well, how can that be? The law was adopted, and published, and signed." And he looked at me, listening with a great attention, nodding, and giggling quietly. I realized at that moment that my previous understanding of the mechanism of Soviet power was wrong: it wasn't Brezhnev or Gorbachev pulling the strings; it was this enormous, immovable boulder of bureaucracy beneath them. That was the first time that I could see it with my own eyes, feel it with my fingers: it was right there, in front of me, giggling in my face.

A few days later, the director came to our meeting at work. After the meeting, he took me aside and told me, confidentially: "What Gorbachev is doing is rubbish, really nonsense." He was talking to me about a general secretary of the USSR, and in such a casual manner, with no fear at all. I realized at that moment that perestroika would never succeed. Either Gorbachev would be overthrown, as Khruschev was in his time, or the whole system would come tumbling down on our heads. There was no third way.

Because of my position, the KGB wanted me to inform on other artists. I was offered a studio in exchange for my services. I remember the KGB officer, waiting for me one day near my car after work, telling me: "Oh, great, you're driving today, why don't you give me a ride?" I had to give him a ride. On the way, he said, "And, by the way, the studio we were talking about—it's right around the corner. Why don't we go up and take a look?" And I had to go with him and take a look. It was torture for me because the studio was stunning—it was really gorgeous. The only problem was that I could never agree to accept it. I could have run into big problems with the KGB. But perestroika happened, and the KGB officer disappeared. He dissolved in the air like a ghost at dawn.

When I came to New York, one of the first things I bought was a kiln. My second day here I noticed an ad: "Artists to make porcelain flowers needed." I decided it might take me some time to become a famous sculptor. Meanwhile, this thing might help me to get by. So I called the number in the ad and went to Hoboken to see those people. They showed me a picture and asked, "Can you do it? Do you know how to work with porcelain?" "Yes, of course," I said, lying once again. After that I went home and experimented for a month and a half, until I learned how to make porcelain flowers. Of course, I could have gone to the library and found a book on porcelain technique and read it, even with a dictionary; it would have made my life much easier. But I decided to reinvent the whole thing.

So I made my samples and took them back to Hoboken to show to my potential employers. They seemed absolutely shocked, and I thought it was because they didn't like my work. But I was wrong. They had been looking for four years for the right person until I showed up. After I started working for the company, I brought in a bunch of Russian artists. Soon, the entire staff was filled with Russians: they asked for less money and did more work. Doing those porcelain flowers was my main income; it was how I made my living for years. In between the porcelain, I did my sculpture.

As soon as I got to America, I realized that everything I had done before as a sculptor was provincial and sloppy. I saw a new world, and it changed my vision entirely. It was like coming out of a greenhouse into the open air—suddenly seeing the real sun shining. Everything is different here, somehow; the sky is vaster. Everything is bigger, even the soda glasses. These things affect you.

I learned how to cope with the new world artistically. At first, I was completely confused. When I now look at the sketches I made at that time, I have no idea what it was I was thinking. They look so bizarre and crazy. But, little by little, I was getting somewhere. In 1992, I finally made my first decent work, entitled *Kouros*. It was bought by the museum at Duke University. It's still my best work, I believe; I haven't done anything better.

I'm happy I left Russia for two reasons. The first one, and it's something I've come to realize very recently, is that America is a great country, an exciting country to live in. Some Russian immigrants complain that Americans are not intelligent enough, that they're vulgar. They just don't know this country well enough. Or they haven't met the right people. Sometimes people who complain don't even know the language, so when they complain it's like saying: "We couldn't find any mushrooms because it was too dark in the forest."

Also, I'm glad I left Russia because the tremendous shakeup of moving was the most important thing that happened to me in my life. Nothing can compare to it—threats of being thrown in jail, or anything else I went through in Russia, and I've gone through some serious stuff. Nothing can be compared to this feeling: you stand alone, and you own nothing but what you wear. I believe that only pressure—be it moral, physical, or intellectual—can move a person forward. Immigration involves all three. What doesn't kill you makes you stronger.

We Russians always have to judge everything. Something Americans would never do. Americans classify things, but Russians judge. When a Russian sees a bad show on TV, he thinks: "This is an awful show. Children in this country watch those shows, which is why they join gangs, kill their parents, and so on. This is an awful country, because there are such awful shows on TV." An American watches a bad show and thinks: "Well, this show is pretty bad. I would give it a C." And that's it.

This desire to judge makes the life of Russian immigrants here much harder. Being thrown into new surroundings, and not having the time to get to know them, they immediately jump to conclusions. It's like trying to guess what's under the blanket by lifting a corner. But those of us who read, watch, and listen soon realize that life here is diverse. One of the most important things for every immigrant to understand is that there is no such person as an American, just as there is no such person as a Russian. There are many different kinds of people. And a big country like America has everything in it; you can find everything for every taste. You just have to find your own niche. And after you've found it, you discover it's much deeper, cleaner—intellectually and ethically cleaner—than the most comfortable niche you had in Russia. Because this society is much more honest. Despite all the lies you have to listen to here, it's more honest than Russia ever was.

Eteri Shkodua
Painter with an Attitude

ETERI lives on Bleecker Street in New York. Her studio is the living room of her first-floor apartment. One of her paintings is on the wall: two large naked figures, a man and a woman, he is black, she is white. Solid colors, bold composition. The painting is simple, yet enigmatic—passionate and alienating at once. Originally from Georgia in the Caucasus, once part of the Soviet Union, Eteri married an American years ago. When she and her husband separated, she moved to New York to make it on her own as an artist. Her first show—in Chicago—opened to great reviews. Now thirty-five and a meticulous painter of noncommercial works that "are not easily sold or dealt," Eteri is still determined to earn a living from her art. "In America," she observes, "you have to be a salesperson: everything is for sale. And I'm just an artist."

My life was pretty good back in Georgia. I grew up in Tbilisi, where I completed the Arts Academy as a painter. I was supported by my parents, so I didn't have to worry about money or an apartment, as did most young people in Georgia. But in 1988, I met and married an American linguist. We met in Tbilisi. You see, if I didn't happen to marry my husband, I would never have left Georgia, because I had no reason to emigrate. My family wasn't Jewish, so we wouldn't be able to leave as Jewish emigrants. And I wasn't politically oriented. Life was pretty exciting in Georgia at that time. Perestroika had just taken off. I remember the demonstrations in Tbilisi. People were trying to change things, and that was exciting.

I was twenty-three years old when I left Tbilisi. Through my friends there I had met this very wonderful person. So I never had to look for papers or for a place to stay. We lived at his father's place in Chicago. My husband made a good salary, and we basically lived like normal young people starting out in life.

We loved each other. It was not a marriage made for the immigration papers, or anything like that. He was my first great love and an ideal one: everything was the way it should be. When my husband was invited to work at the University of Tokyo in Japan, I followed him and stayed for a few months. But the culture was too different. I couldn't learn Japanese. Most of the time, I stayed in the apartment and painted. I felt very isolated. It was difficult to live in a society where I couldn't speak the language, where I had no friends except my husband's colleagues—and they weren't big entertainers. It was great to be with my husband—just the two of us, in a different country. It brought us even closer together. But then, in 1989, I had to return to Chicago to meet my father and brother, who were coming to visit. I thought I would stay just for a few months. But I stayed longer. My husband and I saw each other less and less.

Then I had my show in Chicago, and it was very successful; there were great reviews in the Chicago newspapers. All the paintings in the show sold for a total of about $153,000. And then I got a teaching job at a college in Santa Barbara. So, things were looking very good for me. I became very spoiled. I didn't worry at all about how to support myself since it had all happened so easily—I mean, not easily, I was working a lot—but there was such a great response to my work. So I moved to New York.

I lived on this money for three years. But now the money is gone. You see, I don't produce a lot of work. I do about three or four paintings a year. And that creates certain problems. My manager keeps telling me—and other people say the same—that the paintings are expensive because of the amount of time they consume. I have to make out somehow. I have to pay for studio space, for materials. I have to be able to create noncommercial art. My paintings are not easily sold, or easily dealt, and I don't make enough of them. But all I do is paint. This is my daily life.

Sometimes I manage to put money together by selling a painting, and I can live on this money for a while. I don't really care about the money when I have it. But there are times when I don't have enough money to buy food or to pay for my apartment. Life is expensive in New York.

After my first show, I thought I'd make so much money that I could raise the price of my paintings. I thought I'd be able to hire people to work for me. But now that seems impossible. The paintings are not selling well in New York. Now I'm talking to my Chicago gallery about doing a show there.

When I first came to America, I didn't have expectations. I was observing life and learning, moment by moment. One thing I resented from the beginning, though, was the work ethic here—the attitude toward work. People push so hard here. Living becomes so much about working. This work ethic is an American myth constantly held up to me, regularly discussed in newspapers and magazines. From the beginning, I felt it was fake. I don't think that work deserves so many sacrifices: time, friendships—eventually everything—just so you can get your own car and your own house.

I look at my friends who immigrated and had to take any odd job. They come from very good families. In Georgia they always had something to eat, nice apartments. I know they were very disappointed, because they thought life here would be even easier than in Georgia, but it isn't. I saw people going out of their minds desperately trying to balance their psyche and pay their bills at the same time.

But they don't want to go back because they still have hope—this dream of America as a wonderful place. Besides, they grew accustomed to the internationalism, the universality, of life in New York, where you can get to see everything, and so much is going on. It's hard to leave this place. Once you get involved in this culture, any other place would seem like going back to the Middle Ages. But this feeling of being in the center of events is fake, too. Because you may end up just sitting in your room, not seeing what's happening around you, just sitting in your room and working. Still, you have this illusion that you're getting something—some information you'd be missing somewhere else. So, if it's important for you to know what's happening in the world, you wouldn't want to leave New York. But again, it involves such sacrifice to live here, such constant work, that an individual who does try to achieve this American dream eventually becomes a slave.

There are some people who are much better skilled at making money. They will do anything for money—compromise friendships, compromise everything, not care about anybody. Their culture, their families, taught them how to bargain. For Georgians, such a way of life is disgusting. In Georgia, we were taught to spend money, not to save it, not to bargain. Bargaining was considered low. So now, when I try to negotiate, it ends up being to the advantage of the other person, because I give up. I'd rather not bargain at all. But, in America, you have to be a salesperson. Everything is for sale. And I'm just an artist. I don't have business or marketing skills. I don't want to do any of this stuff. But maybe I have to change if I want to stay here. Maybe I should start thinking of marketing myself. Or maybe I should leave.

But my life is here. In the time I've lived here, I've met a lot of different people. I have had friendships, relationships, with all kinds of people—people of different races, different social and economic backgrounds. Like me, people who come to New York were often foreigners in their own culture. You end up in a place where everybody is like that.

I was always accepted and loved back in Georgia. But I was never an ordinary Georgian woman—maybe because I've painted since early childhood, and that spoiled me in a way. I was much freer than most other women in the way I talked and behaved. I found a lot of the values in Georgia old-fashioned. Georgia is a small country where people lived mostly to enjoy life, and not to work hard. Work was a small part of life: you had to do it to survive, but you didn't have to overwork yourself. You could meet a lot of people there who didn't make much money, but they read a lot. You could spend your life just thinking or talking. Here, even if you're a big lawyer or something, you work your ass off. I don't think it's necessary. People should have time for home and friends. I think there is a large deficit of human values here.

Language changes your personality. When I speak English, people feel that I'm exotic. My accent and the timbre of my voice are so characteristically Georgian, this deep, low voice. My behavior is more emotional than is the custom here. For a Georgian person, this is nothing; it's just the way we express ourselves. But, here, it brings unnecessary attention and compliments—like when you really are up to business matters, and you're speaking with a man who is attracted to you because you talk in this peculiar way and you're from a country that he can't even find on the map.

Or welcoming guests, for instance. When I have guests, I take it as my responsibility to entertain them. That was always a big part of Georgian culture, the Georgian mentality. Georgian life was a lot about hospitality, how to make guests feel welcome. This hospitality of mine makes some people feel special. People who understand that enjoy it, and they eventually become good friends. But with some people, you have to be defensive. You can quickly attract someone's attention, but it can be the wrong kind of attention.

When I think of the future, there are a couple of things I want to have: I want to have health insurance, that's for sure. And I want to have a place of my own. I don't want to be without a child when I'm an old woman. That's what I want. It may not happen. As an artist, it's hard to predict anything.

Mark Kopelev
The Tailor

MARK lives in Washington Heights in New York City. Photographs hang in abundance on the walls of his big, comfortable studio apartment: portraits, still lifes, abstract compositions. He turned to photography to fill in a creative void in his life. He is in his fifties now. Having become a tailor in Russia with the help of the KGB, he currently works in the costume shop at the Metropolitan Opera in New York. From theater, film, and TV director to tailor and photographer, he finds joy in life's twists. "One of the big discoveries I made about myself as an immigrant," he says, "is that I can live without recognition."

To be frank, in the seventies, when everybody around me was talking of emigrating, I didn't think about it at all. I was doing my job, directing films. Of course, there was some friction with the KGB. That was inevitable for any more or less intelligent person. Because an active mind, a sense of irony with regard to what was going on around you, that was already a potential threat to Soviet power. No jokes on these grounds were acceptable. And I happen to like jokes. During my college years, I used to participate in what we then called "cabbage shows," very popular satire, quite biting at times. I moved to Ryazan, 140 miles from Moscow, after my graduation. The Ryazan Children's Theater requested that I be assigned to them. I directed a couple of shows, all of which were closed down by the city authorities.

All of my work for theater seemed to have some kind of ideological flaw. One of the shows I directed was "Konyok Gorbunok" (The Little Horse-Hunchback) by Yershov. It's a fairy tale, and as such seems quite harmless. Well, I guess it's not as harmless as it seems. I remember the quotation from Belinsky, "A tale reflects the soul of a nation." I began to think about the tale from this point of view: what does it say about a nation's soul?

Take "The Brave Tailor," a German tale. The tailor there is doing his work, then he sees flies on the table, hits them, and kills seven flies with one blow. So he thinks for a while and comes up with a slogan—"Can kill seven with one blow"—embroiders it on his belt and takes off on a journey. Or take a French tale: "Jean the Simpleton." Jean is working in the mill. His father dies, and the three brothers divide the inheritance: one gets the mill, another gets a donkey, and Jean gets a cat. He's out of business, so what's the use of a cat? So he goes off on a journey with his cat, and the cat helps him out along the way—but still, he does everything on his own.

Now, what does Ivan the Fool in the Russian tale do? He sits on the wood stove. That's all. He's a good fellow. When asked, he'll bring water or look after the fields. He won't take the initiative, but he will do what he has to do. And in doing it—in taking this one-time action—he manages to catch fortune by the tail, be it a Horse-Hunchback or a Pike-Fish or the Gray Wolf, or Vasilisa the Wise. The essence of any Russian tale is to catch the bird of luck by the tail, without putting any effort into it. Then, there's this thing about brothers. Jean's brothers, you see, don't try to harm him. He's doing his thing and they are doing theirs. But, in a Russian tale, Ivan always has two malicious brothers: the envious, smart one and the envious, dumb one. And they do all sorts of bad things to him, like stealing his magic horse, for example. They never leave him alone.

Ivan, as usual, doesn't do anything. The horse does everything for him. All Ivan does is cry, or make trouble, like picking up the Firebird's feather when the horse tells him not to. So that was my concept: the horse is working for Ivan, and Ivan is building a good career, moving higher and higher, to the very top, and getting more and more spoiled along the way. Because, like any career that hasn't been earned, it leads to degeneration. That came across very clearly in my production. Ivan was becoming increasingly presumptuous and impudent in using his horse's services, losing any sense of shame. And, in the end, when Ivan was sitting next to the Czar's throne, the horse was forgotten and forsaken. It had done its job; Ivan didn't need it anymore. When the show opened, it created a big scandal in the city, and the theater broke out into two opposing camps—those who supported the show and those who opposed it.

I decided that it was time for me to leave Ryazan. I thought I would go back to Leningrad, where my parents lived at the time. But then I was summoned by the KGB and warned that I could live anywhere except major cities like Moscow and Leningrad. So I couldn't return to Leningrad. I went to Chita, in eastern Siberia, instead. And I started to work for a television station. Chita was a small city, and I soon became a big person there: I was a TV director, a rare profession at the time, and I came from Leningrad. People knew me. Soon the director of the Film and Television Committee transferred me to the film division. He liked me, or at least valued me as a competent professional. That was always the case in my relationships with authorities: they never liked me, but they respected my work.

So I began making films—documentaries mostly. I liked it. Unlike theater or feature films, documentary filmmaking allowed me to do what I wanted, without having to make compromises with my conscience—to do it quietly, so to speak. This was because the authorities controlled documentaries less strictly than other media. I was winning prizes for my work. Then, one day, I was brought to the KGB right from the studio and held there for the rest of the day. At first I didn't understand what was going on. They were asking me questions, like "What do you think about Solzhenitsyn?" or "Is it true that you were talking about anti-Semitism in Russia?" So I answered them: yes, anti-Semitism exists among some people, but not as a state policy. I had read Solzhenitsyn's works, but only those that were published in the official press. But, all the while, I could sense that there was something else.

When I was about to leave, they suddenly asked: "Have you seen Litvinov lately?" Litvinov was a dissident, whose trial had just taken place. He happened to be married to my cousin. I was making a documentary around that time, a film about miners. We were shooting it at a small mine, near a village called Ussugli, an isolated place surrounded by prison camps. And it happened that Litvinov was doing his time in one of those camps, right near Ussugli. But the thing was, while he was serving his term in this camp, in a place so remote that you couldn't get there by plane or any other regular transportation—there's no direct road leading to the place—the Voice of America, a radio station, was providing daily updates on his life in the camp. So, naturally the KGB suspected an information leak, and was looking for its source. I didn't know anything about it. But they made the connection right away: I was doing my film in Ussugli, Litvinov was in the camp in Ussugli, and he was my relative. It could not have been a coincidence. Anyway, I was interrogated—again and again. After my first "visit" to the KGB, I was fired from my job. I mean, I was asked to resign. That's the way it was done in the seventies.

I went into amateur theater. And I suddenly started to make big money. I worked with a group of students from the Professional Technical School. We had a musical director, a choreographer. I was writing scenarios and directing the shows. We put together a couple of shows, performing them in six or seven locations at once—at amateur art festivals that were held at big local factories.

It paid very well. A regular salary for any professional at the time was about 100 rubles a month—150 was considered big money. Directing amateur shows, I was earning about 300 rubles for each show. We produced about five shows in different places, so I made 300 rubles the first month, 400 the next. When I was making 1,000 rubles a month, I decided it was time to move on. I mean, I did my job well. I brought our group to the level of national competition, but it wasn't a very exciting job.

Another factor made me want to leave Chita—my marital problems. It was common infidelity on her side. My wife, Olga, had been working as a music editor at the radio station in Chita. I was often out of town. One day, I came back from a trip and found her in bed, bruised and injured. She told me that she'd gone for a ride with some Slava, on his motorcycle, and they'd had an accident. I thought, who was this Slava, anyway? I had never heard his name before.

We kept separate archives at home for correspondence. One day, I discovered a strange letter in my box. It was from her lover. It had gotten into my box by mistake; she had misplaced it. Their motorcycle crash was so serious that he'd broken both legs. Now I faced a dilemma: what to do next? I could have divorced her, but at that point it would have made me look ridiculous: I was a deceived husband; my wife was cheating on me. Anyway, I made a move that, I thought, was the most appropriate in that situation. Slava had a wife—Lina, a real beauty. She looked like Raquel Welsh. So I went after her. Soon I discovered that she had her own suspicions about her husband. We started having an affair.

You see, first I tried to seduce her just to get my revenge; but when I actually achieved my goal, I realized how silly and malicious it was. So I told her everything one day while we were in bed. She had also suspected her husband. Maybe that was part of the reason she was so cooperative. It wasn't just that I was so irresistible. Anyway, I showed her the letter, and she recognized her husband's handwriting. And I said, "well, at least we've got our revenge." "No," she said, "this is still not revenge. Let's do it for real, without hiding." So we began partying.

Chita was a small town, and it didn't take long for the rumors to spread. We were collecting apartment keys from four friends at a time, although, in fact, we didn't need any keys; my own apartment was empty. We made sure to be seen together at every restaurant in town. So, eventually, everybody knew. Everybody but Slava, who was lying at home with casts on both legs. My wife happened to be in the hospital, too. The day that she was released, I was at home, expecting Lina. My wife showed up unexpectedly. I had received a call from work, so I had to go out for a while. And Lina was coming. I couldn't reach her. So I told my wife: "Someone is coming over, tell her to wait for me." And I went out. When I got back I saw my wife and Lina sitting at the table. When Olga went to open the door, she recognized Lina, of course. But Olga thought Lina had come to talk to her about Olga's affair with her husband. When Lina asked for me, she understood everything.

It was a scene from a vaudeville farce. I grabbed Lina, and we went out. I spent some time with her, and then we both went home. Now, imagine the parallel scenes taking place: I'm telling my wife, "Let's talk in the morning," and we go to bed. Lina is at home with her husband, Slava, who's grown more and more suspicious, because his wife has been coming home later and later each evening, and she's exhausted. So he calls his wife a slut, and asks, "Who is he?" "Mark," she replies. He's stunned, of course. And she tells him she knows everything. Then Slava asks the most ridiculous question a man can ask in this situation: "Was he any good?" Her answer: "Yes, better than you'll ever be."

Enraged, Slava picked up a hammer and ran out on his broken legs, intent on killing me. But while he'd been confined to bed, he hadn't communicated with my wife. She was in the hospital and couldn't call him because there was no phone. Chita was a province. Hardly anybody had a phone. Anyway, he had no idea that we had moved. He went to our old address, waking up the neighbors. And Lina, at this very same moment, knocked at the door of our apartment, trying to warn me. Eventually, Slava found our new address. And while he searched the neighboring yards with his hammer, trying to find me, Lina ran to military headquarters—we lived right next to the commandant's house—and brought back two soldiers, who managed to grab the hammer from Slava. The next day I left for Novosibirsk.

I had arranged some job with the film studio in Novosibirsk, a major industrial city in Siberia. The first film assigned to me was about an industrial process. After I completed it successfully, I was given a second film to do, this time a serious documentary. I shot it. But when we came to editing it, something happened. I was refused a camera. It had never happened before. I realized that my record with the KGB had finally caught up with me. It took some time for the information to reach Novosibirsk, but it had finally arrived. That was in December 1976.

Novosibirsk had a TV station. When I had first arrived in the city, they invited me to work there. But film work was more interesting, and I refused. After the KGB had notified authorities at the film studio, I called a guy at the TV station to find out if the job was still available. He said that it was. The KGB didn't come after me immediately. That happened three months later, when I was fired for being "unlawfully hired on the job," which is how they phrased it. I then took a step that seemed absolutely insane at the time. It was 1976, long before perestroika. I sued them. And I won. The issue didn't even come to trial. My lawyer looked at the papers and simply said, "That's nonsense, it's completely illegal." She called the district attorney, who called the studio. I was given back my job the same day.

They left me alone afterward. I worked in TV for another nine years. Then, in 1985, came perestroika. Aside from my responsibilities as a TV director, I also produced discotheques. I was one of the first people in Russia to realize that Soviet rock music was a serious thing. In 1985, it was just beginning to emerge from the underground. So, as an expert, I was invited to the conservatory in Novosibirsk to give a few lectures on Soviet rock. First I refused, knowing it could cause problems: Soviet rock was interesting then for ideological rather than purely musical reasons. But finally, I agreed. They talked me into it. I gave a lecture, which was followed by a discussion. I was asked about DK, a popular punk rock group, famous for their obscure lyrics.

An old woman in the audience asked me if I thought the rock lyrics were appropriate. "Appropriateness is a relative term," I replied. "It depends on the situation: it wouldn't be appropriate, for instance, to show up at the conservatory dressed in a swimming suit, whereas such an outfit would be entirely appropriate at the beach." But the old woman picked up on the word "relative," adding, "There are some absolute, unconditional things—like fascism, for instance. It is unconditionally bad." I said, "Yes, of course, fascism is unconditionally bad, I agree. But if the entire country adopted this ideology and has followed it for more then twenty years, it means that other points of view are possible." From this brief discussion, an entire case was fabricated. I was accused of trying to lecture on fascism to the conservatory students. The letter was sent to the Central Party Committee of Novosibirsk. It was signed by forty people, although the lecture was attended by only fifteen people. I was told later that many of the students were forced to sign that letter. It was written in the best tradition of writing of that kind—meant only for the eyes of party officials, who would take the appropriate sanctions after reading it.

I was expelled from the journalists' union for "being ideologically immature," and a recommendation was made to the director of the TV studio that I be released from my responsibilities. The recommendation, in this case, was an implicit order. I decided not to wait to be fired and left my job. I found myself in a bad situation. There weren't that many directors in Novosibirsk, maybe a total of twenty. And they were in the public eye. So people knew me. Which meant I couldn't find a job anywhere—not a professional job, anyway. What was I to do?

My second wife was a seamstress. I could sew a little, too. So, I decided to become a dressmaker. I started making trousers, a Russian variety of jeans. This was the time when private enterprises were allowed for the first time. My wife and I made a bunch of trousers every week, selling them on the weekend. It brought in a good income. I somehow turned tailoring into an exciting process. I made jeans, and later coats, and sold them at flea markets. I liked the process of making the product more then selling; I felt a little ashamed of selling. But I was making good-quality stuff. I believe people in Novosibirsk are still wearing the coats I made. They looked like the coats manufactured by prestigious foreign firms. I created my own label and put it on each item.

I knew it was important to have your own brand. My business was going well, it was growing: the monthly sales were about twenty-five, thirty thousand rubles. At first I worked on my own, but later I brought other people into the business. Soon I obtained a license. I studied the criminal code carefully. When I was picked up at the flea market by the police and taken to the police station, I knew how to protect myself. There were four articles in the criminal code under which I could have been arrested. The first one was speculation. The coats I was selling were expensive, selling for about 500 rubles each. That was how it usually started: "You've been caught while speculating on consumer goods." "Wait a minute," I said, "I wasn't speculating. I made these coats myself. Here's my license." They wouldn't believe me. They called in an expert. And after studying my coats, the expert said, "Yes, these coats are made by foreign manufacturers." I said, "Maria Ivanovna, look at me, do you remember me when I was a director? Remember, you invited me to direct a show for you once." "Yes, I remember," she said. "You're an experienced person, you know how to tell a manufactured coat from a handmade one," I told her. "You should look at the waistband." And she looked at the waistband and admitted, "Yes, this coat is handmade, but handmade very well."

Next the police would accuse me of fraud: "This is a fraud, then. Because you deceive your customers by making them believe those coats are foreign-made." And I'd say, "No. I never told anyone the coats were imported." And that was true, I never did. When asked by customers if the coat was foreign-made, I usually replied, "Can't you see?" or "What do you think, I made it myself last night." Then the police would try something else: "You forged the brand of a foreign firm," they'd say. And I'd say, "No. This is my own brand. I invented it." "Then why hasn't it been registered?" And I'd reply, "Who said it hasn't been?" So they'd call the National Copyright Agency and receive an answer: "Yes, we have an application for this brand. We didn't know how to register it, but the application is here." Well, the law was on my side. So the police could do nothing but let me go. After a while they asked me to make coats for them—free of charge.

Perestroika was taking its course. It was a time of repentance. Suddenly I was termed a person who had suffered under the regime, a fighter for human rights. A film was made about me. A documentary entitled *The Tailor* was produced at the Novosibirsk Film Studio. And this film took a couple of prizes at the first International Non-Feature Film Festival. It was sold abroad, shown on TV. I was reinstated in the societies and unions that had expelled me earlier. But the thing was, I was already fed up. I began seriously to think of emigrating. I realized, despite my business success, that difficult times were approaching. The Mafia wasn't yet in existence, but I could sense it coming. Nobody touched me in the flea market. I was one of the first. People took it as an honor to make deals with me. But I could see that a new generation was going into business—people who didn't care much about anything, who were capable of everything.

I mentioned that I was restored to the Professional Union of Journalists. After participants in the meeting voted to return my membership, somebody stood up and said: "OK, he got his membership back. But now, what shall we do about his membership dues, for the five years he was absent from the Union? Shouldn't he pay this money back somehow?" And they began to discuss, quite seriously, how to obtain these dues from me. Then I stood up and said: "Let's do it this way. Today I was reinstated in the Union. Now, when is your next meeting? Thursday, next week? So, I suggest, next Thursday, let's vote to expel me from the Union for systematically failing to pay my membership dues over a period of five years." And with that I walked out. I realized nothing had really changed in the country, and nothing was going to change. Shortly afterward, I made my final decision to leave.

When I arrived in New York, I went to NYANA (New York Association for New Americans). It's the organization that helps Jewish immigrants in the country settle, find jobs, apartments, and the like. When my caseworker asked for my occupation, I told him that I was a tailor. I didn't mention anything about directing, I thought it was unnecessary. I was starting my life anew, and with a good profession on my hands: I was a tailor, a dressmaker. Soon afterward, I bought my first TV. And when I turned it on—imagine my surprise—the first thing I saw was my own face looking at me from the screen. PBS was showing the documentary *The Tailor*. Of course, I wasn't the only one who saw the documentary. People from NYANA saw it, too. The next day, my caseworker called me: "Why didn't you tell us you were a famous film director?" he asked. "I used to be one," I said. "That was in the past."

Then they called the Metropolitan Opera, the costume shop. They mentioned I was a theater person and, on top of that, a tailor. We went to the Metropolitan Opera for an interview, my wife and I. They didn't have jobs at the moment, they said, but if something came up—the usual story. Surprisingly, in a week or two they did call us and asked us to start right away. They offered us $17.50 an hour, which is pretty good money for anybody. To us, at that time, it seemed a fortune. So we started working. Of course, I didn't have the proper training in couture. I was self-taught. But I can learn really fast. Anyway, they took us on a temporary basis, but after a couple of months offered us permanent positions. That was how my life in America started. It was a good start. I've been working at the Metropolitan Opera costume shop for six years now.

Back in Novosibirsk, when I was preparing to leave the country, the team of filmmakers who made *The Tailor* decided to make a sequel to the film, *The Tailor 2*. They shot part of the film in Novosibirsk, including my preparations for departure. They also added another character in the film, my old friend Gennady Alferenko, who came from Novosibirsk and became an important political figure in Moscow after perestroika.

The film was supposed to end with a scene of Gennady and me meeting each other near the fountain at Lincoln Center in New York. The idea was something like this: one of them (meaning me) is doing an ordinary job and is a free person in a free country, and the other (meaning Gennady) has reached the very pinnacle of power, but is completely dependent on his position. Gennady had some problems with his wife and daughter. Like any functionary of the highest rank, the first thing he did was to send his daughter out of the country. He had made connections with American senators and millionaires. And one of these people offered to take Gennady's daughter into his family. So, the girl was taken into this really wealthy, Waspy American family. She went to the best private school, dressed properly, shopped in the most expensive stores; her English was exquisite. And then, imagine, her parents come from

Moscow and they speak bad English, they're not dressed neatly, and they smell bad. She came to be ashamed of her own parents. Anyway, the moral was that Gennady had achieved something he had always dreamed of, but he hadn't found happiness. And I, on the contrary, had overcome suffering to eventually find peace and happiness. And here we are, meeting in this plaza in New York City.

When my friend, the director of this film, decided to come to New York to finish it, he called to ask me to buy a professional camera for him. He said he wanted to try some photography. So I bought the camera. He happened never to use it. But I decided to give it a try. As a film director, I knew a thing or two about photography. Very soon, I began taking good photographs. Now I am mostly known in the Russian community as a photographer. My photographs appear in publications in Russia and in Russian-speaking publications in America. The recent collection of Joseph Brodsky's poetry included the photograph of Brodsky that I made. I've participated in a number of exhibitions. I even had a one-man show. Photography is an expensive occupation. Almost all of the money I make at my day job I spend on buying materials and equipment for my darkroom. I don't have an agent. But I'd like to have one—to have somebody help me because he likes my work.

One of the big discoveries I made about myself as an immigrant is that I can live without recognition. In Russia, if you were an artist it automatically made you an exceptional person. A person who wrote one play in his life expected to be known by everyone. Here, in America, artists expect and gain recognition, but only within a small professional circle. It's the other side of freedom: There is too much of everything.

But there are not that many good photographers in America for a number of reasons. First, America is a pragmatic country. Most of the photographers specialize in the one thing they know how to do the best: like taking pictures of a left boot exclusively, or of a right boot exclusively. They can be really good with that boot. And they know that if there's a demand for photographs of a left boot, or of a right boot, they will be called on to do it. So, there is a narrow specialization in photography. You can't make money on art, on doing what you want to do. You can make money only in commercial photography, on doing what you are asked to do. Of course, there are great masters, like Avedon. He manages to bring something new, even into commercial photography. But, generally, art is commercialized. That's why there aren't that many great photographs.

There are plenty of technically excellent works. They impress you the first time you look at them. After a second look, you discover that there's not that much in there. They're technically well done, but nothing really touches you, surprises you. Often when I go to a photo show, I feel intimidated after taking the first look around. But the second look brings relief: I realize I can probably do something they cannot.

Aaron Kanevsky
A Documentary Filmmaker

AARON puts a bottle of vodka, fresh from the freezer, on the table. Then he fills a plate with salami, cheese, and a few delicacies from the Russian shop a few blocks away. In 1990, he and his wife followed their son to America. But most of Aaron's memories are of Russia. Once he begins to speak, we're transported a world away from this Washington Heights apartment. Now in his seventies, he spent his life as a documentary filmmaker. He invented the genre of documentary comedy in Russia, but it was his film on the K-701 tractor that brought him a big official award. Aaron smiles, "It's always been that I had to throw one bone to the Bolsheviks in order to be able to make two or three films that I really wanted to make."

I was deprived of many freedoms in Russia and I couldn't always do what I wanted. But what a person wants doesn't matter. After all, all of great literature is based on that conflict between the desirable and the possible, the struggle between what you want and what you can do. So, of course, as a film director, I suffered from not always being able to shoot what I wanted to shoot or to show my best films to the public. I had to wage the never-ending war with the authorities—all that is true. But the other truth is that there was a thrill in that struggle. I actually enjoyed it. And my best films were often born from that struggle.

I've never done anything in my life but documentaries, I never was able to do anything else. I started making films pretty late in my life. I did not have a professional education in film. I had a degree in automotive engineering. But I abandoned my first profession after World War II. I happened to work as a reporter during the war, writing for a field newspaper, and I remained a journalist after the war.

Journalism led me to filmmaking. I worked for a TV station in Kharkov. I was a senior editor, in charge of one of the film groups. Once I picked the script for a new documentary, but it happened that the director of the film had to travel to Moscow. Deadlines were approaching, so I suggested shooting the film myself. I tried, and the result surprised everybody. Ironically, my first experience in filmmaking happened to be a film about Lenin, intended for his centennial, which was celebrated that year, in 1970.

I was so engaged in the process of making my first film that it came out fresh and alive. Because nothing else in connection with Lenin's anniversary showed any signs of life, my film was noticed. Afterward, I was allowed to make my second film, which I consider to be my first. It was an eighteen-minute film titled "Two Times Two Makes X." That one was noticed by Alexey Kapler, the host of a popular TV program called "Kinopanorama." He showed the film on TV as part of his program. It was intended to teach algebra to first-graders. However, the film was not about algebra, but rather about how kids learn how to think. The day after the film was shown on TV, I woke up famous. My next film was an even bigger hit, but that didn't prevent my new boss, who arrived at the TV station in Kharkov in 1974, from laying me off. In a way, I'm grateful to him for doing that, because it pushed me to leave Kharkov and move to Leningrad, where my career really took off. It happened that the Leningrad Film Studio had two openings for film directors on its staff around that time. I applied for the position.

I got it. The only problem was that I had no place to live in Leningrad. Trying to exchange my apartment in Kharkov for an apartment in Leningrad was a hopeless venture. So I couldn't start the job until about six months after. The director of the film studio then offered me a deal: he promised me an apartment in Leningrad if I would make a documentary about a tractor—the K-701 tractor. The film was intended as a personal gift to Brezhnev. The leader of our Party happened to be a big fan of this mighty machine, in part because he had worked as a tractor operator at the start of his career. Later in life, he made it his hobby to collect automobiles. By the way, this wasn't the first time that I had crossed Brezhnev's path. During the war, when I worked on the field newspaper of the

Eighteenth Army, Brezhnev was the commander in charge of that particular division. Anyway, I made the film, entitled "Champion of the Fields," and to my big surprise, I got the apartment. I never quite believed that my boss would keep his word, but he did. Moreover, that film was shown on TV, on the main Moscow channel—and not just once. When my wife saw the film for the first time, she called me to say, "If I ever see anything like *that* again, I'm filing for divorce."

The film was a finalist in the First National TV Festival in Vladivostok. I remember the announcement of prizes before the festival began. The first prize was a crystal vase of an enormous size, and the second prize—and it caught my eye right away—was a cube of Plexiglas with blue coral inside, unbelievably beautiful! I remember telling my friend jokingly: "Well, you know I can live without the first prize, but I'd settle for the second." And guess what? I won the second prize for that tractor! I was amazed. But, I guess the members of the festival jury had to take care of their careers, too. Right away, I went to a post office and telegraphed my wife: "Darling. Got the second prize at the festival. You don't understand a thing about art." Such are the tales of my life in Russia.

It's always been that I had to throw one bone to the Bolsheviks in order to be able to make two or three films of my own, films that I really wanted to make. I invented the genre of documentary comedy in Russia. And, of course, these comedies were always aimed at this or that ridiculous aspect of the Soviet reality. It was a very creative time because I had to come up with so many tricks!

When making a film about the book-subscription boom (subscriptions took place when there were acute shortages of published books), I announced—through one of the book stores in town—a subscription to the works of three writers: the first was Olga Forsh, a Soviet writer, not widely known; Alexander Dumas was the second; and the third was "Rasinant, the distinguished French novelist" (actually, Rosinante, Don Quixote's horse). Eight out of ten book fans subscribed to the works of Rasinant. Only one of the subscribers, a young man in glasses, came up to me and said: "Don't put me up for Rasinant—I don't have a stable." Another time, I was filming part of a documentary in a kindergarten; it was about the shortages in stores in Russia. As soon as I shouted "store!" all the kids formed a line.

One film I made was about the ridiculous job discipline campaign initiated by Andropov. During the day, people were stopped on the street, in restaurants and stores, in buses and subways. Their papers were checked—all to detect absenteeism. Here I came up with another trick. We were filming the line of people near a beer kiosk. I dressed some of the crew members in working clothes, so they could pretend that they'd just sneaked out from work. I put them at the head of the line, right next to the kiosk window, and had them address the people on line: "Brothers, let's buy a couple of beers, we have to be back at work right away." And the chorus of voices from the crowd replied, as I was filming: "Just what do you think we're doing here? You think we don't have to be back at work?"

Despite these problems, I never considered emigrating. After all, I kept on working, I was never without work. But it just happened that my only son, Vladimir, emigrated to the United States in 1989. And as reluctant as I felt about leaving Russia, my wife and I decided to follow him. The idea that we might not see him again was simply unbearable. Still, leaving Russia was a tragedy for me. It was 1990 when we finally got all the papers together. I had just finished yet another film, a documentary that many of my friends consider my best. And suddenly I had to leave. It was a real tragedy.

As I was leaving, my friends warned me: "What are you doing? You'll spend the rest of your days on a bench with the other old Jews, recalling how much you were cherished by the Bolsheviks!" Thank God, that hasn't happened. From my first days in this country, I tried to lead an active life, writing for the Russian-language newspapers in New York and organizing a movie club, first in Manhattan. We show old and new Russian films—it's maybe the only place where people can see them. Then, there's is a Russian TV station—two stations, in fact—formed shortly after I arrived here. Of course, I've been there from the start. I have my own program, once a month. It doesn't bring in lots of money. It's not something I can live on, but it's something I can live by—it keeps me alive.

I wasn't surprised by America. I had a chance to travel before I left Russia; I've attended many film festivals around the world. It's still a mystery how I got such a privilege, being a Jew and an artist. Maybe my association with Brezhnev played a certain role, after all. I remember an interview before my first trip abroad, to Hungary. After being questioned on the situation in Russia, I was asked to tell a little about myself. "What did you do in your life?" The man asked. "Well," I said, "I did many things. I fought the Germans next to Brezhnev." "That's enough," he said. "No more questions. I believe you're well enough prepared to go on this trip." And after that, I was never denied a visa to a foreign country. My friends used to asked me about Brezhnev: "what kind of man was he?" Well, he was a nice man, actually—good-natured, pleasant. He'd be a real find as a head of some collective farm, I'm sure. I never saw him after the war, never talked to him. But once I almost did. I was invited to a reunion of the veterans of the Eighteenth Army held in the Kremlin. Brezhnev loved these kinds of events. He was very proud of his heroic past.

I happened to be in Moscow at the time, so I was invited. After a few drinks, I decided to go to his table and chat a bit, about how we fought together, you know. His table was in the center of the room. So I started in that direction and was immediately approached by two veterans, suspiciously young-looking. They took me by the hands and whispered sweetly: "Where are you heading, brother? To him? How about another drink, first?" So, our conversation never happened.

Yevgeny and Larisa Ryzhik
Freedoms Lost and Found

YEVGENY is in his mid-forties. He lives in Houston with his wife, Larisa, and their daughter. Once an artistic director of a theater company in a small town, he left his job to move to St. Petersburg. From there, in 1990, he moved again—to the United States. In Houston, he had to soon abandon his hope to make a living as a stage director. He switched gears, and went to work as a translator for oil companies. He and his wife have found many freedoms in America—just as they had hoped to. They have also lost a few, like the freedom to talk back to your boss.

Yevgeny: The first year of immigration is a very curious experience. You feel vulnerable, completely insecure, in a new country, surrounded by new people with unfamiliar customs. It's a shock. Then, little by little, you begin to adapt.

Larisa: In Russia, we used to judge people by the way they spoke. The test of someone's intelligence was his ability to express himself. And I think that's how Americans judge us, too. So, I can imagine what they thought of us.

Yevgeny: Being inarticulate is a burden in any language. Because we all think in a particular language. And when you can't speak the language, to some extent, you lose the ability to think, too. And then, there was another powerful factor that entered our lives here—fear. Fear of not finding a job, fear of being fired. Fear of not having a place to live, enough to pay rent. In Russia, our life was free from this anguish. In Russia, you could argue with a boss, contradict him, make jokes, without a fear of being fired. Here, an invitation to a supervisor's office makes you tremble with fear: "What did I do wrong? Am I going to be fired?" Because there's no stability, that feeling of hanging over a precipice never leaves an immigrant.

In Russia, there was a different kind of fear. I remember a story that the late Georgy Alexandrovich Tovstonogov, a celebrated theater director in Leningrad, told his students. It happened when Stalin was still alive. Back then, they used to organize those big concerts attended by members of the government: ministers, their wives, and sometimes even Stalin himself. The show was usually followed by a party, with food and dancing. It was a big deal; everything had to be right. At one of these shows, Tovstonogov served as a kind of stage manager: he opened and closed the curtain and made sure that the performers were on stage on time. He was a very young man back then.

One of the groups performing that night was a new dance company formed recently by Igor Moiseev. It was one of their first major public presentations. So, imagine: they've just finished their number, and the audience applauds wildly. It's a huge success. The program director asks Moiseev, "Do you have another number?" Moiseev shows him the piece. It's a burlesque number danced to foreign pop music. The director thinks for a moment, then says, "No, that won't do," and leaves. Tovstonogov, the stage manager, and Moiseev stand backstage in confusion: they don't know what to do. The audience is waiting. Stalin himself is clapping from his box, waiting for the dancers to do their encore. Finally, Moiseev decides to perform the number. "I take responsibility," he says. And the piece is performed, to the audience's great enjoyment.

And, right away, the party begins: music is playing, people dance. But behind the curtain, Tovstonogov witnesses the following scene. The program director appears from out of nowhere, furious, runs to Moiseev, and begins to shake him, yelling: "Just who do you think you are? What is it that you allow yourself? I'll show you! You'll rot in prison for that. You'll go to Siberia for that!" At that moment, from another wing of the curtain, stepping quietly in soft Caucasian boots, enters Stalin. The two men don't see him. Red and sweaty, they keep shaking each other, yelling. Moiseev keeps repeating: "What was I supposed to do? You didn't say anything. I had to do something." The two are almost reaching for each other's throat. So, Tovstonogov sees Stalin walk past the two men, turn to them, and say something quietly. The two men give the Leader of the People a stony look; then they suddenly embrace each other tenderly and begin waltzing. "I had never seen anything like that in my life," Tovstonogov said. "After the party, I approached Moiseev and asked him: 'What was it that Stalin said to you?' Moiseev told me: 'Why argue? It's better to go and dance.'" Fear is inside us. People create it themselves.

I think here, in America, people live within boundaries that are much more strict and narrow than in Russia, even in the worst of times. They live in constant fear; they wear themselves out with hard work. Nothing is stable here. The competition is high, and no job lasts forever.

One of your painful realizations after coming to America is that you are not the citizen of the world that you thought you were, but a product of a particular system and its generations of slavery. And this slavery shows itself in little things like scent, for instance. Russians are not concerned with personal hygiene that much. And there are other things—the way you behave, the way you laugh. Our jokes are not acceptable here. You suddenly feel like a boor, even though you've read all of Dostoevsky, and millions of other writers that Americans have never even heard of. Despite all that cultural baggage, you behave like a gorilla.

Larisa: Americans are often called insincere. But I personally prefer American insincerity to Russian sincerity. I remember when our daughter, during our first year here, performed at a school concert, playing the piano. And after the concert, other parents came up to us, complimenting her, telling us how well she played, how much they enjoyed it. And we replied, "Oh, no, no. Don't say that. She wasn't good at all. She made this and that mistake." And they looked at us as if we were idiots. They couldn't understand why a parent would say anything bad about their child's performance. But in Russia, it's the natural thing to do. We were all used to humiliating one another.

Yevgeny: We all were spoiled in a way by the peculiar work ethic known as the "dictatorship of the proletariat." From that perspective, a simple workman had the power to scoff at his supervisor, tell a workshop foreman to go to hell, and the like. Supervisors, on the other hand, had much less freedom and were burdened with more of a moral responsibility than workers of the lowest rank. Work relationships in Russia were democratic: there was no strict hierarchy, as it exists here. Different levels of the hierarchy here are even physically separated, situated on different floors in the organization. In the company where I work, there is a ninth floor where I have never set foot, and probably never will. Everything is different on that floor—the length of the receptionist's legs, the thickness of the carpets, the suits people wear. It's a different world. And this is hard for a Russian to take. You begin to think: Is it really a free country? What kind of freedom is this?

Larisa: Friendship for Americans is a different thing. Here, family always comes first, and friends come later. The family is more important for an American than any friend. In Russia, it was the other way around. Friends were always the first priority. But I am getting used to the new American ways—in friendship, too. And I actually like them. Most of my American friends are simple people, not particularly sophisticated intellectually, but, all in all, they're much happier than we are. Happiness has become my religion lately. You see, I've lived more than half of my life in Russia, I have read all the books you can think of, I learned things that I maybe don't even need to know. So what? All this knowledge—did it help me in the end? Did it make me a better person, a kinder person? Did it make me happier? No. And, here, I am beginning to get some feel for it, the happiness. It's still very blurry and maybe that's how it will remain. Maybe that's how it should be. At least I can reach for it.

Vadim Shron (*left*), 1950

Vadim Shron, 1981

Semyon Slutsky, c. 1998

Alexander Bolonkin
in exile in Siberia, 1976

Mela Tannenbaum

Vladimir Kanevsky (*left and center*) and Aaron Kanevsky (*right*)
(photo by Mark Kopelev)

Vladimir Kanevsky, sculptor

Mark Kopelev
in Russia

Julia

Julia, dominatrix

Boris Kardimum, in New York City (photo by Mark Kopelev)

Gennady Katsov (photo by Mark Kopelev)

SCIENTISTS and DOCTORS

Boris and Tatyana Girshovich
Astrophysics and Politics

BORIS AND TATYANA *are physicists who have followed their granddaughter to America in the wake of a family tragedy. They spent their entire careers in the Russian aerospace program. Boris started out in the 1950s in the Lavochkin Lab, a center of cutting-edge rocket science and then, ironically, a haven for Jews denied entry to other research venues. He helped design intercontinental ballistic missiles in the late 50s and moon landers in the 70s. Tatyana worked at the Moscow Aviation Institute, an expert in the field of dynamic gases. They currently live in the outskirts of Houston. Boris's involvement in the space program is limited to translating and editing documentation for NASA. He is amazed at NASA's way of managing scientific projects. He observes: "Everything is done according to instructions. There are even instructions on how to assemble a bookshelf written so that even a complete idiot could do it." He found much more personal responsibility in the Soviet Union, just one of the attractions of science.*

Boris: Ours is not a typical immigration story. We came here for personal reasons, not political or economic ones. Although we never bore tender feelings for the Soviet regime, this fact doesn't make us political refugees. Our reason for coming here was not particularly exciting. We had two daughters once. One of them, the older one, died in 1992, in Russia. She was thirty-four years old. When that happened, our second daughter was already living in Chicago. She had always wanted to move to America and eventually she did. She had come to the United States with a business visa. Through her sister and her sister's husband at the time, she learned about some American company in Riga, Latvia, that was hiring young Russians to work in American summer camps for kids from poor families.

Getting that job was extremely competitive. She had to travel to Riga for an interview, and she passed it mainly for two reasons. First, as a kid, she had studied at an English-language-oriented school, so her English was quite good. Second, she held Master of Sports certificate in gymnastics, so she got the job. She was working essentially for free. She earned only about 300 dollars for the entire season. But she received room and board.

She returned to us that year. And the next year, the camp director invited her to come back. She took along her husband and two kids. Her husband started out as a kitchen aid in the camp, but as he was a highly qualified computer programmer, he was able to write a couple of record-keeping programs. The camp director introduced him to a friend. Shortly afterward, he was hired by the computer department at McDonald's, in Chicago. He and our daughter soon applied for refugee status and it was granted to them. That was in the summer of 1991. Exactly at the same time my wife and I stood in the line of people defending the White House in Moscow against the tanks, protecting democracy during the coup of August 1991.*

When our older daughter died in 1992, she left three children: the boy and the girl from her first marriage, and a daughter from her second marriage, our youngest granddaughter. The older two,

---

* During four or five days in late August of 1991, Gorbachev was arrested in his summer residence in Crimea. The Communists attempted to take power in Moscow: tanks had surrounded the Russian parliament, the House of Soviets, known as the White House. Crowds of people from all over Moscow had gathered near the parliament building to defend it with their bodies. Boris Yeltsin was there making inspiring speeches. The image of Yeltsin, then president of the Russian Federation, climbing on top of a tank to address the people, became an important and inspiring symbol. Although people stood all night ready to defend the White House, nothing happened in the end; the tanks never attacked. Gorbachev was released and returned to Moscow. Still, it was the beginning of his fall and the rise of Yeltsin.

the boy and the girl, were taken by their father. And they still live with him and his family. But the youngest girl remained with us. Her father didn't express any interest in her future. We were both pretty old people. We were afraid that we wouldn't be able to raise our granddaughter on our own.

She was one-and-a-half years old when she came to live with us, and emotionally scarred, as you can expect in such a situation. She stayed with us for three years. And all that time we continued to work. Tatyana Alexandrovna was working in the Moscow Aviation Institute. My wife has a post-doctoral degree in physics, and she's an author of a couple of books, and many dozens of articles. Her field is the dynamics of gases.

We decided to bring our granddaughter here, to put her in the care of our younger daughter. She wanted to adopt her niece. So, we got permission from her father and we finished all the adoption paper work in Russia. Then, we had to deliver the girl along with the papers to our daughter in Chicago. That was not easy to do.

Tatyana: We knew, in fact, from the start, that we would never leave Asya, our granddaughter, once she was here. We knew we wouldn't go back to Russia. She meant too much to us, we couldn't leave her behind. So, basically, we pretended that we were going to America for a short visit.

Boris: We went to Pittsburgh, to visit my old friends who lived there. A couple of friends from my school years were living in the United States: one is in Pittsburgh, one in Dallas, and one in Boston. We went to a very special high school in Leningrad as kids, one of the most prominent schools in the city at the time. After I graduated from high school, I went to study at the Polytechnic University in Leningrad, in the Department of Physics and Mechanics, one of the most difficult to get into.

Tatyana: That's where we met. His life in Russia was quite rich in experiences, but not always pleasant ones. When he graduated from high school in 1949, he came to the graduation ceremony expecting to receive a gold medal, but he didn't get it. The reason, they said, was that his final paper failed to sufficiently show why Nekrasov's poetry is ideologically more mature than Pushkin's poetry. So, he got a B on the paper.

Boris: And with a B on a final paper one couldn't hope to get any medal, even though the rest of my grades were A's. Then, I had to pass the entrance exams to the Polytechnic. There were nine exams. I got A's in all of them. Afterward, the chair of the Admissions Committee invited me for a chat. I had the same last name then, which didn't leave any doubts regarding my national identity. In 1949 Jews were still accepted in the department, although already in limited numbers. Later, the doors of the Physics and Mechanics Department would shut completely to people of my kind. Even then, I was the only Jewish person in my group.

Tatyana: And a year earlier, there were plenty. So that was the very beginning of it.

Boris: So, the chair of the Admissions Committee who was also the director of the office that handled student profiles tried for about an hour to convince me not to enter the Department of Physics and Mechanics. "It's a lot of pressure", he told me. "A lot of hard work. After the first semester you'll fail if your grades are not good enough, and then what? You will be kicked out of school. Why don't you go to the Department of Electrical Mechanics instead. It's a great department. Some terrific people are teaching there, really lovely people." But I kept repeating stubbornly, "No, I want to study here." We kept talking like this for an hour. Finally, he turned crimson red and said: "All right, but you'll regret it later."

Tatyana: He didn't receive a single B during all his years at school, only A's.

Boris: Again, for some reason, they didn't give me a Stalin Scholarship.

Tatyana: I remember that I kept asking him why he didn't get the Stalin Scholarship.
I was so naive, I had no idea whatsoever about anti-Semitism. It never even crossed my mind. We studied in parallel groups in the department. I studied with Professor Laschansky.

Boris: I studied with Professor Lurie, among other things the theories of resiliency and elasticity. When I graduated from the department, the chair of the committee that assigned jobs to students invited me in for a talk. "There are two job possibilities for you," he told me. "The first one is workshop foreman at the watch factory, but in Leningrad." So, I got a chance to stay in Leningrad. The other one was in Lavochkin's lab in the suburbs of Moscow, with no housing guaranteed.

Well, Lavochkin was famous for designing fighter planes during the Second World War. After the war he did a number of things. Since 1945, his lab was the leader in the Soviet aviation industry. This was the lab that developed the first automated space stations, such as Luna, Mars, and Venus. Of course, I didn't go to work in a watch factory. I went to Lavochkin. I couldn't understand at the time why I was offered such a dream job. Later I understood.

The reason was quite simple: Semyon Alexeevich Lavochkin was Jewish. He was a Jew from Smolensk. And because of the closeness of his lab to the top circles, he, the last and only one in the country to be so favored, was allowed to hire Jews. He had a mandate, from Beria* personally that allowed him to take in all the Jews who had been kicked out of all the other places: the Central Institute of Aviation, Korolev's laboratory in Lipki, and the like. He gave jobs to these people, and soon his Control Systems team became the best in the country, and so did his Aerodynamics team. The kind of work done in his lab was ten or fifteen years ahead of its time. He died in 1960.

In his lab in 1959 we conducted the successful testing of a rocket that flew a distance of 8,000 kilometers. It was the first in the world to use a system of astro-navigational correction (navigation by stars). It could hit a target with an error of less than 1 kilometer. We continued to test the rocket in 1960, but soon the project was closed down, partly because of Lavochkin's death and partly because of changes in the government. Khruschev had come to power, and other engineer-designer-in-chiefs happened to have a big hand in the new government. Personal connections decided everything.

But what an amazing rocket it was! All of the Soviet PVO (Air Defense Forces) failed to detect the rocket in its flight from

---

* Lavrenti Pavlovich Beria was head of the secret police and national security under Stalin from 1938 until Stalin's death in 1953.

Vladimirovka, near Stalingrad, across the entire country to Kamchatka. None of the aircraft in existence at the time would have been capable of destroying it. The rocket was shot from a railroad platform. It was huge, weighing about 100 tons. It resembled the later U.S. space shuttle in its design. Two accelerators, shaped like a plane: a rocket with wings. When he came to inspect the rocket in the plant, Marshal Zhukov would ask a single question: "You think it would make it to America?" "It would, Georgy Konstantinovich," we would reply, and he'd leave satisfied.

Anyway, I came to the lab right after graduation and I worked there until my departure from Russia. After Lavochkin died, the lab switched from aviation to work for Cosmos, the space program. The reason was obvious: Sergey Korolev, who had initiated most of the Cosmos programs, couldn't cope with all of them in the end. Other firms were called in to help. And some of Korolev's jobs were passed on to us. Korolev, for instance, couldn't ensure the soft landing of a space station on the moon's surface. He attempted thirteen shots, none of them resulting in successful landings. But, a year after the project was passed along to us, we made it work.

I've always enjoyed my work. But I never felt that it was particularly appreciated by my country. The Soviet regime collapsed in the end because the system failed to recognize the disparity among people. Gifted people, those who were capable of doing something special, weren't getting what they deserved for their work. Still, I was in a privileged position. As a friend and colleague put it when I ran into him, in 1993—things were already falling apart in the space program and in the country—"All our lives we were paid big salaries for doing what we liked. Now it's payback time." That's true. We did the work we enjoyed doing. But was it ever appreciated?

We delivered the first soil from the moon in September of 1970. We had designed a spacecraft that picked up a sample of soil from the moon and delivered it to earth. The whole thing was done on the first try. Afterward, we attempted to patent this particular method of delivering soil from the moon. Eleven people were involved in the project, and cited as authors in the scientific papers. I was one of them. It took many years for the papers to get registered. Babakin, director of the firm after Lavochkin, was already dead. Then the whole thing bogged down, because Babakin's successors were not among the list of authors. They hadn't taken part in the project, so we didn't mention them. Anyway, the invention was finally registered and we got paid for it. Each of us received one month's salary as a bonus. We are talking about the first spacecraft to bring soil from the moon.

I knew I could never get official permission to leave Russia, because of the kind of work I was involved in all my life. They simply would not have let me go. When I applied for a visitor's visa to come to America, it was denied. My wife got her visa in a month. But I could not get one. Then I wrote a letter of resignation from my job. We had to solve the situation with our granddaughter, one way or another. "I'll wait as many years as needed until my knowledge of my country's military secrets will reach a harmless level," I said. "Then I'll leave." Of course, in some cases, even a period of fifteen years proved not to be enough. It all depends on the people who decide how much knowledge is considered harmless. But then my boss told me: "If you don't quit, if you stay on your job, we'll put your name on the list of employees considered for business trips abroad. This way you'll get your foreign passport. And then, whenever you need to go, we'll give it to you."

So, I agreed. They put my name on the list. I was sent to the International Space Exhibition in Thailand, where our firm organized a couple of exhibits. I stayed there for a month, working as a guide. The following year I came to America for a visit. And the year after that, for another visit. The third time we all came—and stayed. I never officially quit my job. I kept extending my stay, even after living here for a year. They expected me to return to Russia. Then my wife had to undergo surgery and one thing led to another. I couldn't drag it out forever. Finally, I called my boss. He's a good friend of mine, and recently had become an engineer-designer in chief of our enterprise. "I'm not coming back," I told him. " I'm sorry things turned out this way. But there's nothing I can do. It's just the way it is." "That's life," he replied. "I understand."

Here we applied for green cards, as part of the program for outstanding scientists. We got them. When we applied for the work permit, we had only to present a proof of a job offer. Later, when we received the green cards, we had to present evidence of employment—which we didn't have. Luckily, a friend helped us to find jobs as translators at Technical Translators International (TTI). It's a translating agency contracted by NASA, that is translating from English into Russian the documentation on the shuttle-MIR program. I've been working there for almost a year, as a staff editor. My wife works there on a contract basis.

We knew English in Russia. For the most part, it was passive knowledge. We were able to translate scientific documentation and some articles. We used to make extra money in Russia this way. Our conversational English was always bad, and it remains quite weak. But the fact that we know the subject, and know it, unlike many other translators, from the inside, helps a great deal in our present job. I don't do too much translating myself. I work mainly as an editor. Sometimes, I see mistakes in documentation that I have to revise, but not translator's mistakes—rather flaws in the design, engineering mistakes. At first, when I discovered them, I would report them to my bosses. Later I realized that I'm not supposed to do that. My job is simply to verify the translation, no more than that.

A few of my friends tried to help me find a job in my field. I sent my resumes to a couple of places. There was no reaction. Well, I did have an interview at NASA once—for an engineering position—and I was promised a second interview. I could see that the person interviewing me was very interested in getting me in—but nothing happened. I believe I know the reason. First, it's my age. Then, my bad English. The third reason is that I'm overqualified. That's a big obstacle. I can't hope to obtain a position in my field at the same level that I had held in Russia. All these positions are taken. And the people who occupy them would only view me as a competitor. Maybe I made a mistake by writing the truth in my resume. I should have just written "engineer" as my occupation.

The irony is that I'm translating the documentation being read in Russia by people whom I know very well, people I've been working with for many years. I try to keep a philosophical approach to it all. I realize I probably won't have a chance to work in my profession anymore. And I'm glad I've found at least some kind of job here, a steady job. One has to be realistic. My biggest hope is to achieve a certain stability, not to be afraid of tomorrow. And, also, I want to be able to travel, including back to Russia.

If not for our granddaughter, I wouldn't have left Russia. I could have worked for another ten years, maybe. But after that, we'd be left with nothing. Surviving on a pension is impossible. We didn't save anything. The money we earned was hardly enough to sustain an average standard of living—pay for the apartment, keep a car, buy groceries. We couldn't save money. Here, ironically, our situation is quite similar. We are not refugees, so we're not entitled to support from the government, such as welfare. We can only count on ourselves. If we manage to save enough money to support ourselves when we can't work anymore, I'd consider us lucky.

Tatyana: I have no hope of finding a job in my profession here. Age is a big obstacle.

Boris: Of course, if I were offered a professional job here, I would take it without hesitation. Particularly, because most of the upcoming projects in space are joint Russian-American ventures. In 1970, our company designed the *Lunohod,* or Moonwalker, operated from Earth. It landed on the moon in November 1970. The American Marswalker, which is on Mars now, is basically a copy of the Moonwalker we produced. The basic technological ideas are the same. Of course, all our designs and drafts were published.

The situation in Russian science and industry now is tragic, not only because funding has been and continues to be reduced—that's happening all over the world. The entire field of space studies is too closely related to the defense industry; in fact it grew out of it. That can't be ignored. But what makes it particularly tragic in Russia is the loss of the best minds, the drain of young specialists from science into commerce, or emigration. One generation is already lost, and if the next is lost, too, there would be an empty hole. The chain would be broken.

Of course, this growing cooperation between Russians and Americans might give it a chance to survive. We've always competed with America. Actually, there are quite a few amusing episodes that I recall. For instance, our first attempt to land the Moonwalker coincided with the arrival on the moon of the *Apollo II.* These two events literally coincided in time. Unfortunately, our Moonwalker crashed on landing, due to some flaws in the program. At that very moment that it crashed, Armstrong was already walking on the surface of the moon. And the seismograph he installed registered our fall. So, the Americans were the first to know about it. What an embarrassment! Here's another funny episode: when our *Luna-9* captured the first full panorama of the moon, the picture was transmitted to Earth through an open channel, which anyone could receive. The first to receive it happened to be Bernard Lovell, the British astronomer. He published the panorama two days earlier than it was published by *Pravda* in Moscow. That happened because transmission of the photos took place on Friday, and our entire Politburo was resting on the weekend. There was nobody available to sign the letter permitting publication of the material.

When perestroika arrived, I couldn't help feeling somewhat suspicious. It was hard to believe that we had a general secretary capable of walking and talking on his own. He was not a half-corpse and he gave speeches without prompting, without constantly having to look at the paper in front of him. I think Gorbachev's role is strongly underestimated now. If not for him, everything could have turned out differently.

It's amazing—once it became apparent that the Communist party couldn't last much longer—how many signs appeared on the doors of all the executive committees: such and such shareholders' company. In a day, the entire enterprise became the property of the party bosses, those dullheads. They grabbed all the money.

By 1995, there was a complete end to lawfulness, of any kind. People who had money could do whatever they wanted. There was nothing and nobody to stop them. One night—it was winter—we were driving home after having picked up our granddaughter at her day care. It was already dark, and snow was piled up on the road. Only one narrow lane was available. So, I was pulling out of the day care, driving on that narrow lane—it was maybe 100 meters long. I was halfway through, when, suddenly I saw another car enter the lane and drive directly toward me. I gave a signal, which meant: "Let me get out first, then you can drive in." But the car kept on moving. I stopped my car, and so did the other driver. I was waiting for him to back up and let me pass. He did not. Then I opened the door of my car, slightly. The door of the other car also opened, and a huge fellow—2 meters in size, with his head shaven—came out. He walked right over to me, shouting: "Pull back!" I tried to explain: "Can't you see? I made it almost to the end. Let me get out, and it's all yours." "If you don't pull back, I'll throw a grenade," he said, very calmly. Well, I pulled back. I had a child in my car. And I believed that he would have thrown that grenade—without any hesitation.

Sometimes the violence didn't seem to have any reason behind it. In the building where we lived, someone blew out all the windows in a hallway. The janitors patched up the holes with cardboard. About a week later, they blew up the cardboard. Then the janitors covered the holes with lumber. In a week, the lumber was gone, too. Afterward, the windows were left wide open to the wind.

Living in Houston and translating for NASA, I have a chance to observe their system at work and to compare it to ours. Some things seem very strange to me. People working at different stages of the process perform their particular functions, but usually have no idea of the process as a whole. The first time I noticed a mistake in the original documentation, I called a publisher at NASA. The publisher had no idea what I was talking about. He called a NASA expert, who had no clue either. Only after four telephone calls—to Washington, then to Canada—were we able to find a person who confirmed that there was a mistake and that it should be corrected. Documentation passes through a number of official channels, and those who deal with it, typically have no understanding of its meaning. That can lead to a disaster.

In Russia, we have a different approach. One person is responsible for the entire project, from the beginning to the very end. That scientist developed it, performed all the calculations, issued all the documentation, tested the project, and followed up on performance—making all the necessary adjustments and corrections along the way. The project leader worked alone or with the help of a staff. When something went wrong it was the leader's responsibility to fix it.

Here, everything is done according to instructions. Maybe that's why the instructions on how to assemble a bookshelf are written so that even a complete idiot could do it. But there are some situations that require decisions to be made in a matter of seconds. How they can handle situations like that here is a mystery to me. Here the person who presses the buttons on the operating console and controls the flight of a spaceship is not the one who designed that ship. That person doesn't know all the intricacies of the design, he or she simply has read the instructions. To me, that's complete nonsense. Well, here it's the rule.

Konstantin Likharev
The Decline of "Big Science"

KONSTANTIN *built his career as a first-rate physicist at Moscow University, eventually becoming the director of a national laboratory. During that time, he enjoyed beating the vastly wealthier Americans in fundamental technology. Unable to obtain funding for his innovative research in cryo-electronics in 1990, he managed to move the core of his staff to the Physics Department at the State University of New York at Stony Brook. Now, in his fifties, he describes the desperate situation of scientists in Russia, who have lost their jobs and life work; some have even committed suicide. "Big science was just a toy in the hands of the military-industrial complex, and when that fell apart, nobody needed big science anymore." Still he remains captivated by his work, putting in more than seventy hours a week. If not for his work, he would return to Russia. "America is a good country, but it's not mine. What really helps, though, is that I'm not really living here—I'm working here. I joke sometimes that I have simply moved from Room E11901A to Room B135."*

I lived in Moscow and worked most of my adult life at Moscow State University, in the Department of Physics. During my final two years I served as a director of the Laboratory of Cryo-electronics (low-temperature electronics). For a time we did very interesting work, but then in June 1990, when the

Soviet Union became bankrupt and lost all of its hard currency, we were told quite clearly that the laboratory had lost its funding.

It was a high-profile laboratory. In 1988, I once presented findings to the Politburo of the Communist Party Central Committee, and I even shook hands with Gorbachev. Anyway, the whole thing burst like a soap bubble. By June 1990, we literally had no work left to do. So, I went to America to see if some of our research could be moved over here. I took quite a tour. I visited twenty-six places in two and a half months—universities and different companies. I was looking for a job not only for myself, but for the core of our research group, which made it much more difficult. Employers in America have a personal approach to hiring: they like to interview people, look them in the eye, find out what they are like. I was trying to sell people nobody could see, and nobody knew in person, though they were known by their work. Finally I was able to create what they call here a package: three people were hired by the Department of Physics at Stony Brook, and three others by a small firm called Hypress, not far from Stony Brook. We formed a cooperative agreement, meaning basically that our groups would work together.

Soon afterward, I went back to Moscow, packed up my lab and moved. Now, we have a large team of Russians here, what my secretary calls a "pipeline." There are two full professors: Dima Averin and me. There are also quite a few Russian postdoctoral students, some research scientists, our students. Some study here all the time, and others who are based in Moscow travel on a regular basis to do work here.

The research that I do lies somewhere at the intersection of solid state physics and electronics. We create new electronic devices based on the most innovative concepts in physics. We often say proudly that there are two major trends in our work: we create the fastest electronic devices in the world; and we create the smallest, the most compact, electronic devices in the world. Both of these trends, which we had put forward some time ago, are becoming increasingly popular in America today.

For many Russians scientists, coming to America isn't easy. I was in a better position than the rest because I had already had the experience of living abroad. Back in the eighties, despite the fact that I wasn't a party member, some good people—at first Khokhlov, a rector of Moscow State University, and then Velikhov, a vice president of the Academy of Science—gave me two big breaks. Without asking the permission of the Party Central Committee, they pushed me out of the country to America, where I spent a couple of months during each visit. It was almost a miracle at that time: to be able to visit America twice and not be accompanied by KGB officers. Anyway, I had this experience, and I knew what life here was like.

All the same, people should stay in their country, where they have cultural roots and share a cultural background—all these little things that you absorb from childhood. There is nothing good about living in a country that is not yours. America is a good country, but it's not mine. What really helps, though, is that I'm not really living here—I'm working here. I joke sometimes that I simply moved from Room E11901A to Room B135.

I didn't know Russia that well, either. I was working too hard. In some ways, I know America better. Here, at least, I can travel. In Russia, it was impossible—all these problems with hotel reservations. The cities I knew in Russia were Leningrad, Kharkov, and Kiev, that's all. I was in Novosibirsk once, but I never got to Lake Baikal. And here I travel often: at least once in two weeks I take a little vacation in the United States. So, factually speaking, I know America better than I knew Russia. But it's only a surface knowledge. Because there's also the culture, the layers of it that you begin to absorb from the time you're two weeks old. I can't say that I understand American culture. And, considering the amount of time I spend at work, I feel pretty hopeless about ever knowing it. I miss Russia. I often see it in my dreams. I see a ski track I used to take, near Moscow. I often follow it in my dreams. I can count every little hillock on that route. Well, those are just small, insignificant things.

The great tragedy in Russia is what happened to people. I speak mostly for the scientists, since I know them the best. They had been told in a loud and compelling voice: "You guys, just keep on learning and everything is going to be fine. We need you. Our science and industry can't survive without you." And then it came about that nobody needed them. Big science was just a toy in the hands of the military industrial complex, and when that fell apart, nobody needed big science anymore. The country's industry wasn't developed enough. Even America no longer needs it that much anymore. Science here was also a toy in the hands of the military industrial complex; and now when that has shrunk, science has suffered. The situation here—particularly in physics, in fundamental research—is terrible. There are not many jobs.

So, even in America, science is in a desperate situation. In Russia, the situation is much more serious. Scientists are unemployed. There is no work for them at all. Some are luckier, because they know other languages, or they have connections. They've managed to leave. Young people, like my son, changed their occupation and went into business. Some did it gladly. They're young and limber; they actually enjoy the change. But those who are older than thirty-five are stuck. And it's not only a question of money. People feel useless. You can't keep telling a person for thirty years that he's an important member of society, and then suddenly tell him he's obsolete. Some well-known scientists have committed suicide.

In Russia today scientists are like fish out of water; they have lost their life's purpose. Because for people like me, work is almost everything. Recently I've counted: I'm working seventy-six hours a week. You can work in this way only if you believe that your work is necessary. If you're told one day that nobody needs you, it's a tragedy. I heard of a person in Russia who recently went on a hunger strike, because salaries weren't being paid. I think it was the director of the Physics and Earth Institute in Moscow. They all laughed, because nobody cares. Who needs these physicists and earth scientists nowadays?

What I'm trying to say is that there are two ways of looking at the situation. On the one hand, this is a positive and inevitable process of achieving balance. Because the truth of the matter is that Russia can't have more scientists than America, because it has much less wealth. On the other hand, the decline of big science is causing millions—literally, millions—of personal tragedies.

Only a small percentage of Russian scientists left the country. For one thing, only a few scientific fields were considered world class: some areas of mathematics, most of physics, and some fields of engineering, for example aeronautical engineering. But even in the most highly developed fields, like physics, the percentage of actual emigrants is very small. Actually, even those who remain in the country become emigrants—because they leave science.

They can't survive on their salaries. The average salary in a governmental institution is about $48 a month. Even if a person keeps his job, he has to constantly search for other sources of income, and his work becomes inefficient. Science requires concentration: you can't afford to think of other matters. So, basically it doesn't matter if the person emigrates out of the country, or "internally"—in either case he leaves science. And if I try to count the percentage of scientists who have left science, well, I can say almost all of them did. Nobody is paid enough to be able to work as a scientist—almost nobody. I know some really good scientific teams that have been erased from the face of the earth. As for my own laboratory, not long before leaving Russia, I counted the number of Ph.Ds in my laboratory: there were twenty-six. Only four of them are still in Moscow.

Science is a funny thing. If you work only a little bit today, tomorrow you won't remember what you've done. If a physicist works less than forty hours a week, I think that he's wasting his time. But after putting in a certain amount of time, there is an abrupt increase in outcome. You invest only 2 percent more effort, but your work makes twice as big an impact. It's an engaging, intoxicating process—and a little nightmarish. You can keep going for a long time, and then, suddenly, come to a halt unable to go on any further. One can easily go crazy. Some people actually have to enter mental institutions. In Moscow, right across the street from the Physics Department at Moscow University is the Soloviev Mental Hospital. And sure enough, about one-third of the physics faculty spent their vacations in that lovely place. You can joke about it, but it's serious.

Here, I can stay focused on my work. I don't have to stand in line to buy potatoes, or anything else, as I did in Russia. But, again, there is such a thing as cultural space. You may not notice its presence, but you always feel its absence—and you suffer as a result. In Russia there was a theory that if, at least once a week, you didn't take a walk and look at objects that are not rectangular—like trees, leaves, birds, or people—eventually you would go crazy. I don't know if it's true, but it certainly doesn't contradict what I have observed. The thing is, nobody ever tells you a thing about the importance of things other than work, like your cultural or natural surroundings—things like a chat with a friend, which you often think of as a waste of time. But when you lose this cultural support, you feel bad. That's why Russians are forming groups now in America, just as before perestroika, Jews clustered together in Russia. The reason for organizing such groups is obvious: people were protecting themselves against anti-Semitism. If someone happened to build a nest someplace, he or she immediately started to bring his own people into that nest, to protect the nest from intruders.

Here, it's different. Nobody is attacking you. There's no anti-Russian or anti-Soviet mood. It's simply easier for people to be with their own kind. Take our Russian pipeline here: the reason why it was created and why it keeps working is probably the unconscious desire of people to re-create a Russian cultural atmosphere in which they can breathe. In Russia we didn't need a special Russian community. You could go anywhere—to a bar, a café—and talk to ordinary people. Here we don't have the opportunity to communicate with common people. We're locked into our small, rather select circle. I could go to a bar here, too, of course. But I wouldn't understand a word around me. My English is quite good; but there are cultural references I don't understand. You have to start in kindergarten in this country to understand those references.

Stony Brook is a good place to work. People are friendly, and the atmosphere is free of intrigue. They're strong professionally. You have to work hard if you don't want to fall behind, but I like it. In Moscow I was a little bit spoiled. I was considered a star, maybe a quasi-star. Here I have to keep running with my tongue out simply not to be left behind: the average standard here is much higher than in Russia.

Another thing I like about American science is the funding. In Russia, all the money came down from the top, from the government, and it was distributed by the presidium of the Academy of Sciences to the research institutes. The director of each institute would then distribute the money to individual departments and laboratories. The entire system was based on a false premise, that if a director of some institute was a Nobel laureate, that automatically made him capable of managing the work of thousands of people. Landau, one of the greatest Russian scientists, used to say that a person couldn't have more than three people under his supervision. And that was a rule in his institute. Unfortunately, not in all the others.

Anything but science determined where the money would go, factors like who is whose friend, or who was better liked by the boss. So, when I look at what's happening now in Russian science, along with a feeling of great sadness, I feel a certain satisfaction. The Academy of Sciences is not in a healthy state right now, and the academy members are miserable. They don't have any money, so they wander along the corridors and complain. Nobody is kissing their feet anymore, which gives me some satisfaction. In the United States, the system is different: it all depends on getting grants. Of course, it's also not an ideal system. There's a lot of stupidity and envy involved. But at least you can compete for your money. That's why you won't find the kind of obscure, dark, outdated science that existed in Russia. That would have no chance of survival here.

Some people complain that the grants system allows for all kinds of speculation, that the people who more often and loudly repeat the words *new, newest,* and *advanced* are given the best opportunities. That's true, in a way. No system is ideal. But at least you must stay up-to-date. All the same, about 20 percent of the people in each department cannot obtain grants. They're usually given a bigger teaching load. In order to teach undergraduates here, you don't have to be an innovative scientist. They teach about what happened in the eighteenth and nineteenth centuries.

Another good thing is that you compete for grants in Washington. So if you're on bad terms with colleagues in your own department, if there was a personal clash, it won't affect the decision. And it's easy to stay on good terms with your colleagues because you don't compete with them. In Russia, you had to fight for funding. Every director had his favorites and black sheep among the laboratory chiefs. This constant bickering was making life miserable. Here it doesn't really exist. And that's nice.

My future largely depends on the situation in Russia. If I were to decide to go back now, there would be nothing for me to do. Russia will have use for my work in another fifty years, maybe. It makes me feel sad, but not guilty. Of course, I wish it hadn't happened this way. I wish that Russia was a strong country with cutting-edge science and industry. I wish I could work there and beat the Americans with our results. That would be wonderful. I remember those times in Russia—I attending a conference and giving a paper that caused Americans to turn green with envy, and then white with shock. I'd prefer it that way. I'd prefer to live in my own country.

My son is in Moscow. He went into business. It's difficult, of course, but things are happening. New companies come up and go bust. People are attempting to establish new industries. It's a struggle. And it's life. My daughter lives in the States and she's married to an American. She's spent a significant part of her life here. I don't think she would ever go back.

I'm too old to change my occupation, start out in an entirely different field. If I were younger, though, I'd probably do it, without reservations. I believe that Russia is a country of immense opportunity right now. If you want to believe in a great future for Russians, you realize that its foundation is being laid now. These years will be later remembered as legendary. People will write about them, as they write today about the period of J.P. Morgan or Vanderbilt. Those days in America were fantastic times—violent, crude, greedy—but they were big times.

I went back to Russia in 1993. It was great. For the first time I saw the expression of freedom on people's faces. Previously, they had worn an expression of misery, as if they were beaten up or walked over. It was the expression of people who can't control their lives. And now it's an expression of independent, sovereign people, busy people. They may not smile much—smiling is rare in Russia—but they're doing something important, they're building their lives.

I liked that a lot. That was in 1993, still a very difficult year in Russia. I remember stopping to buy a book for my grandson. I paid for it, picked up the book, and suddenly something I heard caught my attention, something very unusual. I tried to figure out what I had heard, and realized it was "thank you." The saleswoman had said, "thank you." For the first time in my fifty years in Russia, I heard a salesperson say "thank you" without a nervous strain in her voice. It was fantastic.

Anatoly and Olga Borisov
Science Pure and Impure

NOW *in their forties, Olga and Anatoly lived and worked most of their adult years in Academtown, a huge academic and science research center on the outskirts of Novosibirsk, in Siberia. Consisting of a university and a total of about sixty academic research institutes, it was a community created specifically for the pursuit of science. Since 1993 they have lived in Houston, where Anatoly is a physicist in a small company. They have a son and daughter. Their son is a skilled tennis player, having played for Texas in a national tournament. Olga and Anatoly still miss the unique and intense community that they left behind. "But I like Texas," Anatoly says. "It reminds me of Siberia—vast lands, a free spirit among the people, an atmosphere of internationalism."*

Anatoly: I came to America because I was invited by a university. It was the end of 1993 when I arrived and I lectured until May of 1994. I found out later that I could extend my grant if I managed to find a job. So I wrote a few letters to colleagues of mine in the United States. Two of them were Russians: Professor Bochnik and Professor Shtern. They helped me to find a position at the University of Houston, where I worked for two years. Then I was invited to join a small company that's involved in my field: the mechanics of liquids and gases, the proccss of ignition. The company is called Equadyne International. I've been working in research there since then.

I did the same type of work in Russia, though I was mostly dealing with theory then, more of a pure science. The place where I worked, the Institute of Heat Physics, is one of a kind. It's the biggest in the world. There's nothing like it here. It's part of a large science center in Russia called Academtown, in Novosibirsk, Siberia. It's a very special place.

Olga: Academtown was founded in 1958 by a member of the Academy of Sciences, Lavrentiev. He was a prominent mathematician and also a very influential person.

Anatoly: The best scientists in the country, including Moscow, Leningrad, and Kiev, were invited to work there. It became a major scientific center, encompassing all the sciences. Consisting of twenty-five basic science research institutes and a university, it also includes the so-called implementation ring, made up of thirty-five institutes and technology companies responsible for the practical implementation and application of the scientific research conducted in the core academic institutes.

The university also holds annual national Olympiads in physics and mathematics for high school students. The purpose of those Olympiads is to discover particularly gifted kids, who are then placed in the university's boarding schools in Academtown. The schools emphasize mathematics, physics, and other scientific fields. Kids study there from seventh to tenth grade and then enroll in the university. There are also summer programs.

I've lived in Academtown permanently since 1973 and as a kid I attended one of the summer schools. The town is isolated geographically. The nearest urban center, the city of Novosibirsk, is 30 kilometers away.

The ring of implementation—technology companies—was the first to drop out of the entire complex. The trouble started even before perestroika: the institutes of the implementation ring were controlled by the Ministry of Industry, and the academic institutes were subject to the Academy of Sciences. Science and Industry were often in conflict, and a few firms departed from the ring. Then, military programs were downsized, some of them shut down completely, and, as a result, major scientific programs also shut down.

As a result of the economic reforms brought about by perestroika, many industrial enterprises in the country stopped functioning. Before perestroika, these enterprises had a direct interest in new scientific developments: they received funds from the government for implementing advances in technology. But now when major plants were closing, the ties between science and industry broke down. And as science was stripped bare, students went elsewhere. They went into business instead, looking for ways to make money. Scientists weren't making money. Since the advent of perestroika, our salaries had remained frozen. Because of inflation, it means that they effectively went down. We could no longer support our families on those salaries.

Olga: I miss Academtown. We had a great life there.

Anatoly: And the place was so beautiful. Our houses stood in the pinewoods. The Obskoye Sea was close by. In the summer, you could go fishing or boating. And social life in Academtown was always very animated.

Olga: Except in recent years, when people became involved in things like growing vegetables and fruits on their balconies. The food shortages had already begun. But previously, it was quite lively. It was a great community of scientists.

Anatoly: People were easily excited. Once scientists are enthralled by something new, they go to all kinds of extremes. I remember reading in some magazine an article about windsurfing: a board and a sail. I immediately decided to build one on my own. My friends and I shopped all around town for materials: we got material for the board in one place, fabric for the sail in another, something else from a pharmacy. And we built a beautiful windsurfer and surfed on it in the open sea—to the great amazement of many people. They had never seen anything like that before: from a distance one couldn't see the board; it looked like a person and sail moving on the surface of the water. Boats changed direction to approach us and take a look.

There was another thing, too. There were those who hadn't succeeded in science. And when they suddenly realized it at the age of thirty or thirty-five they redirected their energy into all sorts of strange hobbies—like growing cactuses. For example, a person in my lab was growing cactuses, and he became really good at it. He kept up correspondence with other cactus fans all over the world.

Botanists from Australia wrote to request some seeds of the rare cactuses that he cultivated in his apartment. There were 3,500 cactuses sitting in his tiny room.

I've remained in America for professional reasons, mainly. I wanted the opportunity to work here for a while. My plans for the future are still pretty vague. I keep in touch with my institute in Academtown. I don't rule out the possibility of going back to Russia. But then there's another side to the problem: my children. I'd like them to stay here. My son plays tennis and he's really good; he played for the state of Texas in a recent national tournament. He's totally American now—much more so than the girl, who is a little younger. The boy doesn't want to go back to Russia.

Olga: Recently, he overheard a conversation we had about maybe going back to Russia. He became really frightened, couldn't sleep. He's a very emotional child. He knows there is a war going on in Russia; he hears about Chechnya all the time. He's worried about his life there. I'm worried about his life, too.

I went through a personal tragedy there. My sister in Moscow was killed two years ago. She was one of these people who had left science and turned to business: She had gone to work in a bank. Things were going very well for her. I guess she had the right qualities for that kind of work: what you call a sixth sense, an intuition. But it cost her her life. They still haven't found her killers. Nobody's really looking. It was clearly the Mafia's doing, but nobody knows why, and it's too dangerous to even try to find out. She left two children, and it would put them at risk.

Anatoly: Children hear everything. When that happened, our son became frightened. But if we have no choice, we'll have to go back. After all, we've lived there all our lives, we'll get by somehow. But we'd prefer our children to grow up here.

I like Texas. It reminds me of Siberia: vast lands, a free spirit among the people, an atmosphere of internationalism. People from different cultures coexist here peacefully. The sea is also close. Of course, it was a little colder in Siberia.

Olga: I like the people here. Americans are very open, very innocent. They've managed to keep a childlike approach to life. Maybe it's because they weren't burdened with too many problems in their lives.

Alex and Masha Feoktistov
Starting Over

BACK *in Riga, Latvia, Alex and Masha had been well respected members of the medical community. Still, being Russian in Latvia meant being an outsider. So they learned how to be outsiders even before they came to America. When Baltic nationalists took over in 1990, they decided to leave the country. Settling in New York, both Alex and Masha worked at menial jobs before they could once again practice their professions. They have few complaints. "We never got anything for free, nothing came easy to us. We've earned everything we have. And this is what makes us proud," says Masha.*

Alex: We came to America almost by accident. We had lived in Latvia, and life there had its peculiarities. When glasnost came on the scene, everyone who was not Latvian became unwelcome in the republic—Russians, Jews, Poles.* I wasn't even sure which group I belonged to: my father was Russian; my mother had a Ukrainian father and Jewish mother. Suddenly, all the Russian doctors were required to pass three special exams, including one or two exams in Latvian language and history. Of course, doctors of

---

* *Glasnost* is the term for Gorbachev's policy of supporting the relatively open discussion of ideas in the press, arts, and sciences. Freer speech encouraged the diverse nationalities living in the Soviet Union—as in the Baltic republics—to express their demands for national sovereignty, leading to an eruption of ethnic strife and, eventually, the collapse of the Soviet empire.

Latvian nationality didn't have to take these tests: they were given only one medical proficiency exam. Then we found out that we were about to lose our apartment in Riga. My wife had come to Latvia in 1978, from Moldavia.

But this was 1990. One day a friend called me during my shift at the hospital. He was close to government circles, the kind of person who knows not only the latest news, but also what's about to happen. So he told me, "You'll lose your apartment." "Why?" I asked. "Privatization is coming," he said. "Those who haven't lived in Latvia for sixteen years prior to the date of privatization will lose the right to become proprietors."

I had already known that we would be denied citizens' rights in Latvia. Now I realized that also we'd be left without a place to live. So, that day I came home and I said to my wife, "Let's go to America." And, to my great surprise, she immediately said, "Okay, let's go." I didn't expect her to agree that easily. I was prepared to have an argument, to have to persuade her. But she simply said, "Let's go."

The first thing I did was to call my friends in New York. We knew a couple of people who had immigrated earlier. "Yes, come over, don't even hesitate," one of them told me. "You'll find a job, you'll get a green card, no problem." Another friend was more cautious, less optimistic: "Well, if you think that's what you should do, come," he said. "We'll figure something out."

So we sold the apartment. And with the money we received, we paid for one American visa—for myself—and a plane ticket. We couldn't go together. Since we were a family without children, there was no way the Americans would give us a visa. Our intentions would be too obvious. So I applied for a visa just for myself, and picked it up at the American Embassy in Moscow. I left less than a month after that conversation with my wife.

I had $800 in my pocket and a small suitcase in my hands. Or maybe it was $400 and two suitcases. They were so small, these suitcases—filled with the things we wanted to carry from our old life to a new one. There weren't that many things. We sold or gave away almost everything.

So, I came to my friend in New York, the one who was so optimistic. He put me up for one day. Then he told me: "You'll stay with an old woman, a relative of mine. You can share the apartment with her." The old woman lived on Social Security. She didn't mind having somebody to live with her and pay some cash for the room. I paid $200 a month for the room; it wasn't even private. I started working for cash. The idea was that I go to the United States, get by somehow, find a job, prepare for my medical exam, and wait for my wife. Masha was still in Latvia, with no apartment and no money. She was selling whatever was left of our belongings in order to survive. In two months she applied for a visa. By that time Latvia had separated from Moscow. Masha didn't have to go to Moscow to obtain a visa; she could do it in Helsinki. The computer in the American Embassy in Helsinki hadn't found my name. That's why she got her visa.

She arrived on March 13, 1991. The two of us lived in the same room I had lived in before. The old lady we shared the apartment with was a real bitch. One of those people who had had everything in Russia, she had been a chief accountant at the Kirov Ballet Theater. And here she was living on Social Security. She wasn't happy at all. I told her once, after listening to her complaints, "But, no matter what, you don't want to go back to Russia, do you? Life is hard there, food is rationed with coupons." And she replied, "What are you talking about? I was the one who distributed those coupons."

We had to decide what to do next. Our friends advised us to go to an organization for Jewish immigrants, which gives help to Jewish refugees in the United States. Both of us were born to Jewish mothers.

Masha: In Russia we were often harassed for being Jews. So, we thought finally we're with our own people, and they'll help us. We hadn't applied yet for refugee status. We came to the Hebrew Immigrant Aid Association for advice. I still remember that young woman, a social worker, saying: "You're not Jews." I was shocked. All my life I'd been scorned for being a Jew. Finally I was here, in America, and what did I hear? "You're not Jewish enough."

Alex: We decided not to apply for political asylum, the way most of the Soviet Jews did. I had never fought against the Communist regime. I didn't want to lie about it. True, I had never respected the Soviet system, but it's also true that I had a pretty good life, a good position as part of it. The real problem we had encountered in Latvia, what eventually caused us to leave, was Latvian nationalism. Nobody wanted to hear about it. America supported the emancipation of the Baltic republics; it was considered an unconditionally good thing. How could there be refugees from Latvian nationalism? I even know of some Russians who have been deported from America and sent back to Latvia. The reason for deportation was that "Latvia has a democratic regime."

So, I decided to apply for a work visa. I am a doctor. From 1986 to 1989 I was head of the Central Laboratory of Immunology in Latvia, involved in research on AIDS. It was one of the first laboratories of its kind in the Soviet Union. The reason it came into being was that one of the top Communist Party bosses in Latvia returned from a trip to Tanzania with AIDS. When I decided to look for a job here, I went to a library and compiled a list of laboratories in the United States that were doing AIDS research. I sent my résumés to all of them—more than a hundred résumés, in total. Then I waited.

Finally, I got my first real job in Harlem: they took me as a medical assistant in the ambulance corps for the underserved population. I worked on a trial basis, for one month.

I put in four hours a day, and the trip to Harlem and back was taking another four hours. But after working there for three weeks, my boss called me into her office and told me, "Sorry, you're not the right person for us." I asked why. "You're lucky you weren't sued for what you did," she replied.

"What for?" I asked. "For abuse," she said. I was so naive, that I asked: "What do you mean by 'abuse'?" She explained. Once I was giving a shot to a little boy, a really nice kid, so I joked with him a little. After I finished I slapped his bottom slightly, the way we used to do in Russia as a way of saying "bye." His father saw the whole thing and I was accused of sexual abuse. They said good-bye to me.

A couple of weeks after I lost that job, I was invited to the research laboratory at New York University for an interview. After the interview, they told me, "We'll give you a call." Two weeks later I called them myself. "We are still interviewing people," they said. "We'll call you in two weeks." Two weeks later I called them again and asked, "Can you give me an answer?" "No, not yet," they said. "We'll call you back in two weeks."

On July 12, 1991—I remember that day very well, my visa was expiring that day—I called them again. We had just moved to a new apartment. The telephone wasn't hooked up yet, so I went outside to make the call from a pay phone. "This is my last call," I said. "I need to know right now. Are you taking me or not?" And they said, "Yes. We are taking you."

I began working in the lab at the medical school. At the same time, Masha worked as a home attendant, taking care of an elderly woman. Our life finally began to take some shape. Then, most unexpectedly, a true miracle happened. Masha became pregnant. In Russia, we were told it could never happen. She underwent surgery, a serious procedure. But the doctors told her, "Forget about having children. Don't even think of it. It can never happen."

We had a son. Of course it was hard in the beginning. I spent all day in the laboratory, she stayed at home with the baby. For about a year, we had to live on only one salary. I was making $27,000 a year. It's not that much, particularly in New York. We had to borrow money every month. Our friends kept a hundred-dollar bill always ready for us. On the first day of each month we'd take it, and on the fifteenth of each month we'd pay it back—and then we'd take it again. So, one day I went to talk to my boss: "Mark, I know you need a lab assistant. I suggest you take my wife." He said, "Let her come in for an interview."

She was hired. She's a dentist. But, I thought, it's harder to fix people's teeth than to handle paperwork. It wasn't easy, of course. She was hysterical the first couple of months, because she was afraid to make a mistake; she couldn't afford to make a mistake. I showed her everything. And she had to take care of the child, too, waking up in the middle of the night to calm him down. She was exhausted. I couldn't give her help. I was preparing for my exams. And I also was promoted—from research assistant to associate research scientist. My schedule went like this: I left home at five in the morning so that I could study in the lab before everybody showed up. Every evening after work, I spent hours in the library. The year went by. I passed my exam, and with a very good score, too. I got a residency at Roosevelt Hospital. We now live in hospital housing.

When we came to America—our first months here—we were in a state of shock. And thank God that we were, because we didn't understand what we had done. We had burned all our bridges. We left behind everything: our professional positions, apartments, cars. We came to America with literally the clothes we had on our backs. And we had to live, somehow. So, we couldn't afford any problems—emotional, linguistic, or cultural problems. We pushed forward, didn't look back or around. We had one goal: survival.

We had to live on $400 a month. We paid $200 for rent, and we were left with $200. We had to live on that money for the whole month. I had to walk to my job and back, because I couldn't afford to buy a token. All night long, I lugged a paralyzed man on my shoulders, and in the morning I went back home, totally exhausted.

Masha: In Latvia, we had been respected and quite wealthy members of society; we were doctors. You know, many Russian immigrants keep talking about their past, about what big bosses they were. Somehow, most of these people had been big bosses in the past. It's really quite funny. But, unlike these people, I felt more proud and satisfied sweeping floors and cleaning toilets here than being a dentist back in the Soviet Union. Sweeping floors was something I did for myself, for the first time in my life. In the Soviet Union we were used to somebody always standing on top of us, telling us what to do. We were raised, and lived our lives, in humiliation. Our lives mattered only as long as they were of use to society. None of us mattered as individuals; we were part of a whole, a much larger entity. But here, suddenly, my long-dormant sense of human dignity was awakened. And this reborn sense of human dignity could be expressed even in cleaning toilets. Anyway, we don't know this country too well, we only know New York. But we love this country and are grateful for what it has given us, and it has given us a lot.

Alex: I lived in Latvia most of my life, for thirty-two years. Even though lots of Russians lived in Latvia, it was not Russia. Russian culture in Latvia was not the same as it was in Moscow, or in any other city in Russia. Even the Russian language I spoke was not exactly the same Russian language that was spoken in Moscow. It had the quality of a learned language. So, being Russian in Latvia meant being an outsider. And that was how I felt. And that feeling had increased with time, reaching the level of absolute despair in the end. So I learned how to be an outsider even before I came to America. In the United States, this feeling was never as desperate and hopeless as it had been in Latvia. Here I felt that once you have a goal, and you're working hard to achieve it, you'll get there—and if not exactly there, then some other place. It's another thing I have learned here—to be flexible. You can always try something else, change your plan a little bit, revise it.

Masha: In the Soviet Union, you didn't have much of a choice. Your life was determined from the beginning, a path was laid out for you—once and forever. All you had to do was follow it. No variations allowed. Our lives didn't belong to us. Here we have a choice. And one of the most important things we've learned here is how to live in the present. To live not for the sake of the future—that wonderful and beautiful future which is to come—but to live life day by day. And to enjoy what we have today. And we have a lot, actually: we have a healthy child, we have an apartment with a view of the Hudson River, and we enjoy that view very much.

Alex: I feel easier here—in a moral sense. I feel that I can do what I want, and nobody can tell me: "This is not the right thing to do." That's how it was in the Soviet Union, where everybody spoke to you on behalf of society, telling you what you are, what you should and could be, what is right or wrong. Nobody judges you here: people don't force their opinions on you. Nobody puts limits on what you can do. You, yourself, set the limits, define your own boundaries or you can accept the boundaries established by society, but only because you agree with them, not because they were forced upon you. I am not talking about the limits imposed by the law. I'm talking about personal freedom.

Masha: We feel particularly proud of what we've done, because we've done it with our own hands. Nobody helped us. And we don't have a lucky star. I mean, some people can get away with certain things, but not us. We never got anything for free, nothing came easy to us. We've earned everything we have. And this is what makes us proud. We were completely on our own, and we did it.

Alex: Coming here was like coming to a new planet. We expected everything to be different. We didn't look for similarities between the new and the old worlds.

My previous boss is a very wealthy man; he owns his own company and lives in a duplex apartment on the Upper West Side. He is an established scientist, too, with more than 200 published works. But, talking to him, you'd never even guess it. He is the nicest person. His parents were immigrants.

I remember once talking with him at a party, and he asked me, "What do you think of me?" And I said, "I think of you as my son."

"What do you mean?" he asked. "Well, I'm a first-generation immigrant," I said. "You are the second. You are my son."

Listening to his stories about his parents, how they first came to America, how they lived in poverty, I couldn't get rid of this weird feeling of time moving backward. It felt like we were his parents. Because their experience was so close to ours. He told me about his father, who had been a doctor, who immigrated to America, and found his first job as a scientist. It was as if he were telling me a story about myself. He is twice my age, my old boss, but at such moments he felt like my son. Probably, that's how my son will talk about me, thirty years from now.

Masha: Life here has made me tougher, but also more open—more open to everything new. And if somebody asked me what the most important thing newly arriving immigrants should bring with them to this country, I'd say that they should bring some soap—wash their eyes and ears as often as possible—so that they could see and listen better. That's their first priority.

ENTREPRENEURS

Tatiana Alexa
Winners Don't Cry

Now thirty years old, Tatiana was in her early twenties when she entered the world of business.* A young physician with a husband and a small daughter, she left medicine at a time when many doctors and scientists were losing their research funding and their jobs, and were unable to live on their salaries. She rose quickly to become a partner in a Moscow firm that controlled a variety of business and commercial ventures. In spite of the high stakes, she views her world with a certain detachment: "It was the game that mattered to me; money was merely a measure of one's success in this game. Money meant that I was good at what I was doing." This game has its dangers. Maybe it was Tatiana's common sense that helped her to survive situations that proved to be fatal to many strong and overconfident men. Tatiana now runs an Internet business based in New York.

In Russia my life was rolling down a smooth, pretty much predictable, path. At least in the beginning.

I grew up in a big, loving family. I had a very happy childhood. I graduated from high school with a gold medal. I was

---

* The collapse of the Soviet Union in the end of 1991 brought about a new business climate in Russia. Previously the Communist Party had controlled all aspects of the economy. With its fall from power, there were no controls in existence to regulate the boom in private enterprise. Business was being done at an incredibly fast pace in an atmosphere of lawlessness, bribery, and corruption; organized crime also played an important role.

accepted into the best medical institute in Moscow. It was one of the best medical schools in the country, the hardest to get into. Things became interesting after my graduation, after I finished the six years at college and received my long anticipated medical degree. It was 1989.

The situation in the country had changed, and suddenly, it turned out, neither I nor my professional education was in demand. In1989, the state was still assigning the jobs across the country to every college graduate, but it was the last year that the government was involved in job allocation.

I was among the last to have my "fate" determined by the State Allocation Commission. I didn't come from a medical family, so I didn't have any strong connections in the field. The best I could hope for was a position as a regular staff therapist in one of the many district clinics in Moscow. But that wasn't what I wanted to do. I was a very ambitious student. In fact, in my last year at school, I became involved in scientific research, assisting one of my professors. The project was interesting, and very promising. If successfully completed, it could have had a shot for a Nobel Prize. It dealt with what's known in medicine as lung shock, a condition caused by a stress situation, like trauma or intoxication, that results in the swelling of a lung and often causes death.

Our laboratory's approach to the problem was innovative; the research lab was predominantly composed of young people like myself. It all seemed very exciting. Unfortunately, I could not persuade the Allocation Commission at my school to assign me to the laboratory. But I found a way around their decision, working closely with the lab without being assigned to it officially. The fact that I could get away with it—doing something I wanted, and not what the state ordered me to do—was a sign of changing times. Before, it would have been simply inconceivable.

Those were the last years of the Soviet regime—its twilight. Although most of the government rules and procedures remained, they were emptied of content. They had turned into pure formalities. The system was dead.

My graduation coincided with the beginning of a period of severe inflation in the country. In 1990, six months after I began to work as a doctor in a hospital, while continuing my research, I found that my salary was not enough to buy food. It didn't happen in a day, of course. In the first month or two, my salary, 110 rubles, seemed like pretty good money. After a year, it was nothing. Those years after college turned out to be the most financially difficult years of my life. I had a family by then. My husband was also a doctor, both of us were employed, but we could hardly survive on our salaries, especially after our child was born.

When my parents came to visit us, I often had nothing to put on the table but tea and jam. It was making me feel very uncomfortable. I was raised in a hospitable, generous home, and I wanted my home to be the same. The fact that I couldn't do it, that I had nothing to offer my guests, was torture for my pride, my sense of self. That was the second reason why I decided to leave medicine. The first was that our laboratory was shut down due to lack of funding, despite the fact that our research was so important. On top of all that, my work as a doctor brought me a lot of disappointment. I often had to cure my patients with the power of words rather than with medications; there was simply no medicine available. I'm not talking about a lack of complicated medical or surgical equipment, but of a simple first aid kit, even pain relievers. I had to write prescriptions based on what was in stock at the hospital or pharmacy, not what my patients needed.

All the big changes in the country coincided with my entering adult life. Before that I was simply a student, a mama's girl, who had spent ten years in school, then six in college. I had taken a route charted in advance. My life was completely predictable. And then, suddenly, it all stopped.

I was out of school and nobody was imposing any deadlines or schedules. I was completely on my own. I had to make my own decisions. I was a doctor. I had patients for whom I was responsible. And the fact that I couldn't help them in the way I wanted, the way I was supposed to, hit me very hard. And, still, even though I didn't have the proper means at my disposal, I had to account for their health and well-being as if I did. Recently, I spent a couple of days in an American hospital. The difference was shocking. Here the examination of a patient involves a series of tests. Only after all tests are completed, and the results are in, can a doctor present a final diagnosis. In Russia, equipment was so poor that most of the time doctors came up with a diagnosis not after, but before, or even instead of testing. In fact, a doctor's talent was measured by his ability to diagnose a patient with a minimum of testing, or merely by touch. Another reason for the lack of proper diagnosis was the need to reduce the length of a patient's stay in the hospital. Hospitals were so overcrowded that patients often had to stay in corridors and hallways.

The first medical cooperatives started to form around that time—the first private medical enterprises. I got a taste of it. During the summer of 1989 I went to Samarkand with one of these first cooperatives. From Samarkand we were sent to a small village right on the border between Uzbekistan and Tajikistan. We spent three days there. An entrepreneur has decided to make money by bringing young doctors from Moscow to this remote place, equipped, as the advertisement said, "with the most modern, most advanced, most up-to-date medical equipment." Except we didn't have any modern, up-to-date equipment. All we had brought with us was an ultrasound device for examining the heart, which was useless in this environment, where the main health issue was stomach pain, a liver disorder caused by fatty food. We took along the ultrasound because it was the only portable equipment we could find.

The villagers called us "Moscow doctors with a TV." The whole purpose was to show off, to make an impression on the villagers by examining their stomachs not with our bare fingers but with some metallic device instead. So we examined stomachs with this heart diagnostic device: what we were seeing on the screen had nothing to do with what we told the patients. We simply told them what we knew was the problem. In the end, the treatment we prescribed was the right one. But the whole thing reminded me of a cheap show. You had to perform certain procedures in order to win the patient's trust. If you didn't lie to him, he would not believe you. Anyway, that was my first and last experience with medical cooperatives. The good thing about it was that after I returned to Moscow, I went to a restaurant for the first time in my life. We all went to a restaurant called Prague, where we spent almost all the money we had made.

I had to take a break from medicine when my child was born in 1991. It gave me time to think. I realized that I didn't have much of a chance to do what I wanted if I stayed with medicine. My husband worked as a surgeon. For a while, we had to live on his salary and my maternity-leave compensation. We couldn't even afford to buy new clothes for our daughter: she had to wear used clothing. Everything she wore or used—her stroller, her diapers even—came from my girlfriends who already had children. A few times I received humanitarian aid packages. There was some dry milk in each package, and disposable diapers: Pampers. I stretched that one pack of Pampers for quite a long time. I used them on holidays or for doctor visits.

Some of my friends—doctors who were unemployed after our laboratory was closed—went into business. They started a business that had no relation to medicine, and they invited me to work for them. My child was seven months old when I went to work as a secretary in their office. My first week at work, I had to clean the entire office: they had just moved to a new apartment. There was no office space available for rent in Moscow at the time, so apartments were used as offices. For a week I cleaned the apartment. It was the first step in my business career. But new commercial enterprises were developing so rapidly then; changes in business law were so rapid that it was a time of great opportunity for anyone who could think unconventionally. In less than six months I made my way from secretary to one of the firm's partners.

Our business operations varied from residential construction in Moscow to all kinds of financial operations. We created a financial holding company that served as a liaison between banks and new commercial ventures, seeking both financing and investments for our clients. We weren't exactly middlemen, since we were financially responsible to the banks and the companies we worked with. But our financial activities allowed us to grow very quickly. By the time I left the company, in 1995, there were about ten firms under our umbrella, including a construction company, an airline, a freight-transportation company, a small trade company involved in retail sales, and a number of smaller firms. We didn't own all these companies outright: we were shareholders, holding from 10 percent to 30 percent of the shares.

I was responsible for coordinating the financing of these companies, and all funds passed through my hands. I made decisions on investing, reinvesting, distributing profits, tax allocations. All that had to be done in light of the inflation and changes in the currency rates. I learned quickly, but the laws changed very quickly too. I had to keep up. I took a course at the Finance Academy. But it didn't teach me anything new; it simply provided a theoretical basis for what I had learned from experience.

The main thing was to know the rules of the game. The first rule was: people. Business is made by and between people. It's about relationships, about knowing how to communicate with people.

Here, in America, the general rule is that business is about sales. It's about the ability to sell yourself, your product, the firm that stands behind you. In Russia, at the time, business was about knowing how to make contacts quickly—literally on the spur of a moment. You had to evaluate the situation quickly, deciding how useful you could be to the other person—and how useful he could be to you. And it was about knowing whom to trust. It was impossible to check a person's credit history. Nobody had any credit history. The oldest businesses were hardly a year old. There was no way to know for sure with whom you were dealing, who was telling you the truth and who wasn't. It was all about intuition, your ability to read people's minds, to take risks—but only justified risks. Of course, I had to trust the people I worked with. Without trust I couldn't have done anything. It was all so scary: you knew you could be deceived, robbed, killed, your child could be kidnapped. Anything could happen. The entire business was based on intuition and luck.

Another important rule, I learned very fast, was not to make enemies. Never take any disagreement to the point of confrontation. Because there's no way to protect yourself, there's no way to be safe when there's no law to protect you. The only way I could protect myself was to avoid hazardous situations if possible; but, if I did get stuck, the only way was to go for a settlement. Always. It was scary, of course. I had a small child. I didn't have a bodyguard in the beginning.

Business was like a game to me, a game in which I could win or lose. Losing money didn't bother me much. The worst case would be that I would end up where I had started. The money came easily and went easily. It was the game that mattered to me; money was merely a measure of one's success in this game. Money meant that I was good at what I was doing. It was like a prize for my good work. When I was involved in medical research, I aimed for a Nobel prize. Now it was money. The fun was in building the house, not making the money. Of course, I knew the house could fall apart any minute, because it was a house of cards.

Money changed my lifestyle significantly. I could afford to keep a personal car with a chauffeur six days a week. I could afford to buy an apartment of the size I wanted, and in the part of Moscow I liked. I could afford to travel. Every three or four months I would leave the country and take a trip. I traveled all over Europe in those years. In the meantime, most of my friends made barely enough money to survive.

Members of my own family were left without jobs, including my parents, cousins, uncle, and sister. I have a big family and we were always very close. I felt responsible for them. Anyway, I did something quite silly from a business point of view. I gave jobs to every member of my family that needed them. Later, I found myself a hostage to this situation. When you're working with people close to you, it's hard to make the same demands that you do of ordinary employees. Besides, every one of their mistakes hits you harder than any other employee's mistake. It's terrible to think that you've been set up by your relatives. There were a few times when a relative would give out information that shouldn't have been disclosed, putting me in a difficult position. Confidentiality was a big issue in business at the time. Who you are, what you own, who your allies are, whom you trust and whom you don't trust—it was important to keep all of this confidential, not to leak any clues to the wrong people. It was a matter of security.

Another very important rule that I discovered for myself was to keep out of the wrong places. I could always sense those dangerous, forbidden areas, as if some voice were telling me: "You can go here, it's all right, but not there, never go there, under any circumstances don't go there." And I never did.

Being a businesswoman in Russia was not easy. My enemies gossiped that I was successful because I slept with the right people. That was never my intention; I never slept with anybody. I didn't think I was less smart than the men I met in business; rather, I believed that I was smarter than many of them. My abilities, my skills, were my only privilege, and I didn't need any others.

I had a partner, and he and I owned the company together; each of us had 50 percent of the shares. We made every decision together. There was a veto rule, which meant that a decision could be made only if we both agreed on it. If one of us was against the decision, we had to persuade the other partner. Because my partner was a man, the gossip was that we were lovers. We weren't. We were very close, soul mates, and we spent a lot of time together. Nobody was as close to me then as he was, and I trusted him completely. Our situation was full of danger, and it brought us closer.

On the other hand, there were some issues that I, as a woman, could resolve more successfully. When we needed to get a quick and positive decision from someone, being a woman helped. There weren't that many women in business; besides I was a young woman of twenty-five. One time I managed to obtain a loan for one million dollars, and at a very reasonable interest rate, too. My partner had tried, but couldn't secure the loan. Credit in Russia was given without a pledge, or collateral to secure the loan; it was merely a matter of trust, of your ability to make arrangements with people. I managed not only to secure that loan agreement, but to receive the money from the bank in less than a week. The bank was on the verge of bankruptcy; nevertheless they stopped all other payments until we received credit in full. That was a million-dollar victory, but there were smaller ones every day. That was the nice side of being a woman in Russian business.

The dark side of being a woman had to do with security. When bandits come to your office, and you try to talk to them, and you think, maybe, you could reason with them—if they had more than one neuron in their brain—but they don't. You can't have a rational conversation if there is no mind to appeal to. And once they see a woman—that's it, you've already lost. They look right through you. You have no chance. You can be insulted and humiliated. It all happened to me. Fortunately, I had my partner to handle these situations. But, of course, as a result, his share in all that dirt was much greater than mine. If I managed to preserve my integrity, it's because he had to shovel more dirt.

One way to avoid contact with bandits was to stay away from competitors' territory.

That was another unwritten rule I formulated for myself. It was best to start something new, something nobody was doing before you did. This way you could have all the advantages of being a pioneer, plus the advantage that you didn't stand in anybody's way. If you don't have competitors, there can be no conflict of interests. You are in your own territory. And there were plenty of opportunities to be the first in many ventures, to start your own thing. Everything was new in Russia. For example, the financial schemes we developed were "know-how" schemes.

Nobody was doing that but us.

Doing business affected my marriage. Things weren't going well with my husband. I guess this situation has been described hundreds of times. When you spend twelve hours at work, mostly giving orders to other people, it is hard to stop giving orders when you get home. My husband continued working as a doctor; he remained in what had become my past. The gap between us was growing. A lot of people worked under my supervision. I had to make decisions at work, and very important ones. It was not how many flowers should we plant in the backyard, but decisions that had weight, in terms of the amount of money that was at stake and in terms of the risk, too. These were dangerous games that I played. I couldn't be frank about it with my husband. I couldn't have discussed these things at home, because if I had, he wouldn't have let me return to work the next day. Besides, he couldn't help me in any way, so there was no point in sharing my fears or doubts with him. It would have just made his life more complicated, that's all. As a result, I felt I couldn't be myself at home, with him. I had to play some role. I couldn't allow myself to relax even for a minute, because if I did, I would have burst out crying, I would have said something or complained, and what would be the point of that? This didn't make the family stronger. It created tension, and tension accumulates.

Besides, knowing that you're the one who supports the family, that everything in the household was bought on your salary, that you support not only your immediate family, but a lot of relatives, too, turns you into the family patriarch, the provider, which adds to your years. Immediately, it makes you feel so old. And the responsibility is so heavy, too. When I finally left the company, all of my relatives also lost their positions. And they felt it was my fault. It's strange, but when you do some good to people, they don't praise you for it. They take it for granted. But if something is taken away from them, you're the one to blame.

Those were hard times. Before I left the country, I left my husband. I bought myself an apartment, and I fixed it up. But I lived there for only a month. My business activity was coming to an end. I felt I had reached a dead end. I knew everything about my business. It no longer interested or excited me. I knew everything about the people with whom I did business. I felt like an old woman—who had experienced everything, who knew everything about life, who could not be surprised or moved by anything again. I felt enormously tired and empty.

By that time, we had opened a branch of the firm in New York. I had sent my sister to manage the branch, to serve as a company representative. Soon we started an Internet service business. I became a partner in the business while still in Moscow; and then it occurred to me that I could resolve my situation in Moscow easily and gracefully by sending myself on a long-term business trip. And so I did. In August 1995, I went to New York for three months.

Then I returned to Moscow, stayed for two months, and left again. This time I decided to take my daughter with me. It wasn't easy. The American consulate wouldn't give her a visa. I had to return to Russia. Finally I got lucky. My daughter is with me now. I didn't make a final decision to move at that time, and I still haven't made such a decision. I'm keeping the apartment in Moscow. But my business trip turned out to be much longer than I had planned it to be.

Once I decided to stay here for a while, I encountered certain problems. I came here with no knowledge of the language. I knew German, but what use was that to me here? I didn't have any business connections in this country. What did it matter that I opened a branch, if I didn't know anybody and nobody knew me? And the rules of the game are different in America. My Russian experience was of no use, either. To do business here, one needs a credit history, good references, a guaranty from the bank—all that didn't matter in Russia. What had helped me so often in Russia—my personal charm—didn't work here: I had no language to make it work. And I didn't want to do business with Russians; the kind of business they did here was too petty. It meant I'd have to come a few steps down from the level of business I did in Moscow. So, it was pretty hard. But the most important thing for me is and always was to set a certain goal for myself and then to work on achieving that goal. Even if the goal is mistaken, you get a thrill along the way. You find meaning in the process of achieving, whether or not you actually achieve your goal. In Moscow, I managed to achieve success. It cost me a few moral losses. But I proved I was capable of something. I made it there. Now I wanted to try and prove myself in New York, in the context of real capitalism—real business. The question for me was: Can I make it here? I started proving to myself and others that I can. I haven't reached the happy ending, not yet. I'm still in the process.

I like the security of doing business in America. I mean it's physically secure, safe. But the competition is so intense, it keeps you in suspense. Here it's not your personal security, your life, that's under constant threat, but your business. There are too many competitors. I know that if I fall, I'll be smashed, walked over. And it's not a very pleasant feeling. In Russia the struggle was physical, here it's economic. It's also hard to be new. You have less of a chance in this country when you're new in the game, with no family standing behind you, no connections, traditions, roots. I don't enjoy the bureaucracy here—too many papers and numbers. All this stops me from believing that I live in a free society. I don't like feeling like a second-rate person, and an immigrant to the United States is a second-rate person.

Immigrants are not loved. I don't consider myself an immigrant, and I never label myself that way. But I see how people's eyes change once they learn I am from Russia, once they suspect that I'm not a visitor—because it's okay to be a guest—but, God forbid, an immigrant. Then they'd never forgive my bad English. I feel it constantly, whether talking to prospective business partners on the phone, or shopping, or simply catching the eye of the doorman in a building. I feel it particularly in my business relations. I am in alien territory. But the stronger that feeling, the stronger is the temptation to make it mine. I've decided that if "I can make it here, I'll make it anywhere." What drives me first is ambition. And second, ambition.

But no matter whether I succeed or fail in achieving my goals, I think I'd like to change my occupation eventually and do something not at all related to business, or to money. Perhaps make movies or go into publishing. Whatever I do, I don't want money to be the only measure of my success.

Ella Kozhevnikova
The Twelve Chairs

LIKE *her sister Tatiana Alexa, Ella was a star student who became a doctor. In Moscow, a chance encounter led her to abandon medicine for a much better paid job—as a waitress. Working in a trendy, private restaurant, Ella found herself in the hands of racketeers and influence peddlers. She arrived in New York in 1993 with her husband and child and eventually became an owner of The Twelve Chairs, a small café on Macdougal Street in Soho. It is named after a Russian satirical novel written in the 1920s.* *

In Russia I studied at the Moscow Medical School, as did my sister. It was my father's influence. He was an engineer specializing in computer science. He worked in Zelenograd, a Moscow suburb. Built as a city of the future, it housed about thirty large plants and research institutes. Most of them developed advanced technologies for the space program.

My sister Tatiana and I were born in Zelenograd, and we lived there for most of our lives. When I was about eight years old, my father became interested in medical engineering. He soon began to

---

* *The Twelve Chairs* was written by Ilya Ilf and Yevgeny Petrov. It is set in Russia in the 1920s during the time of NEP (New Economic Policy). It follows the adventures of two small-time swindlers in search of a hidden family fortune. In 1970, Mel Brooks made a film, *The Twelve Chairs*, based on this novel.

work in this field professionally, founding a laboratory that developed new medical equipment. His laboratory designed a new hearing device for the deaf based on bone conductivity: it was a tiny device that could be implanted in the nasal bones. The lab also invented a defibrillator for the heart and a device to measure blood pressure in the eye. My father's love for medicine influenced my sister's and my decision to become physicians. We both graduated from the best medical school in Moscow. My sister worked as a doctor for only one year, and then became involved in business. She never returned to her profession again. I worked in a medical polyclinic in Zelenograd for three years. I was the first in our large family to contemplate emigration.

I don't know why exactly. But I sensed that something was wrong in the country right after I graduated from medical school. I could sense the danger in the air. Around that time my mother saw an article about a firm in Latvia that handled the emigration of professionals to South Africa. This was in 1990. It was still impossible to emigrate from Russia, at least for people like me and my family. We are not Jewish, and we didn't have any relatives abroad. Suddenly, here was a firm that might be able to help us to emigrate. We contacted them.

I was so passionate about this new idea that I infected my sister's husband with my enthusiasm. We went to Latvia together to apply for visas. My husband did not really want to leave Russia at the time, but he didn't object much to my decision. He never believed it would work out. Anyway, we went to Latvia to fill out our applications and were to expect visas to South Africa in about three months. But it was already 1991. In August of 1991, Gorbachev was overthrown. Soon the Latvian firm ceased to exist. South Africa was no longer interested in doing business with Russia; it was frightened by the unstable political situation in our country.

By that time we had already paid for our applications, and of course the money was never given back. That was the end of our first attempt to emigrate. I say "our," although in fact I was the one who really wanted to leave. Now when I try to analyze why—I can hardly formulate the reasons. Neither I nor my family had experienced persecution—because of nationality or anything else. I had a wonderful childhood. We belonged to a privileged circle, and I received a good education; I always had a lot of friends. But even before the events of August 1991, I began to feel uncomfortable in my country. I was always very afraid of any kind of physical violence; and even though in 1990 it hadn't happened yet, I could feel it approaching. It was the fear that I felt, even though I couldn't explain the reasons for this fear. It was an irrational feeling.

So, my first attempt to emigrate from Russia failed. I was working as a doctor by then. And so was my husband. He graduated the year before I did, and was soon hired by the Research Institute for Artificial Organ Transplants in Moscow. He was a cardiosurgeon, a very prestigious profession in Russia. He worked until 1993 in the Division of Heart Rhythm Disorders.

They often tested new equipment, or new procedures, directly on patients. Some patients would come in for surgery, standing on their feet, and they would be carried away from the operation room with their feet forward, dead. Of course, there is always a certain risk in heart surgery—but still some things were not ethically clean. And then there was another issue—bribery. The director of the cardio center was known to be taking money from patients. All the staff doctors received a standard salary of 140 rubles regardless of how many hours they spent in the hospital, or on a night shift. Most of them were young doctors, right out of medical school. All these things eventually led my husband to leave the clinic. Afterward he went to work as a doctor in the Emergency Ambulance. It was as if he'd become a dishwasher after having been a chef in a fancy restaurant.

I was still working in the polyclinic in Zelenograd. I took the job in the first place because it came with an apartment. At age twenty-four, I was the first among my many friends to receive my own two-room apartment. The administration hoped to attract college graduates in this way: working as a doctor in a public clinic was not considered a prestigious career. But I didn't care much about prestige—not after my family had to share an apartment with my parents for four years. My husband, our son, and I lived in one room of 9 square meters. I took the offer without thinking twice.

When I came to work in the polyclinic, I hoped that I would be working with an experienced doctor, so that I would have the opportunity to learn. But, in fact, I had to start entirely on my own. Luckily, a nurse who worked with me showed me how to fill out prescriptions and the like. I didn't know that I was supposed to prescribe only those medications available in the pharmacies. I had no idea what was available. I had taken a course in pharmacology at school, but theory had nothing to do with the actual situation in the pharmacies—that nothing was available. After my first day at work I came home crying. I was convinced that I could never become a real doctor. But after a couple of months, I felt pretty comfortable in my position. The clinic had made a real doctor out of me.

Life was not easy for me at the time. I remember having only one pair of high-heeled sandals for the summer and one pair of boots, also high heels, for the winter. I couldn't afford to buy a second pair of shoes. So, I walked miles in the dirt and snow, and climbed to the top floors of twenty-story buildings in the new housing developments when I went on house calls. Occasionally, the building would have a freight elevator, but there were no lights. It was scary to take those elevators.

When I started working, my boss warned me: "When you do a house call, don't ring the doorbell right away. Wait and listen to the sounds in the apartment to make sure everything is fine." It was 1990, and there were some incidents. Once, a young doctor was locked in an apartment, held there and threatened. A man wanted her to give him a note proving that he was ill, so he would be excused from work. I had an incident once. I was barely able to escape. You see, anything can happen when you are alone in an apartment with a man who is older and stronger than you are. You never knew why a person called for a doctor.

My salary was 160 rubles a month. I received no overtime pay, no holiday pay, even though sometimes I had to work on weekends doing emergency visits. It all was all covered by my salary. I worked like this for three years. And, then, one accidental meeting changed my life. My husband's brother's wife worked as a waitress in a restaurant. I met her at my husband's birthday party. I had never even seen her before. Anyway, she mentioned that she was taking a new job at a Chinese restaurant in Moscow. She simply mentioned it, didn't give it too much attention. At the time, I was sick and tired of my life, of not having any money. The last straw was that I had to borrow money for that party, to celebrate my husband's thirtieth birthday. I couldn't allow myself not to celebrate it.

Anyway, a few days later, I remember thinking, I should call Sveta—my sister-in-law—to find out if they needed another waitress at that restaurant. Quite miraculously, that same day she called to ask if I wanted to work with her. The man who had recommended her said she could bring another girl.

The restaurant called Panda was located in midtown. It was the first privately owned restaurant in Moscow. In 1993, nobody had ever heard of anything like it. So, Sveta instructed me in the car: I was to say that I was an experienced waitress, that we had worked together in the Red Dragon, a big Chinese restaurant in Moscow, for three years. Of course, I didn't have a drop of experience as a waitress. I had been in a restaurant only once or twice in my life. And I had no idea what Chinese food looked like.

When we arrived at the restaurant, there was a long line near the entrance: girls that were applying for waitressing jobs. But we didn't have to wait in line. We were expected. Somebody had made a call to the manager, and we were admitted right away, without any questions. This somebody, as I found out later, was a big political figure in Moscow. He knew Sveta from the Red Dragon. When she decided to leave that restaurant, he said he'd help her find another job. And he did.

Panda was about to become a very fancy restaurant, one of the most expensive in Moscow. It was a hard-currency restaurant. At the time, I had hardly ever seen a dollar bill. The first time was in Latvia where I went to fill out an application for a visa. The fee for one application was $35, which was then equal to 700 rubles—six months' salary.

We were hired in a moment: nobody even asked if we could speak English. As a hard-currency restaurant, and a very expensive one, it was meant mainly for foreigners. The cheapest appetizer cost $19.95. Chinese restaurants are the most expensive in Russia. The three owners of Panda were quite interesting, too. One of them was Chinese, and all the chefs came from China: they worked on contract. Some of the hostesses were Chinese, too. Another owner was Russian but had lived for twenty years in America. The third owner was a Russian who had always lived in Russia. And, of course, the restaurant had supporters among the top officials, powerful people, without whose influence it could not have been opened.

One of these top officials was an assistant on economic issues to Khasbulatov, the parliament leader who was still in power at the time. This person—his name was Misha—had recommended both of us. I don't think that we'd have been hired without his recommendation—the competition was so fierce. So, we began to work at Panda. We were both made managers from the start: each of us had five girls under our supervision. That was a big disappointment for me, because I was hoping to work with Sveta and learn from her. I didn't know a thing about waitressing. I didn't know the names of the Chinese dishes in the menu. The menus were written in English, and I didn't understand a word. I was scared.

I decided not to quit my job as a doctor, but rather to take a leave and give my new job a try. I got a release from work supposedly because of my son's illness. I didn't tell my parents anything about my new job. Only my husband knew. I told him I wanted to give it a try.

My first day at work I was asked to help with the cleaning. They were behind schedule and needed help to open on time. I was put to clean the toilets, and I remember cleaning and crying, "Is this going to be my life now?"

But when the day of the opening arrived, I was suddenly bursting with energy. I did such a good job that I was asked to serve in a private room, meant for the most important guests. Misha, who had recommended me without ever having met me, happened to be among those guests. Sveta introduced me to him. He told me that I was an even better worker than Sveta.

At the end of the day he asked Sveta and me out for a drink with him. Since he was our benefactor, I thought we couldn't refuse. I had never been in such a situation, so I didn't know how to behave. I looked at Sveta and said, "Yes, why not? Let's go someplace for a drink." He invited us to a casino. I'd never been to a casino before; I didn't even know they existed in Moscow. Misha asked the manager to let us go early that day. The manager didn't object. Misha's word was taken as an order. Even though he didn't have a share in the business, it was by means of his will and political influence that it stayed in existence. He could do whatever he wanted. So, he went to the manager and said, "I am taking these girls with me." Nobody said a word. We went out with him. I was wearing a fur coat and sandals; I didn't have time to change my shoes.

We got into his Mercedes—the first time I had seen a Mercedes in my life—and took off. He was driving. We sat in the back seat, chatting; we were in a good mood. I didn't know Moscow too well, but Sveta did, and suddenly she said: "I think we're going the wrong way." "I changed my mind," he replied, "We're not going to a casino, we're going to my dacha." Before we had a chance to realize what was happening, the car was driving down a highway at a great speed. We stopped chatting and sat there quietly.

He had brought us to his dacha, a big house in a suburb of Moscow. He wanted to make dinner for us. I tried to explain: we were not what he thought, what he took us for. I made an effort to make it clear to him. I told him I was a doctor. Although he had known Sveta longer, I felt that he'd taken more of a fancy to me. So I would be the one to pay the most. I confessed everything: that I had no experience as a waitress, that I was a doctor. "My husband is waiting for me," I said. In response to these confessions he simply said: "I could tell you are a smart girl. Go take a shower and come to bed." He said it to both of us. First he took out champagne, whitefish, other delicacies and set the table. Then he went into his bedroom. "Come and join me," he said. I didn't know what he was going to do with the two of us. At this stage there was nothing else to do but go for an open conflict. "No. We won't," I said. "It's all a mistake." "Why did you sit in my car?" he replied. "We thought we were going to a casino," I said. I could not play games anymore. I think he had never been refused before. I knew how much power he had; I was scared. But there was no way I could do what he wanted. It was impossible. Finally, he left us alone and retreated to his bedroom. We couldn't sleep, we didn't even undress, we just sat in that room all night. We couldn't leave the house on our own. It was surrounded by snow, we were hundreds of kilometers away from Moscow, we didn't even know exactly where we were, and I was wearing summer sandals. Where would we go?

In the morning, he woke up, and went jogging. He didn't talk to us, didn't say a word. As if we weren't even there. Then we heard him making a phone call. He came into the room and told us: "Somebody will come to pick you up." "We should leave here immediately," I said to Sveta. "He probably called his boys, and they'll come and slaughter us." He saw us putting on our coats. I said: "Sorry, and thank you, but we better go now." I kept repeating: "Sorry, sorry." I did not want to get him mad again. "Why don't you want to wait?" he said. "We are late for work," I replied. We were supposed to be at the restaurant by eleven that morning. He thought for a while, and then told us: "OK, I'll take you to the patrol post." He didn't insist that we wait for the car that was supposed to pick us up. So, he dropped us off at the patrol post, and from there we walked—a few kilometers in the snow, in summer sandals—to the train station. When we finally arrived at the restaurant at 2 p.m. that day, nobody asked us any questions. They had seen us leave with him.

Thanks to this incident, we had a privileged position in the restaurant. Nobody dared to touch us, or fire us. We were "his" girls. Misha, on the other hand, didn't say a word to anybody. He showed up in the restaurant a couple of times afterward, and each time I saw him I shook. I was afraid of revenge. I talked to my sister, Tatiana, the same day that we escaped from his dacha. She was already in business and knew some influential people—not as influential as he was—but still I was hoping they would help us if anything happened. So, the same day, I called her, and she arrived at the restaurant with her friend and business partner. I told them the entire story. Tatiana's friend gave me his cellular phone number, and told me to call him if the guy ever showed up. "You can't joke with these people," he said. "It's amazing that he let you go, just like that. You simply don't realize what a serious situation you got into. Never go outside the restaurant alone. People have simply disappeared."

Panda was a very expensive, trendy restaurant. It was quite common for the waitresses to receive propositions from customers. The waitresses were all young; and all wore the same uniform: short, red Chinese-style dresses. Nobody stayed for a long time. There were too many conflicts and a lot of stealing. They hadn't yet developed a system to regulate employees. Later, management installed video-cameras. But at first, everybody was stealing. And they fought over tips. Tips were supposed to be divided among the staff—waitresses, bartenders, and kitchen workers, but waitresses often tried to hide their tips. Or when some customers paid their bill by check, it often wouldn't reach the register, disappearing along the way. Some people were caught. Some people caught others. Some girls went out with the wrong guy, or refused to go out with the right one. All this could lead to being fired. In the eight months I worked in the restaurant, the staff turned over maybe three times. Everybody was fired—except for us. Nobody dared to touch us, including the owner. Although he was a big lover, he never made any passes at me or Sveta. We were considered Misha's girls. Even after Khasbulatov went down and Misha stopped coming to the restaurant, nobody touched us. We were untouchable. Besides, Sveta and I stuck together. It saved us from many undesirable situations. We rented an apartment in Moscow that we shared. Since we had to work for two days in a row, and the restaurant closed at midnight—too late to take the train back to Zelenograd—we rented a place to stay in Moscow. The other two days—when we were off from work—we spent in Zelenograd with our families. My husband did not like this situation too much.

He says it's the reason that we eventually left Moscow. He didn't want me working as a waitress. Medicine was my profession and he wanted me to hold on to it. It's interesting that even my parents—who, when they first heard of my waitressing job, were very much against it—eventually accepted it. Our financial situation was so bad. Working as a doctor, I made 6,000 rubles a month when I left.

My starting salary at the restaurant was 25,000 rubles. But that was nothing compared to the tips I earned, and all these tips were paid in dollars. I was making 40 to 50 dollars a day in tips. That was an incredible amount of money at the time. I remember, after a couple of weeks as a waitress, I finally decided to officially quit my job at the clinic. I remember how my colleagues looked at me when I said: "I don't need to wait for my paycheck." They looked at me like I was crazy.

Of course, waitressing was a hard job. I had to stand on my feet for twelve hours. I couldn't sit down for a minute. There wasn't a single chair for waitresses to sit on. Now, in my own restaurant, when I see my waitress has no customers, I tell her: "Go, sit, relax, read a book." My manager back then, if she saw me standing idle even for a second, would shout: "Don't you have anything to do? Go wash the wall." And I'd go wash the wall. It was hard. People at the restaurant were constantly humiliated. I didn't let people know that I was working as a waitress. Except for my sister, my husband, and my parents, nobody else in the world knew, including my closest friends. I told my friends and colleagues at the clinic that I had found a job in a medical firm in Moscow. I simply could not tell the truth. I could not admit to anyone that I—a gold medal student, a graduate of the most prestigious medical school in Moscow—was working as a waitress in a restaurant.

By that time my husband began to think seriously about emigrating. He found an ad in one of the newspapers for a firm—this time in Moscow—that helped people emigrate to Canada. The firm promised Canadian visas for eligible persons who fit certain requirements regarding age, family status, and profession. The entire procedure, if successful, would cost us 15,000 dollars. In June or July of 1993 we went for an interview. My husband suspected that the entire affair was a fraud. We shared our suspicions with my sister, Tatiana. She advised us to wait.

Because Tatiana knew of our intentions, a new opportunity soon came. Her company was opening a branch in America, and she suggested to the board of directors that my husband be their representative. We were invited for an interview, we passed, and my husband was offered the position as director of a new branch of the company in America. It was supposed to handle the export of medical equipment, a field that my husband did in fact know quite well. In November 1993 we arrived in New York. We had no intention of moving to America for good. Nobody in my family had ever been to America. New York seemed to me like a dark, dangerous place—the source from which crime spread around the world.

My husband knew some English, but I didn't know the language at all. During my first year in America, I don't think I had any clear idea of what the country was like. My husband was working and earning a salary. He had to create a whole new business from scratch. It was hard work, but at least he didn't have to look for a job. He had a steady salary. Instructions came from Moscow, but he had to decide many things on his own. Our roles had reversed: he was the active one now, he was the one who was working and providing money for the family. I stayed home with our child. I was happy about this role change.

He became good at his job very quickly, handling all business negotiations and correspondence—all this without any previous experience. I guess you can learn to do anything under pressure. Our biggest problem was our son. He was seven years old, and he felt very unhappy in America. When we were leaving Russia, I remember everybody telling us: "You might have some problems there, but not your child. Children at that age adjust very fast." But the opposite thing happened. He cried every day, remembering Moscow. Before going to sleep, he said "Good night" to ten people: "Good night to grandma Marina, and grandma Valya, and grandpa Stasik . . ."

Three months after we arrived in New York, I started looking for a job. I opened the Russian-language newspapers to the job listings. I did not ask any questions, although we had neighbors who could give me advice. I preferred to do it on my own. And I didn't want to be asked about my husband's job; we were warned not to talk about it. Russian businesses were supposed to remain confidential. My husband did well, and soon after we arrived he bought a used car and was driving it. We had enough money. But I felt bored: I didn't go out much, didn't talk to anyone, I didn't really feel like I was in America. So, I started to look for a job where I could speak Russian.

I noticed a couple of ads in the paper. The first number that I called was a cosmetics firm. They were looking for women, and knowledge of English was not necessary. I felt scared to call this number. What helped me was that the answering-machine message was in Russian. I left my message—basically my name, number and the reason I called. In two hours a woman called me back, and I was invited for an interview. That's how I came to work for the Mary Kay company. It's an American marketing firm that sells cosmetics. By the time I started work Russians made up the majority of sales people and customers.

The way the business works is that you had to buy some product for 50 percent of its price and then sell it at full price. In addition, you had to create your own team, recruit new salespeople like yourself, and receive a percentage of their sales. I had no idea how hard it would be. Before earning any income, you first had to invest money to buy the product. I didn't realize that selling the product at full price would be almost impossible.

But it happened that I had a little luck from the start. Somehow I managed to sell the right amount of product and sign up the right number of people. At the end of the first month, I was promoted and given a car. It wasn't my own car—it was loaned to me—but it was still a big deal. I stayed at the firm for a while. Now, I don't regret it, because, if not for Mary Kay, I wouldn't have my restaurant.

Eventually, I left Mary Kay. It happened that I met a woman, Nellie, through one of my co-workers at Mary Kay. She had lived in New York for four years, and before that in Israel for seventeen years. She comes from Siberia. One day we had dinner at her home. She mentioned to me that she wanted to open a restaurant. It was her life's dream.

Even back in Moscow I had been thinking of opening a small cafe with Sveta as my partner. But that was an incredibly difficult and dangerous proposition in Moscow, because of the racketeering and everything else. Here, it had got to me. I thought about it all night. "You know I met this woman," I told my husband. "What if we opened a restaurant together?" I was completely intoxicated by this crazy idea.

Nellie wanted to open a restaurant in Manhattan, in Soho or Greenwich Village. She loved that neighborhood. She took me there one day, showed me around, gave me a complete tour: that's where Barbara Streisand made her first appearance, that's where O'Henry wrote his "Last Leaf," this is the narrowest building in the world. She was in love with Manhattan, even though she lived in Brooklyn. For me, it was the first time I actually saw Manhattan, the first time I walked its streets. Nellie showed me the place she had picked out for her restaurant. The building was for sale. The next day we went to see the real estate agent, but we didn't have any success. We couldn't explain ourselves: I didn't speak English, and Nellie's English was poor. We were two women, dressed not very presentably: I still wore the old overcoat I had brought with me from Russia. We did not make a good impression. Then I asked my husband to come along. By then, he had experience in business negotiations, he had bought some proper business suits, he knew how to talk. We all went together, and this time they took us more seriously. They showed us a couple of places. One was on Macdougal Street. We loved it right away.

We encountered many difficulties in opening the business. But we didn't become discouraged. We had no doubt, not a single thought, that it wouldn't work out. Nellie had wanted to own her own restaurant since she was seventeen, and I had thought about it for the last three years. We made a lot of mistakes. For instance, we had to buy refrigerators. Of course, I didn't know anything about refrigerators—what we needed, what they cost, or anything. We found a company that gave us what I thought was a good discount. They sold us used refrigerators for $1,000 apiece; the price of a new one is $3,000. I didn't know at the time that the company had gotten these refrigerators for free. Restaurants that go out of business give away their equipment; they even pay to have the old refrigerators removed. These people got their refrigerators for free, then painted and sold them without replacing the motor or any old parts. Of course, the refrigerators broke down in a matter of days. Despite the problems and obstacles, we never regretted starting the business. And it pays well now.

Lots of people pass through our café every day. And we have good relationships with all of them, with our customers, neighbors. Our café was never intended for a specifically Russian clientele, although some Russians come here. They find the place by accident, but we know our Russian customers by name. Some of them have become our friends. The majority of our customers, though, are Americans. They like the place, and they like its name: The Twelve

Chairs. They don't know that it was named after a famous Russian novel by Ilya Ilf and Yevgeny Petrov written in the 1920s. Some people count the chairs and ask: "Why are there more than twelve chairs?" Then we tell them about the book. We keep an English translation of the book in the cafe, so that people can read it. In the beginning we did not advertise the fact that we were Russian. We didn't know what kind of reaction it would get. There was no way to know, and nobody to ask: no books have been written on the subject. We didn't want to lose customers, and it could have happened. Everything matters in this business: who you are, what neighborhood you are in, the relationship you have with your neighbors. This area is predominantly Italian. We get along well with them. Little by little, we got rid of our fears, and we realized that the attitude toward Russian immigrants was positive.

We finally told people that we were Russian. There are a couple of Russians in the neighborhood, and they became regular customers. Many of Americans who come here tell us about their grandparents who had come from White Russia, Ukraine, Georgia. Recently there was a small article about us in the *New York Times*. When it came out, the effect was like an explosion. We had tried to advertise, but it was like throwing your money into the garbage. But after this tiny article appeared, the telephone didn't stop ringing for a month: people were calling to find out our address. And all because of one paragraph in the newspaper. Nellie and I were spending more time in the restaurant than at home with our families. Of course, it's getting easier now, but we are far from relaxed. We're not at that stage yet—letting ourselves relax.

If not for this café, I am not sure that we'd stay here. I like this business very much, and it's keeping me in New York. My husband didn't particularly want to stay. When we opened the restaurant, Nellie's husband was still working. The company that my husband started had gone under. So, when we sold our apartment in Russia, we split the money between us. My husband wanted to open a limousine service. So, I invested half of the money in our café, and he put the other half into buying a limousine. We didn't make any profit in the restaurant during the first year. Our husbands made enough to support our families.

A few months after we opened the café, Nellie's husband became ill. He had to undergo surgery, and afterward he became disabled. He lost his job. A month later, my husband had an accident.

We were driving in his limousine when a car crashed into it from behind; the car had driven through a red light. We weren't injured, but the limousine was damaged beyond repair.

We didn't get out of the car when the police arrived; we were in shock. We had never been in an accident before, and we didn't understand how the laws worked. In addition to the driver, there were a few people in the other car. Those people gave their testimony as witnesses, as if they weren't in the car. They said it was our fault. We told the police officer that they had gone through a red light. But their testimony was given more weight, as the testimony of witnesses, and ours didn't count: a passenger's testimony doesn't count. We could not find a lawyer to take our case. We lost all our money, and my husband lost his limousine. So, it happened that Nellie and I lost our family providers almost simultaneously. She has three children, and I have one child. It was a tragic situation, but we managed to survive. We spent days and nights in the restaurant, because we couldn't afford to hire any help. My husband stayed at home with our child. He was very depressed for a while. Later, friends helped him to find a job. Then I persuaded him to prepare for the medical exam. He's a doctor, after all.

I don't miss Moscow that much, but I miss my friends in Russia. We can still go back. My husband wants to return. I'm the one who keeps us here. And it's my restaurant that keeps me here. I've come to like this gutsy city. And I realize that you can't keep moving all the time. Moving is a big deal, it's like a big fire: you can survive it once, but you can't do it over and over again. I've overcome so many obstacles. My life here has not been sweet. But I still feel good, better than in Moscow. I breathe more freely.

Sergey Tchavretov
Business in the New Russia

LIKE *many other physics students who graduated in 1989, Sergey went into business. At first he and his friends wrote computer programs, then he bought and sold electronics, furniture and other goods. Now in his early thirties, he heads the branch office of his firm in New York, which is located in the Empire State Building. "We rented this office space to make an impression on our Russian clients," he noted. "Every Russian has heard of the Empire State Building." In Moscow, the trading business supports a security division of 70 people—it's just how business works there.*

I lived in Rostov. My partners and I started our business in 1989. We worked in Russia for about four years, then expanded to other countries. We bought different products, some in Europe, most in the United States. At a certain stage, business interests demanded that we have an office here, so we opened the office in New York.

We started out as a cooperative. I had been a student at Rostov University in the Physics Department. Many of my college friends went into business, and they're doing pretty well. Maybe it's because commerce is not unlike the natural sciences, such as physics or math. They all deal with numbers, things that can be counted, calculated.

I wanted to make money. I needed to earn money to live. If I were a scientist in Russia, I couldn't have managed. Still, life was kind to me in Russia. I didn't have to work like a slave in a state enterprise, sitting through endless working hours. I went into business right after the university. The year 1989 was a good time to start. People had already been given an opportunity to make money, but the dangerous times had not yet arrived. In 1989 the psychological climate was not much different from the pre-perestroika era.

We wrote computer programs and sold them, and sold the computers as well. Then we started to import other products, which we bought in Europe. The tariffs were low then and we could buy new consumer goods in Europe pretty cheaply, then sell them in Russia at a good profit. Imported products were still rare then. At first, we brought in electronics, then furniture and goods. A lot of people were involved in similar businesses.

It was around that time that I met some of my future partners. We decided to merge our businesses, and we've been working together ever since, which is quite rare in Russia. The most common problem to affect business partnerships is that, at a certain stage, people have to choose between friendship and profit. Most of the time they choose profit. But, to me, friendship, relationships, and trust have always been more important. And my partners share that attitude.

When private enterprise first came on the scene, the general feeling was, "You should do it fast, because tomorrow it could be banned again." In fact, even though it was not banned completely, it became much more difficult and intricate to accomplish. Any businessman will tell you that doing business in 1989 was much easier than in 1996. Take taxes, for instance. In 1989 you had to pay 3 percent of your income to the state. Now it's 70 to 80 percent. When taxes are so high, people simply stop paying them. They find a way around the law. Because it's unreasonable. You just can't explain to people that if they make 100 rubles, 70 rubles belong to the state. Giving away 30 percent of your income—as you do in the United States—is hard enough. So, it's just the typical cat-and-mouse game that our government plays with its people all the time.

Our company has significantly expanded over the years. We opened a few stores in New York, too. We're selling European furniture here as well as in Russia, though our main customers are still over there. We rented this office space in the Empire State Building to make an impression on our Russian clients. Americans don't care so much about where our office is located. But every Russian has heard about the Empire State building. It's the first thing they know about New York. So, by putting our office here, we created an image, and image is very important in business. I guess that our American partners are not indifferent to the fact that we have an office in this building, either. It shows that we're a respectable firm, with some history. We have a good reputation. Now, a lot of companies here have branches or representatives in Russia, so it's actually possible to check out a company's background. Before, it was practically impossible. The information they were getting on us was favorable, I guess. I know some American business people were making inquires about our company in Russia, checking our credibility.

What I like about business here is that it is safe. In Russia there are more ways to make money, and they are easier. Profits are higher, but the dangers associated with business are incomparably higher, too. Business is risky in Russia. And the Mafia is not the biggest risk. Government bureaucracy is. The tax laws change almost every month, and taxes are going up. This means that even if you paid your taxes in full, you could still owe some money to the state. Privatization of government enterprises is another danger. Privatization means that influential people are actively involved in the enterprise, powerful people who have authority, and who want to appropriate it for their own sake. Sometimes, different groups of influential people lay claim to the same enterprise, bringing about a conflict of interest which they resolve through judicial or violent means. Our company, for instance, keeps a security division of 70 people, 20 of them armed. We couldn't work without this security team. To look after our 400 employees, we need 70 guards. But that keeps us out of trouble.

What also helps us to avoid trouble is that we do business honestly. We try to keep our promises. Problems arise when people try to cheat us. For instance, they take out a loan and don't pay it back, or they get a product and don't pay for it. When people intentionally cheat other people, those who are cheated are pissed off. Then they attempt to either retrieve what was taken from them or to take revenge. The party that has been the victim hires someone to collect a debt from the party that conned them, and this person receives a percentage of the amount that he was able to retrieve. You could call it a racket, of course, but in fact it is just a way of getting justice—a way of doing business.

That's because there is no proper legal system in the country that can enforce justice, or reimburse losses incurred through fraud. Here, you have police, the courts, and lawyers. In Russia, racketeering takes their place. It is in fact the only social function that can provide a solution. You see, nobody in Russia would take seriously a threat of being taken to the police station. That does not scare anybody. But the threat of losing your health does scare people. Ninety percent of the vendettas that go on in the country are about getting even.

We started doing business in Rostov. Now we have offices in Moscow, in New York, in Italy, and in Prague. We also have business partners in many other countries. It happens that I was put in charge of the office in New York. I never intended to leave Russia. I still consider myself on a business trip. I work here, in America, the same way that I could have been working in Moscow. This job is my assignment, that's all. My wife and children are with me in New York. But my parents and my sister are still in Russia, back in our native town. I travel to Russia every three or four months and stay for three weeks each time. So, I'm still very much connected to Russia. It's hard for me to say which is my real home. It is both here and there. And, of course, I belong there much more than here.

As one of my friends put it, and I find the description true, "America is a labor camp with a refined diet." It's true that living conditions are good here, but people work very hard. Well, maybe, that's what they want. They have different principles and goals in life, and they are not acceptable to us. Take the relationship between children and parents. In most families in America, children stop living with their parents after high school; and after college, parents stop supporting their children. They assume that their mission is over. In Russia, parents support their children much longer. Parents and children are much closer to each other, and stay close throughout their lives.

I do business with Americans, but I don't have American friends. It's easier with Italians. Italians are much more like us. The way they feel about parents, family, friends is the same as we do. For an Italian, friendship is more important than money. You can't say that's true for an American. Of course, there are exceptions to every rule. Italians respect tradition, just as Russians do. In America, there is no historical ground for a deep tradition—except in business. In business, Americans have achieved unrivaled heights.

What amazes me in this country is how smoothly the system works, despite the fact that the average American working person is mediocre. The average office worker, a clerk in a bank, can hardly add two numbers together. But that doesn't obstruct the system at all. Because it is so well structured, it doesn't matter who's rolling every little wheel. It just keeps running. If you compare the qualifications—the professional and intellectual level—of the personnel of an average company here with that in Russia, I think the Russians are superior in many ways, even though their salaries are incomparably lower. But the system in general is much more efficient here than it is in Russia, and the results speak for themselves.

I have met some smart people here, people in charge of businesses, for example. I often feel sorry for them, because they have to hire these mediocre employees, pay them huge salaries, and still manage to stay in business somehow. This is not a trivial task. The fact that they cope with it successfully deserves respect.

America got lucky by not having destructive wars for a long time, as Europe has had. As Russia has even now. Rostov, my home town, is only 600 kilometers from Chechnya, where the war is raging. It's very close. It's as if you lived in New York, and there was a war in Maine. It's driving distance. And it's not just a war, it's a horrible, bloody war. Much worse than Afghanistan. Of course, it makes me worry. And the notion that in any minute it could turn into a civil war is scary.

Roman Kaplan
Art and Food

> IN *Russia he taught himself English by reading the Dickens novel,* Great Expectations. *Part of a circle of artists, actors and writers, including the poet Joseph Brodsky, he "was always attracted to people who had talent." Driven by both curiosity and persecution, he left Russia and came to New York in 1977. He missed his bohemian hangouts in Leningrad and Moscow though. In his sixties now, a man who enjoys people, conviviality, and a good meal, he owns The Russian Samovar, a popular Russian restaurant in New York. He sees a logic to the turns his life has taken.*

It always seemed a miracle to me, the fact that I'm somehow managing to survive, that I'm still alive, that I'm even making some money. It's a miracle because I was always convinced that only people who can actually do something, possess specific skills, have a profession, are able to make money. I don't have any skills. I'm not good at anything in particular. In Russia, knowing a foreign language was considered a skill. And I knew a couple of them. But here nobody needs it. Here it's the professionals who are in demand. I'm not at all prominent. Well, there is my restaurant. It's turned out to be a nice place. But even the restaurant is not a huge success, at least not commercially. People love it, that's true. But that's pretty much it.

I came to New York in 1977. The idea of living all my life in one place, in the Soviet Union, without ever seeing any other part of the world seemed strange to me. For all of us living in Russia, the notion of "abroad" was a significant notion. All foreigners seemed like Martians to us. They were an entirely different breed of people. And for us, young people raised under a strict and very brutal regime, the possibility of traveling, of seeing the world, seemed very exciting.

I was always fond of foreign languages. But communication with foreigners was strictly forbidden in Russia. You can imagine the difficulties it created for people like myself, who wanted to learn and then practice their knowledge of languages. No publications were available in foreign languages, except for a few paperback books, sold only in a couple of bookstores in town. And that was in Leningrad. There were no magazines or newspapers in foreign languages. So, for curious people, getting some information about the "West"—which seemed to us like a monolith, the "West" with a capital W—was not easy. And the information was often dated and inaccurate.

I remember that my friend and I regularly bought *America* magazine. A woman at the newspaper stand at the Moscow train station often secured a copy of the magazine for us for a special fee. She had only a limited number of copies in her kiosk. We studied this magazine carefully, almost caressing each page. I remember the feel of the paper—heavy, glossy paper. I remember the photographs in that magazine—photographs of cars that nobody in Russia could even dream about. Now every child is familiar with them, but not back then. *America* itself was just an ordinary propaganda magazine, but for us it was a great treasure.

I remember once noticing a group of tourists, black tourists, on Anickov Bridge in Leningrad. They were studying four statues of horses with the horsemen that stood on the bridge, and they were gesticulating expressively. They were dressed in these incredible clothes, bright and colorful: yellow sweaters, green scarves, light-colored overcoats. On the gray street, dirty melting snow on the ground—a typical misty Leningrad landscape—was this bright, beautiful spot, and its primary color was yellow. And they wore these extravagant hats. I never saw a more beautiful picture in my life. So, I approached them: they were Americans, artists, who had come to Leningrad on tour with a theater company, putting on Gershwin's *Porgy and Bess*. I don't remember which year it was exactly—probably 1956. And they were talking together, in English, laughing. I stood there looking at them absolutely stunned. I thought, "America, what a country!"

I didn't know too much about America at the time. I didn't know that in America these people could not eat in the same restaurants as white people, or stay in the same hotels. I remember looking at a glossy page of *America* magazine with its photograph of an unemployed person, and the caption underneath reading, "An unemployed American receives $400 a month in unemployment benefits." And the guy in the picture was wearing jeans, both pants and shirt, clothes that were objects of desire for young people like myself. So, we thought to ourselves, "What a luxurious life those unemployed Americans have!" Of course, what we didn't realize was how easy our life was compared to life in America. Easy and cheap. True, we didn't own anything, but life didn't cost much, either. It was possible to live in Russia with almost no money, which many people did, in fact, do.

When I first decided to learn English, I went to a bookstore. The only books in English that I was able to find were *By the Path of Thunder*, a book about apartheid in South Africa, and some Dickens novels. I chose *Great Expectations*. Maybe it was because I still had some expectations at the time; I was young. And I began to learn English, following the technique I had read about in some book. I read the entire Dickens novel three or four times. At the first read, I would write down the words I did not understand. Then I would try to memorize them, and then to use them in proper context. I learned other languages in this way, too. I always had a great interest in languages. I loved reading dictionaries.

A foreign language was a window into another culture. I loved to read poetry in other languages. We read a lot back then. We copied our favorite poems by hand and passed them around. We copied poems by Joseph Brodsky, and by other poets and writers. We also discovered Russian poets of the early twentieth century: Osip Mandelshtam, Marina Tsvetaeva, Anna Ahmatova. They were suddenly being rediscovered, and this discovery made life so bright. The people in my circle during that time were people who possessed an ability to express their thoughts in the most concentrated, energetic, profound way. They were real poets. Thinking about those people prevented me from becoming a writer. I knew I could never do it the way they did.

I was born in Leningrad, but I had to leave the city eventually and move to Moscow. The same people who had arranged Joseph Brodsky's trial in 1964 had fabricated a case against me a year earlier.

It's not like I was a dissident or anything—but I guess people like me were too different from the masses. We were more educated. We knew other languages. We listened to the Voice of America, to Music USA. We attended underground art exhibitions and screenings. We even spoke our own particular slang. Anyway, I don't know why these people picked on me. The word *stilyaga,* a stylish person, was in use at the time. A typical filthy Soviet word. Of course, we dressed differently than other people you'd meet on the street: we were very much into everything Western. We tried to copy the Western style in everything.

Once I remember I was sitting with a friend in Under the Roof, a restaurant in the Europe Hotel, and a group of foreign tourists suddenly walked in. We were dressed in some checkered jackets that my friend who knew how to sew had made for us. They were made out of some cheap material: old blankets or something. They were too warm, these jackets, and clumsy. And then I noticed these people walk in and sit down at one of the round tables in the room. They were dressed in some light slack-shirts and checked jackets, and they wore these clothes with such elegance and nonchalance. They looked so fresh, so clean—these people—so free. They looked like a living reproach to us, a reproach to the misery of our lives. So, I always wanted to see what life was like there. America interested me the least. I was fond of Europe, and dreamed of going to Italy or France. The United States just happened to be the freest country of all. It was easy to come here, to stay, leave whenever you like. Nobody much cares. Still, everybody wants to come here. It's the last refuge in the world.

I mentioned that I had to leave Leningrad. I was a postgraduate student at the time, studying art history. I was being harassed for having contacts with foreigners. My persecutors wouldn't leave me alone. They published nasty articles about me in the newspapers, accusing me of passing along secret information. But I had no access to any secret information. What I was interested in was information about art, about new books published in the West; I wanted to have this information firsthand. Foreigners came from the entirely different world separated from us by rivers, seas, and iron grids. Everything about their lives was incredibly interesting. So, even after I was warned by the authorities, I never stopped seeking contacts with foreigners, I did not react to the threats. So, they took their revenge. My brother who was then a postgraduate student at the Mining Institute was expelled.

Finally I was forced to flee Leningrad. My friends, Brodsky among them, found me a job in a geological expedition. When I returned from the expedition, I moved to Moscow. I took a course in foreign languages at a teachers college—my English was actually quite good. After I graduated, I began to make a living by teaching English and translating. It didn't make me rich, but it was a reasonable income. I was an ordinary person—not too wealthy, not too poor. I remember back then, in Moscow, how we used to gather in a restaurant, the Eastern; it was a popular hangout for people like myself. You could always find some friends there, join them at their table, sit and chat, hop from table to table. That place saved me from feeling alone in the city. When I opened my own restaurant in New York, much later, I thought of the old times in Moscow.

Moscow was a much more open and free-spirited city than Leningrad in the 60s. Leningrad was a provincial city. The authorities went out of their way to prove their loyalty to the regime, so the ideological pressure was much more intense. Moscow was a cultural center, a metropolis. The international festivals and exhibitions took place in Moscow. All the prominent artists, musicians, and singers lived there. I was always attracted to people who had talent, who were extraordinary whether at singing or painting or poetry. I always had a lot of friends among artists—and among the best of them. I always believed Russian art was the best.

I was curious about the West, but it was the people around me, my friends whom I really admired. I wanted them to be recognized in the West. I wanted the West to know what was happening in Russia. I did everything I could to change this situation by introducing my friends—painters, poets, and writers—to lots of people from abroad, so that they'd get an idea of the incredibly high and sophisticated level of Russian artists. Actually, my life was pretty good at the time. I wasn't being persecuted and I could support myself financially.

If I had been allowed to travel freely abroad, I don't think I would have stayed in the West. The thing is, we didn't have much of a choice. One of my friends had met a French woman, a very nice woman, and he liked her a lot. He wanted to go to France to meet her parents, but he was denied a temporary visa. The Soviet authorities told him: "No, you can't go to meet her parents, but if you want to move there for good, we won't object." He was given twenty-four hours to decide. He told me that he didn't need twenty-four hours. He could decide in fifteen minutes. He left Russia.

If I were allowed to go abroad, I believed I would not have to emigrate. I just wanted to see the world. I applied for a tourist visa a couple of times, but was denied a visa even to visit Romania. This was the main reason that I decided to emigrate. Through a friend I managed to receive an invitation to go to Israel. I applied for an emigrant visa, and I was quickly given permission to leave the country. That was how I left Russia. I was leaving without looking back, but I had no clear idea of where I was going. I found myself in Israel. But I didn't feel right there. I never really thought of myself as a Jew, and I still don't. From Israel I moved to America, to New York where I've lived since 1977.

I did not experience cultural shock in America. New York felt like my city, from the beginning. So much of the world's wealth, material and cultural, is concentrated here. On the other hand, you're completely on your own. You can do whatever you want, and nobody will stop you. Nobody will help you, either. In New York, you have to fight for survival every day. You begin your day early in the morning, and you struggle through the day until late at night. Every little thing takes a struggle, even driving in the endless stream of cars rushing to get somewhere. You struggle to meet the people you want to meet, to do the things you need to do. You fight to earn money to live, to buy food. In Russia they used to call New York "the jungle of stone." It's true in a way.

I found myself in a strange country—with no money, no home of my own, no clear prospects for the future. Of course, I was anxious. True, I knew English, but so what? Everybody in New York could speak English, some better, some worse. Besides, I didn't have working papers, I didn't have the right to work. I had a tourist visa from Israel. I had a friend, an American whom I knew from Israel. He had been my best friend in Israel. I had shown him a book that I wrote in English, and he was very impressed. But when he found out that I'd come to New York just like that, without making any arrangements, he strongly disapproved. He was a very wealthy man, head of a big real-estate company in New York: he owned twenty residential buildings in Manhattan. I asked him if he could give me a job. The only job he could offer was as a doorman in one of his buildings. I took the job. "There are no dirty jobs," I told him. You finish your work day. You wash yourself. And you are clean again. There are dirty souls that can never be cleaned out, but there are no dirty jobs. So, for a couple of months I worked as a doorman. I knew it was a temporary thing. I knew something would happen, sooner or later.

A couple of months later, I met a man called Nakhamkin. He was a Russian immigrant. He was starting an art gallery. He needed someone to help him, although he had no idea what kind of person this someone should be. I was tailor-made for him: I knew English, and he did not. He couldn't write a letter on his own. But he knew a lot about business and the art trade. He dealt in works by contemporary Russian artists. This was the first gallery to present contemporary Russian painting to the world. But working with living artists is not easy. Each one has a temperament, an ego, and you find yourself embroiled in this constant clash of egos. Besides, the interest in Russian art in the Western market began to drop. Times changed, and the market was saturated. Only a few collectors own Russian art. So, after the Russian art market had collapsed, only those artists who had established reputations remained in demand. The larger group of artists whose work Nakhamkin was presenting fell into oblivion. I left the gallery, realizing it was time for a change.

That was when the Russian Samovar came to life in the early 1980s. From the beginning, it was very popular in the Russian community. A lot of my friends knew about the place and supported me from the first day. It hadn't been my idea to start a restaurant. My family and I lived right across from the gallery, on Eighty-first Street and Madison. People were always coming and going, hanging out in our apartment. We were cooking meals every day. There was a lot of drinking and eating—and talking. Of course, this was hard on my wife: everyday after work, she had to receive guests. Finally, she told me in a fit of an anger: "I wonder if your friends would visit you that often if this was a restaurant, not your apartment".

Well, it happens that my friends still visit. They come as often as they did, only now to my restaurant. It's turned out to be a cozy place. What makes this restaurant so different from other Russian restaurants in New York is that it's a warm place, soulful, and people appreciate that. They feel at ease here, as if they fit in. Americans come here, too, but mainly it's a Russian place. We don't care much about the commercial side of the enterprise. It's good enough if we can pay the rent as well salaries to the employees. We don't make that much of a profit.

Back in Russia I never envisioned myself as an owner of a restaurant, but now that I am I see a certain logic to it. I've always liked people, I've always appreciated hospitality, I enjoy a convivial atmosphere. So, I guess there is a certain destiny to what has happened in my life.

SURVIVAL

Boris Kardimun
Itinerant Spirit

> BORIS *is sixty-six years old. His earliest pleasant memories are mixed with the horrors of war. By 15, he knew he hated his country. By 18, he had fallen in with dissidents and began reading occult literature. In Soviet eyes, he was a parasite. He achieved sudden success as an itinerant painter. Emigrating to the United States in the 1970s, he feels he didn't leave Russia in time.*

I was born in Georgia. My parents had moved to Georgia in 1930. Both of my parents come from the Ukraine; my father was born in Odessa, my mother in Vinnitsa. So, although I was born in Georgia, I am by origin a typical shtetl Jew.

My father served in the military as a professional officer. After twenty-five years of service, he was discharged from the army with the rank of lieutenant colonel. That gave him significant career advantages. He was given a civilian position, as the Deputy Director of BelGlavSnabSbit, an organization with a ridiculous name that was nevertheless quite powerful. Basically, his duties were to control the transport and distribution of White Russian timber, vodka, and sausages to the other Soviet republics, in exchange for coal from Kazakhstan and other raw materials. But that happened much later, after the war.

Going back to the beginning: for a while we lived in Tbilisi, in Georgia, and lived peacefully, at least from my point of view. I don't remember much from those years; the horrors of the war erased most of it from my memory. My mother was the youngest of seven brothers and sisters in a big Jewish family. They kept a tradition of annual gatherings at her parents' house. That was how in June of

1941—all of us, a big family of thirty-six people, found themselves in Vinnitsa, a small town in the Ukraine. All my relatives took a vacation to spend the summer with my grandparents in their hometown. Of these thirty-six people, only my mother and I survived the war. (My father was serving in the army at the time.) I was the youngest of the cousins, so my grandparents insisted that we leave the town when the war began.

We were surrounded by the enemy, by shooting and bombing. Here is one of my memories: my mother and I are hiding in a coal wagon, on a barren plain, somewhere in the Don Basin near the Black Sea. We are covered with sweat and coal dust, and it's the middle of July. The heat is terrible. In the same wagon, there is another mother with her son who's my age and has the very same name—Boris. Then the German bombers and fighter planes show up in the sky. People, refugees like us, run out on the open plain to get away from any buildings or structures. But we can't get out of the wagon; the walls are too slippery, soiled with sawdust. We are stuck in the wagon. My mother covers me with her body. The other boy named Boris is right beside me. Something hits him. He dies. I was four years old at the time.

My memory doesn't retain the sequence of events very well. But pictures I see very clearly. We are running toward some steamboat. I don't know why we are running. I step over a railroad track. It's shining in the sun. Then I step on the wooden crossbar of the track. I can see the oil stains on it, gravel around it, and a daisy sticking out. I remember crossing the fragile planked footway leading to the boat. I don't remember what the boat looked like. I didn't see it all. All I saw was the black hole of a hold we were heading to, and then the sacks of potatoes inside the hold. I climbed up one of the sacks to look out the window, and then the bombing started. The boat next to ours was blown to pieces. I remember human body parts flying through the air, smashing against the window. I remember the blood on the glass, and how I slowly slipped down that sack of potatoes to the floor. For years and years afterward I couldn't hear the sound of an airplane without trembling. It took me fifty years to be able to calm down.

In 1944, in Tbilisi, a new bakery shop opened right across the street from our house. There was still a war going on. One could feel its presence in Tbilisi, but it was a distant presence. I don't remember a single bombing of the city. A few times, German airplanes would fly over the city, but they dropped leaflets, not bombs. Still, a pastry was an exclusive luxury even in Tbilisi. For a couple of days, every time I passed the pastry shop, I'd stick my face up to the window and gaze at the cakes on display, fighting the temptation. Finally, I gave up: I opened the drawer where my mother kept the money, and I took out one bill. I still remember how it looked: it was a 30-ruble bill, the color of red brick, with a portrait of Lenin on it. With this bill I bought five pastries; each one cost 6 rubles. I brought the pastries home. I might have been in a trance—because I don't remember how exactly—but I ate all of them. And I left the waxed paper which the pastries were wrapped in on the window sill. And that was where my mother discovered the paper, with a few crumbs stuck to it. She examined it. She licked it. Then she asked me, "Where did you get the money?" I pointed at the drawer. She said only one thing: "Well, you could have left one for me, at least." She said nothing else; there was not a single reproach.

My father went to fight the Germans and he never came back from the war. Although his failure to return doesn't imply here what it usually does. He came back alive from the war, but to another woman—and then another one, and then another one, and yet another one. For a while, my mother tried to get back with him. In one such attempt, she decided to move to Moscow, where my father was at the time. It was 1947. We settled in an apartment on Volkonka Street, right across from the Pushkin Art Museum. The apartment belonged to my father's aunt. She shared it with us.

The day after we arrived in Moscow, I went into the yard where the other children were playing, and the first thing I heard was somebody saying, "Look, there goes *yidionok* (little Jew)." I wasn't raised in a strict Jewish environment. I didn't even know I was a Jew. I thought I was Georgian. But at that very moment, I became a Jew. That's how my real education began—in that yard. They played with me, they talked to me, but I wasn't one of them: I was different, a *yidionok*. That was in 1947. In 1948, Stalin attacked the Jewish Anti-Fascist Committee.* Its members were accused of being

---

* Following the German invasion of Russia, the Jewish Anti-Fascist Committee, led by the Yiddish actor and director Solomon Mikhoels, worked to gain support—in the Soviet Union and abroad—for the Soviet effort to defeat the Nazis. During the Stalinist terror, Mikhoels was murdered and the Committee dissolved in 1948.

traitors and executed. When it started, I heard people around me, including my mother, whispering to each other, talking together in secret. I already knew that I was an outsider. I belonged to a race of strange people called Jews, people with jarring voices, large noses. Once I asked my mother about it, but she evaded the question. And we were still eating matzah for the Passover. It's funny how old traditions kept protruding here and there. Nobody even spoke the word Jew, but there was matzah on the table.

The trial of the Jewish doctors in 1952,* the Doctors' Plot, made an anti-Communist out of me. At fifteen I knew that I hated my country and did not want to live there. But in 1955, I met people who changed my life. They were dissidents. They were mostly in their early thirties. I was eighteen. We read and disseminated work by unpublished writers, including those who had emigrated or died in Stalin's camps. My new friends had access to this literature because they themselves were the sons or nephews or grandsons of people who were opressed.

These people came from families of the old Russian intelligentsia. I was their chance to continue the thread. They wanted to teach me what they knew and what they stood for. My mother knew about my friends, but she did not know everything. I couldn't tell her everything. There were enough reasons for her sleepless nights. I was giving her a lot of trouble, growing up without a father. Even though I loved my mother dearly, she was never an authority fugure in my eyes. I remember that she always worked very hard. She was a pharmacist, and she worked at a pharmacy her entire life. And she was always doing something at home—sewing something, or cleaning, or washing. She was restless, tired, and beautiful.

She and my father never got back together. But she never tried to turn me against him. He did it all on his own. I always had a difficult relationship with my father. Later in life, he refused to give his permission for me to leave the country. I was able to emigrate only after he died.

One misty winter day in 1952, I was taking a stroll in my neighborhood, in Kuntsevo, then a suburb of Moscow, accompanied by three girls. We reached a square near the train station. The girls

---

* See footnote on p. 30.

walked into a pharmacy. I stayed outside, waiting for them, embarrassed to go inside. The word "pharmacy" was linked in my mind to the word "condom". I was fifteen, and everybody seemed to be talking about condoms. At least, that was true of all the teenagers in Kuntsevo, living in the barracks. My friends in Moscow used to discuss different matters, but Moscow was far away. In Kuntsevo, the conversation turned, inevitably, to burglaries, prisons, and condoms. So, I couldn't even think of walking in there with the three girls. And suddenly I heard somebody screaming behind me, "Get the little *Yid!* Knock him down!"

And before I realized whom the exclamation was referring to, the two men knocked me down on the ground. Both were enormous, robust guys, drunk like fish, but still very strong. They punched me and we fell into the snow, rolling there; they were all over me. It was slippery. Because I was a boy and slim at the time, I managed to crawl from under them, like an eel, and I ran. But I could not escape: a crowd surrounded us, people stood close to each other, like a live wall. There was not a single gap in this wall I could escape through. A few times I tried to cut through the crowd, bouncing against the bodies wrapped in overcoats, trying to push through. They would not let me. Their soft mass was so pliant, and yet so hostile. The two men knocked me down again, this time a third person joined them. I was covered with dirt and mud, half undressed and bleeding. I was exhausted and ready to give up, when suddenly I felt somebody, from behind, pressing my eye with his thumb trying to squeeze it out. The pain was so strong, it gave me a burst of energy—I pulled away. This time I plunged between the people's legs, and I was able to break through. I escaped.

I didn't know those people in the crowd. They didn't know me. My only fault was that I was unmistakably a Jewish boy. And that was always my problem, or maybe, my advantage, because it freed me from many problems that some less apparent Jew would have had. Like trying to pass for a Russian, changing my last name, etc. Since my early childhood the opposition between Jew and the others became painfully clear to me. That was the foundation upon which the layer of anti-Sovietism was later added. I never became a Zionist, but I never stopped being a Jew. I was quite stunned to discover, after I came to the United States, that from the point of view of many Jews, I am not a real Jew, because I don't go to synagogue, and I don't observe Judaism. In the Soviet Union my background had steadily secured the hatred of many others. And I had equally strong feelings for them. I always hated them. I don't mean to say I hated Russia and Russian people. But the truth is that the "Great Nation" didn't favor me much. Although, some occasional representatives of the "Great Nation" were eager to admit that "there are some good Jews, after all."

My resentment of the realities of Soviet life caused me to like books. I became interested in literature and philosophy, particularly themes not related to the Marxist doctrine. I became a big authority on the occult, a kind of spiritual guru. But according to Soviet law, I was a mere parasite. Although I graduated from the Teachers' College in Moscow, I never took the job assigned to me upon graduation. I did not want to serve the regime. I never did. Instead, I took all kinds of odd jobs, worked as a freight worker, a baby-sitter. Fortunately, people in my country never ceased having various needs, and somebody had to fill those needs. For a while I worked as a hypnotist. And in my last couple of years in Russia I even became a rich man.

It happened almost by accident. One of my "spiritual" pupils introduced me to his friend from Odessa, a handsome young man, and a great hustler. We liked each other from the start. He was serving his last year in the army. So, soon after we met, he went back to his base. Meanwhile, I went to the county of Kostroma, to gather mushrooms. Kostroma's forests were famous for their mushrooms. Suddenly, I received a long distance call from my young friend. Lev was his name. He said: "There is an opportunity to make money, and big money." "How big?" I asked. "Three thousand [rubles]." That was a lot of money. I didn't believe him. I said: "I'm busy, I'm gathering mushrooms here. It's the peak of the mushroom season and I can't leave now. Call me later." So, I stayed in Kostroma, kept picking mushrooms and canning them. In two days he called again. The business opportunity he was talking about was decorating the walls of a local cultural center in a small town in Altay. That's where he served, and where he called from. Painting was among my many occupations. And I had a lot of friends who were painters, too. He said: "Find a friend, and come over here." Anyway, this time I believed him. I took a friend, we arrived at the place, we did the job. And we made not three, but seven thousand rubles. And that was just the beginning.

Soon the two of us formed a company, a workmen's association. The idea was simple: there were an enormous number of collective farms. And in those many collective farms the children grew up, having everything except for one thing. The walls of their schools and kindergartens were painted in a dull gray. We offered the proud parents, the collective farmers, to decorate the walls with scenes from Pushkin's fairy tales. And that was a killer idea, because nobody could object against helping children or illustrating Pushkin. Everybody was happy in the end: the farmers, we, and the artists whom we were giving a chance to make some money.

The only problem was that what we did was illegal. Our little enterprise was not sanctioned by the government, but there were ways of solving this problem. The procedure was usually as follows. We'd come to some provincial town. Lev, our business director, would make a visit to a third secretary of a local regional party committee. A third secretary was usually the one handling the ideology issues. The average price of a Third Secretary of Ideology in an average Soviet town was 600 rubles. Lev had a gift for bribing. He could handle any bureaucrat of any rank or stature. In the end, our underground, half illegal gang was given a government assignment to decorate the Medeo skating rink, the largest skating arena in the world. The offer came directly from the Minister of Culture. But by that time (1979) I had already left the country.

My wife was a very clever woman, she was much more adept at being an immigrant than I. By the end of our transit period in Rome, she spoke English fluently, whereas I was just beginning to mumble something. Within forty-five days after we arrived in New York, she had already found a job as a computer programmer. Very soon she became successful. I was way behind. At first, I was proud of her success. Then I felt humiliated by it.

In many ways, I kept holding on to the old illusions. I had some friends in New York—American writers, film directors. In Moscow they had taken a big interest in me: I was a dissident, an exotic bird. In New York I became a common immigrant. Suddenly there was a huge gap between us. They all lived in Manhattan, in nice apartments. There was no way we could communicate as equals. My wife didn't have such problems: she had her job, she had a family to support. She became the family provider. In Russia it was the other way around: I was the provider. I was the man, master in the house. Russia is in many ways an Asian country.

Here, the master had turned into a zero. My wife was making rapid progress. I remained where I was. This created certain problems between us until, finally, our family collapsed. Many Soviet families don't survive immigration. And quite often the wives do much better than their husbands. While a Soviet-Russian husband spends his time reflecting on life, a wife keeps working. She has no time to suffer, or contemplate. She has responsibilities. In Russia it was taken for granted that a woman should endlessly stand in lines, cook, clean, take care of her husband and children and yet go to work every day. But here you can't take it for granted. This is the West. The rules are different here. I'm ashamed to say I was a typical Russian macho husband. For a long time I was convinced it was her duty to take care of me and the family, while I sat and contemplated life and death issues. Now I can't believe I was so stupid. And it took me a very long time to realize that, and to admit that despite all my hatred for the Soviet system, I was, in fact, a typical product of it. I was a conformist. Only a tiny part of me had protested, the rest of me had conformed fully.

For a long time I existed in some kind of fog, blinded by my own preconceived ideas of what America was like, not being able to see the reality. I brought too much baggage with me, I mean cultural baggage, which turned out to be a big obstacle in my understanding America. I believed I'd be able to survive and live here the same way I lived in Russia. My logic was: "If I was able to survive in Russia—it'll be twice as easy here." But I kept failing, and I couldn't understand why.

For a while I didn't have to worry about money. I had brought my collection with me—a collection of books and paintings. For a while I was able to survive—even travel all over Europe—by selling the books from this collection. The collection lasted five years. When I ran out of books to sell, I sank into a deep depression. That was when my family fell apart. I had to start working. My first job was as a consultant on Russian avant-garde books. Then I gave private tours all over Europe.

Still, there was not a single moment in all my years in America that I missed Russia. In 1989 I happened to go back—not to Russia, but to Georgia. I had a special invitation from the Georgian minister of culture. The reason for the visit was the creation of the first

Georgian Cultural Center in New York. I was supposed to head the modern art gallery of the center, and I was flying to Georgia basically to select the paintings. It was April of 1989, the beginning of the collapse of the Soviet government in Georgia. I witnessed the student demonstrations in Tbilisi, and the shooting that followed. I saw the wounded. I was in the crowd myself, with a mini-cassette recorder. I was the last foreigner to be evacuated from Tbilisi. I saw the crowd smashing shop windows, destroying cars. Ironically, I was protected from the enraged crowd by a KGB officer, assigned to me for that purpose. I found this fact amusing, given that a number of years earlier I had been interrogated by the KGB. Now they provided my security. In my last night in a hotel in Tbilisi, the KGB officer slept on the floor, outside the door to my room. It was indeed an unforgettable visit.

Now, I'm working in an organization called the New York Association for New Americans (NYANA). Basically I provide professional orientation for newly arrived Russian immigrants. Most of them are around my age. That means they have been entirely formed during the years of Soviet power. They were created by that system, and all the changes happening in Russia hardly touched them at all. They emigrated from Russia essentially because they can't live without the Soviet system. And in America they find this Soviet system preserved intact: they're being taken care of, they can go on welfare, they get Social Security benefits. A lot of these people are engineers, scientists, professionals who had good positions in Russia. Here they find themselves in a vacuum. They can't find jobs, they can't learn the language. They communicate only with immigrants like themselves. Their problem is they didn't leave Russia in time.

Matvey Kanengiser
In His Own Style

Now in his early thirties, Matvey grew up in Kiev, Ukraine. He comes from a family of metal workers. A chance meeting led to a job modeling for a hair stylist. He liked the business right away and soon became a high fashion hairdresser in Kiev. He emigrated to America in 1991. He soon found work in an elegant French hair salon on Madison Avenue in New York, where he learned about style. At the salon, young and mostly foreign workers were paid low wages, working for the experience and the opportunity to make connections with the rich and influential. "In a way, it's the same system as in Russia," he observes. "Only there, you'd shmooze for a slab of meat."

I left Russia in 1991. I had lived in Kiev, and I lived well. There were plenty of Jewish people involved in my occupation, so I never really suffered from anti-Semitism. I didn't look typically Jewish, so that wasn't a problem. I remember a certain period, in 1989, when rumors were spread about pogroms in Kiev. People would find anti-Semitic notes in their mailboxes. Some people really panicked. But the threats never materialized. No pogroms happened. The whole thing just died away. I decided to emigrate because I was looking for excitement.

I began working as a hair stylist in 1985. Earlier, I had worked in a metallurgy plant, where my father sent me after I graduated from high school. My father was a workshop supervisor in this plant. My whole family, including my aunt, sister, and cousin, worked in this plant. It was a family tradition. I started there as an apprentice, but in a year I was promoted. I operated a simple machine, cutting sheets of metal. All I had to do was to move the handle up and down, and then up and down again. Operating this machine didn't require much sophistication, or even thinking. Then, by chance, I met a woman who was looking for people to model for her husband, who was a hair stylist. He needed models to present his work at fairs and exhibitions.

So, for a while, I modeled for him, and I liked the business. I liked the people involved in the business. There were a lot of beautiful people, and I liked that. I thought I'd try it myself. His wife was teaching at a professional school for hairdressers. I took the course and became a hairdresser. The profession suited me, and I suited it. I like change, and that is what fashion is about. It never stays in the same place. Some people warned me, "You'll get bored, standing on your feet all day, cutting people's hair." But it was never boring to me. It's amazing to watch a person change before your very eyes with a change of hairstyle. A person's manners change, the way she or he walks, facial expression, even the voice. It's as if you have created a whole new personality.

I soon became a very fashionable hairdresser in Kiev. I won a couple of competitions. I was making good money. People wanted me to do their hair and paid a lot of money for that. The salary in a beauty salon isn't great. Most of the money came from tips.

People in customer service—hairdressers, directors of retail stores and supermarkets, and salespeople—were all closely connected. We lived by the same principle of ownership—"What you guard is yours." So, if I did the hair of a director of a supermarket, he paid me back in sausages. If I didn't need any sausages, I could go to a person who "guarded" something else, and get something else in exchange for the sausages. After perestroika things changed, but not much. You still had to provide services for different people, so that they'd pay you back in kind. You still had to serve as a sort of go-between. You still had to bend before the people with power. That made life humiliating.

After the Chernobyl nuclear disaster in April 1986, some Americans—who seemed to worry more about it than many people in Ukraine—invited a few children, supposedly victims of Chernobyl, to visit and spend some time in the United States. It was a kind of humanitarian gesture on their part. But the children who ended up going to America were for the most part sons and daughters of the same directors of supermarkets, hotels, and the like, and the children of other powerful people, people with connections. The same old Mafia.

The whole emigration process took me five years. At the end, I could think of nothing but getting away from Russia. All the political and social upheavals in the country passed me by. I came to New York in 1991 and settled in Brooklyn. The Jewish immigrant organization, NYANA, supported me for the first couple of months. I was learning the language and looking for a job. First, I tried a couple of beauty salons in Brooklyn, where I lived. Some of them were run by Russians.

But I was rejected. They needed somebody who could speak English. I couldn't speak English well enough for them. Ironically, the first employment I found was in a fancy French salon in Manhattan. I passed by, I liked the way it looked, and decided to inquire about the job. They took me. The French didn't care much if I could speak English or not. They didn't speak that much English themselves, and they didn't demand it of me. They were French: they believed French was good enough. It was one of the best beauty salons in New York, on Madison Avenue and Seventy-Fourth street. For me, it was a great professional school. I worked there for two years, the best time of my life here. I felt fine among my French coworkers. Their English was not much better than mine, and we often had to communicate with gestures. Our boss was spending half of his time in New York, and half in Paris, where he also had a salon. I remember him talking to clients—a lot of them were wealthy old ladies living on the Upper East Side. Often he would listen to them describe what they wanted in a hairdo, and then say: "I'm going to cut your hair up to here." And that was it. If you don't like it, you were free to go. For the most part, this was what I was required to be able to say: "I'm going to cut your hair up to here."

I was spending a lot of time at work. I was basically coming home only to sleep. A lot of interesting people used to come to the salon, many celebrities—princes, models, actors. It was fun. But I wasn't making much money. In a way, I was exploited. Like any other immigrant business, this hair salon was built on a certain principle: take more from the customers and pay less to the employees. Most of the employees were young people brought in from France. They didn't speak English well—or at all—and while they learned

English, they were paid very little, about 20 percent of the fee charged to customers. The average price of a haircut in the salon was $150. Usually, after a year or two, when workers improved their English and their skills, they would ask for a raise. And they would be told, "Okay, this is not working, you can go." And the boss would bring a fresh batch of people to take their place. That was how the business worked. There were a couple of experienced stylists in the salon. They had their own clientele, and they were paid good money. The rest of us worked our butts off for very little pay. Some got lucky. Take Renat Bakkay, for example. He came from France. He didn't speak any English, either. He didn't know anybody in New York. Then he happened to meet a movie star; she was one of his customers. She introduced him to an executive at one of the top stores, where he opened his first salon. That's how things work. In a way, it's the same system as in Russia. Only there you'd schmooze for a slab of meat, or a sausage. Here, the stakes are higher.

In this French hair salon, I first learned about style. In Russia, there was no real style. Everybody did what everybody else did. No real news about fashion was available, and there was no understanding of "class." The most colorful style was often considered the most fashionable. Chic meant having a foreign label on your garment. Or take the Russian fashion designer who designed dresses in the shape of eggs, Fabergé eggs. And he brought them here. Well, Americans put them in a museum. What else would you do with those eggs? You couldn't wear them. This is not fashion—it's just a desire to shock. Fashion designers here also try to shock, to impress the public. But what they do makes sense as clothing, and there is a simple idea behind the design. In Russia, all the designs are complicated, piled high with decorations. I remember the elaborate hairdos we used to create in Russia: by the time we were finished, the whole thing began to crumble and lose its shape. Here I learned about style, and I found my own style, eventually. Recently, I read this article, an interview with a stylist from Russia. He said he could choose any style he wants; he could dictate style to the public. For instance, he could tell people to wear red today—and they would—and green tomorrow—and they would. That's his idea of fashion. A typical Russian approach: they all want be to be Napoleon.

When I came to America, I wanted to achieve great things in my profession, to gain recognition. My profession is a creative one. You have to be up-to-date in fashion, and you have to read the fashion magazines. Competition is very heavy here, but still it's much easier for me to work here than in Russia. I can't explain why, but it's true. There's an atmosphere of freedom. I knew nothing about America, about New York, when I came here. At first I was shocked by many things I saw. Like all that garbage in the street. I was shocked by the amount of poverty. But now, when I go to Central Park and see all the homeless people lying out in the sun, looking so carefree, I think maybe there's some freedom in their existence, too.

A certain class of clients in New York strongly reminds me of my clients back in Kiev: they're Russians from Brighton Beach. Former managers and directors of supermarkets and clothing stores, here they own restaurants and stores and whorehouses. They haven't changed a bit. They still like being supervisors.

I really don't have a circle of friends. New Russians don't interest me. The old Russians, immigrants who have lived here for twenty years or so, are boring. So, my only circle is my girlfriend, really. She's my company. After I left my first salon, I worked in a couple of others. Finally I decided to work for myself. It's the best. I don't like having supervisors. I am not a collective kind of person. I was not in Russia, and I am not here.

Sergey Artushkov
What's Missing?

IN Russia he was part of the artistic underground doing translations for literary magazines in St. Petersburg. Now in his forties, he works as a network administrator in a large computer company in San Francisco. He came to the United States in 1989 for a visit but soon found himself a job translating the Book of Mormon *into Russian. He decided to stay, partly because he felt a sense of security that he had never felt in Russia. Then again, friendship is different here—much more formal.*

I left Russia to visit a friend who lived in America. I came here in April 1989, after Misha Iossel, an old friend who had emigrated a couple of years earlier, sent me an invitation. Misha was working at the University of New Hampshire at the time. Not long after I arrived, he found me a job.

It was a translating job that Misha didn't feel like doing himself, so he turned it over to me. The job was to translate the *Book of Mormon* into Russian. Our clients were the Mormon Sectarians living in Kansas City. They had split with the official Mormon church in the nineteenth century over the issue of polygamy. The project was meant to last a year. I was supposed to do the rough translation, and Misha would edit it later. But no editing was really needed: the book was written in the stylized language of the Bible. The same expressions and rhetorical figures were used repeatedly throughout the text, and after the first hundred pages I pretty much knew them by heart. So, I ended up typing up the pages, sending them to the Mormons without even proofreading, and receiving the money.

The fact that I had such good luck from the very beginning strongly influenced my decision to stay in America. I could spend the entire day wandering around, then, in the evening, type a couple of pages on the computer, and still make enough money to live on. The Mormons were paying me $20 a page.

The other reason for my decision had to do with the feeling of physical safety that I felt in America. It became obvious to me that my life in Russia was accompanied by a constant sense of physical danger, which I didn't feel while I was here. Every minute in Russia I lived with the fear of humiliation, and with my readiness to accept it. I never believed that the Soviet state could offer me any personal protection.

I lived an odd life in Russia. I lived in Leningrad, repairing computers. The job brought me enough money to live on, as well as a free schedule. In my spare time or, should I say, my primary time, I was actively involved in the life of the cultural underground. I attended all the literary discussions and readings at Club 81. I was doing translations for *Pretext,* the literary magazine published by my late friend, Sergey Khrenov. That was my life—devoted mainly to socializing. Perestroika didn't really change anything. But it did provide an opportunity to make money. For instance, by working in a cooperative, I was able to earn enough money to take my trip to America. Perestroika gave me not only financial opportunities, but the freedom to come to America, and for that I am forever grateful to Mr. Gorbachev, personally. He didn't have to do what he did. Nobody pushed him really.

Subconsciously, I had always wanted to emigrate. What prevented this desire from surfacing was an insufficient level of fear—and confidence. I was never persecuted as a Jew, because I'm not Jewish. Also, I had no belief in my potential, no self-confidence whatever. That's why I had never given the idea any serious consideration.

But, once I found myself in the United States, my decision to stay was made pretty quickly. First of all, I had plenty of friends here, already living in different parts of the country. Some were in California, some on the East Coast. Many of my schoolmates, and even more of my friends from University, had emigrated from Russia. Now they all were telling me, "Don't be so foolish as to go back to Russia." They also explained to me how to apply for political asylum. I described my life in Russia, and my connections to the underground. And I got the status of refugee. So, after I finished translating the *Book of Mormon,* I started to looking for a job repairing computers. I found one, and I stayed at that job for almost four years. Afterward, I took some courses. My next job was much more sophisticated, and much better paid. I'm now involved with computer networks, as a network administrator.

My only difficulty in America is the loss of a social context. In Russia we were used to being part of a larger community. That was the way we were raised. My communication with Americans, for the most part, is very formal. Formality guards against offense. America is a nation of immigrants and its culture is based on an individualistic mentality that values self-protection. The culture has created certain formalized ways of expressing emotions, guarded forms of communication. It doesn't allow you to get inside another person, to know him in depth. It amplifies the distance between people to a safe distance. Historically, I think, this has helped people who come from so many different cultures to coexist in one society and to live in peace. These advantages, I believe, far outweigh the shortcomings of such a system.

We were much less formal in Russia thanks to drinking. Heavy drinking was part of the social culture in which we grew up. Drinking provided a sense of unity within the group, a certain oneness. But it also killed a lot of people, including many talented people. I truly believe that had I stayed in Russia, I would have drunk myself to death by now, like so many of my friends.

THE GRAY ZONE

Yelena
New York Madam

ATTRACTIVE and businesslike in demeanor, thirty-six-year-old Yelena had decided to start an escort service even before she emigrated from St.Petersburg in 1990. She learned the business from a KGB agent, who patronized her underground tailor shop. Yelena's escort service in New York has developed into an upscale enterprise. She now manages only a few select "girls" and attracts high-paying clients whom she vets personally. "The nature of services is never spelled out," Yelena remarks. Although she tries to separate her business and family life, her children are growing up and beginning to ask questions.

I came to New York from St. Petersburg in 1990, seven months pregnant. Like most Russian immigrants, I was not financially well off. I was married, though. After my son was born, we began to search for ways to make money. The idea of opening an escort service came to me in Russia. A friend of mine ran such a business in Russia. He had seven Russian girls working for him. He was a KGB agent, so he could provide them with free access to all the international hotels in St. Petersburg. He rented apartments for them, too. He lived pretty well off this business. The girls were doing well, too. In the 1980s, the average rate on a girl like that was between $100 and $200. That's for a night, not for an hour. But, that was good money. And since he took care of not one but seven girls, he was making about $600 a night. The girls gave him all the money they got from clients. In exchange, he provided them with clothing, food, and places to live. In America this system is known as the "pimp" system. We didn't have the term in Russia, but we did have the practice.

I knew him and his girls for about two years. The girls used to buy clothes from me. I kept a good selection of imported clothes and they were my regular customers. In Russia I owned an underground tailor's shop. In addition to selling imported clothes, we sewed our own clothes, put on imitation foreign labels, then sold them. The business was illegal, of course. Later it became legal, but I had already made my decision to leave Russia.

In Russia, my husband had been the director of a big food storage business. That was a very good position back in Russia, but it was hardly something he could continue doing in America. I couldn't rely on his supporting me and the child. So I decided to open an escort service. I said nothing to my husband. I did it on my own. In the beginning, I worked only with Russian girls. My English was pretty bad at the time. I placed ads in a Russian newspaper, *Novoye Russkoye Slovo*. Back then they were still taking such ads. That's how I found my first "girls." Then I advertised the agency in American and Israeli newspapers. That was my lawyer's advice. It brought us a lot of clients from Israel.

My agency charged low prices. That was necessary in order to survive the competition with other escort services in Manhattan. In this business, a client pays either by the hour or for a package. A package might include limousine service, dinner, sometimes even tickets to the theater. The nature of the services is never spelled out. That's why the escort business is considered a "gray zone" in America. A client pays for the companionship. The word "sex" is never used. It's not part of our vocabulary. I never ask girls what they did, or how exactly they spent the time with my clients. The client pays for the time; all I need to know is how much time. How they spend this time is their own business.

In its first two years, the business didn't bring any money; it didn't even cover the expenses on advertising. But we kept expanding. We began to hire more American girls, then European. I tried to be creative. I added new services, such as fantasy and role playing—S & M, submissive and dominant. So I had to hire girls with expertise. Russian girls weren't particularly popular with clients. There is the feeling that Russian women are cold. Looks are important in this business of course, but social skills are also important. A woman has to be able to loosen up the client. She needs to know how to adopt and to create, you know, a chemistry with him. And Russian girls were not very good at that. They often felt shy, maybe because of the language barrier.

I own this business, but I would never want to work as an escort myself. I never had any interest in that. It's not my kind of thing. Besides, I've always been married. And Russian husbands are not particularly tolerant of that sort of thing. For a long time my husband didn't even know the nature of the business I was running. I told him it was an agency for cleaning and housekeeping jobs. He believed me. Eventually he found out, and it caused a serious shift in our relationship. But we got over it in time. Some of the girls who work for me are also married and keep it a secret from their husbands.

It's not very difficult to keep such a secret. Most people are not very curious. When I started my business, most of my casual friends didn't know what I did. True, I didn't have many friends at the time, so it wasn't hard to keep it a secret. My only close friend knew, of course. But other people, people I was meeting socially, weren't even curious enough to ask me what my occupation was.

My business has grown and became upscale. In 1990, the hourly rate we charged was $150; now it's between $500 and $2,000. We work with the biggest porno stars of Hollywood. Their minimum rate is $1,500 an hour, usually higher. In order to reach such a high professional level in business, one has to listen to clients. Usually it's the client himself who gives you tips on how to improve your business. People ask for a particular product or type of service. And when you don't have such a product, but you see that there is a high demand for it, you begin to think, "Well, maybe I should get it." For example, a lot of clients may ask you about a particular person, or for a person with a particular talent. You shouldn't think of girls as just escorts; you should think of them as talents. Each of our girls is famous for something. It's either a film she did or particular skills she has. We have some European girls who can also work as translators or secretaries on business trips. Because, typically, European women can speak three or four languages, we use them for business trips, domestic or abroad.

The main thing in running a business like this is to be patient. You need to be patient with both the clients and the girls. You sort of stand between the two, and either side can cause you problems. Maybe that's why the escort business is considered a woman's business in America. Most of the services in Manhattan are owned by women. And clients feel more comfortable when they deal with a woman.

Now that my business has gotten the reputation as an established agency, I don't have to place ads to find the girls; they're referred to me. I get calls from all over Europe, and I invite women to work for a week or two. I have six girls at a time—I don't need more—who each work for me about two weeks. Every two weeks I replace them. The clients need new faces. And we have a lot of regular clients. Men like variety. And because we have only six girls, we can really focus on them and give them as much work as possible. So they get a chance to make good money. Some girls come to work for me only one week a year. In one week they make as much money as an average worker earns in a year. Some of the girls have many such jobs. Some simply travel for the rest of year. Sometimes, when I like a girl, I offer her an annual contract. If she signs the contract during that year, it means that she can't work for any agency but mine during that year. If she breaks the contract, I have the right to sue her. It's all official. The contracts are written by lawyers.

In all these years, I have never had a conflict with the law, although that does happen frequently in this type of business. The reason is that I'm very careful in what I say to clients over the phone, how I sell the services. Companionship is a broad term. Every client has his own specific needs and chooses a girl who can satisfy those needs. I have never had any problems with clients, no complaints from either side. I can afford to screen the clients, and I take only people I want to work with. Sometimes, we get so many calls. We get so busy. I don't have to take every single man who calls. I ask clients how they make their living. I ask for their addresses. You can always determine if the client is wealthy just by his address. And I check all the information they give me.

In the long run, I think my occupation has affected my personality. It has definitely affected my attitude toward men. But I believe this business is indispensable to society. If not for us, the streets of this city would be filled with madmen attacking people at random. So I believe we're doing a great service to this city by reducing male stress. We get a lot of calls from stockbrokers, for instance. And I can understand how important it is for these people to relax at the end of the day. Simply talking to someone is important. There are plenty of lonely people in New York. They need companionship.

Some men break up with their girlfriends and have a hard time getting over it. Some have ordered tickets for a cruise, and then break up with a girlfriend or a wife. So, instead of returning the tickets, they can call us and find a companion to go on the trip. Situations like that are very common.

In these situations, a girl sometimes starts a relationship with a client. But it never really leads to anything good. Not in real life. Nothing comes of it. And then the girl comes back to us anyway. Americans marry women according to their status. And even if someone did marry a girl like that, sooner or later he would bring it up. He'd say to her, "Look at yourself in the mirror! Aren't you used up?!" So, in the end, the girls always come back.

Still, most of our clients are Americans. We don't have Russian clients. I'd rather not have them. Russian men are too demanding. They want too much for their money. And Russian men treat women badly. That's why I never work with Russian clients. And, anyway, they never want to pay the full price we charge.

I try to keep my work and business separate. But my business and my private life intertwine all the same; it's hard to prevent it from happening. That's why I think that at some point I'll have to wrap it up. My children are growing up and they're starting to ask questions. I have a small daughter now. Since she was born, I've begun to think seriously about quitting the business. I want to protect my daughter. I don't want her to take the wrong path when she grows up. The only reason I started this business was that it was easy money. I didn't have to go to school. I could start right away and be my own boss. The kind of money I make now, I could never make at any other job in America. But I won't keep this business forever. What I would like is to open a restaurant, a big one, so that I could make as much money as I'm making now. And I would throw big parties at my restaurant and invite a lot of people, including friends. This would be the next step for me. I think I have enough money now to open the kind of restaurant I want.

What I like about my experience in America is that I had to learn how to take care of myself and stand on my own. In Russia I believed that a man could do anything, if he had the right connections and the right position. But a lot of Russian men find themselves helpless once they come to America. They lose their confidence, and their spirits break. That's why a lot of Russian marriages fall apart after immigration. It takes many years for some men to get back on their feet and start a new life. It's easier for a woman. A woman can always find something. At the very least, she could work in an escort service and support herself that way.

I am satisfied with my life. I have never had a moment when I felt too sad, or unhappy, or desperate here. Neither have I experienced a moment of real happiness. My life has been neither black nor white—just gray. I like traveling. I went recently to the Mediterranean. I loved it there, Egypt in particular. It's a virginal land. It's not modern, not developed in our sense of the word. Everything is ancient, and it wants to stay that way. I felt comfortable in Egypt, as if it were my country, more so than Russia or America. I think I could actually live there. The time I spent there made me happy.

Lana
Topless Dancer

THE *daughter of a Russian airline executive, Lana lived in Paris until she was fifteen. When her family returned to Moscow in 1983, she was bored and resentful. After a brief marriage, the birth of a daughter, and work as a translator, she left for New York, ostensibly on a visit. Bold and good-looking, she decided to stay, walking into a job as a topless dancer. Now thirty-three years old, she dances in a club in New Jersey. When asked what she wants from life, she answers, laughing: "Love, sex, money." She is not sure which one comes first.*

My background is unusual. I was born in Moscow, but my family moved to Algeria and then to Paris because my father worked for the Russian airline, Aeroflot. So, I basically grew up in Paris. When I turned fifteen in 1983, we moved back to Moscow.

I couldn't stand it in Moscow. I didn't like the regime and I didn't like the culture. After I finished high school, I entered the Foreign Languages Institute in Moscow. But I was in constant conflict with teachers who put me down at every opportunity. I remember getting bad grades even though I could speak French fluently. After three years, I dropped out and I began to work as a translator. My life in Russia was not too hard: I come from a well-to-do family. We had an apartment on Gorky Street, right in the center of Moscow. Later I got my own apartment, which was a big deal in Russia at the time. But in spite of it all, I resented my life in Moscow.

And later, with perestroika, it didn't seem any better. I didn't think much of the freedoms given to us.

I never liked the men I met in Moscow. I got married when I was seventeen to a man eighteen years older. He also happened to be a Jew, a big disadvantage at the time. My family didn't approve of him, but I moved in with him despite their resistance. We had a daughter. In the end, I couldn't live with him anyway. He had a heart attack at the age of thirty-eight. I stayed with him until he recovered, and then I split.

I decided to leave Russia. My friends helped me get an American visa. I went to New York, supposedly to take a two-week flight-attendant course. I had no intention of taking the course, but it enabled me to spend two weeks in New York. From the first moment I got a glimpse of the skyscrapers, I knew that New York was my city. I am a social animal by nature. I enjoy living. I love men and wine. I love all of life. So, right away, I fell under the spell of New York.

I came to New York with a French businessman, a friend of my family who was supposed to keep an eye on me. But soon after we arrived, he had to go to Israel. I was left in New York all by myself. I began to explore the city, wandering the streets, meeting people. I couldn't speak English. All I could say was "My name is Lana, and I'm from Russia." But even with such a limited vocabulary, I managed to meet a lot of interesting people. The Frenchman came back to New York. "You should go back to Russia," he told me. "Your visa is about to expire in a few days." Having said that, he took off again. But I had no intention of returning to Russia.

One day I was walking on Thirty-third Street, near Seventh Avenue. I was in a state of confusion. My visa was about to expire, and I had no money. I had brought only $600 with me. Suddenly I overheard two big guys with shaved heads speaking Russian. They were standing near the door of the building with a sign overhead that read: "Club." "What kind of club?" I thought to myself. Looking closer, I saw a picture of a naked girl in the window. I got the idea. I walked into the nearest café, put on some makeup and tousled my hair. Then I knocked at the door of the club. When one of the guys opened the door, I spoke to him in French: "Is this a topless dancing club? Are you hiring?" "Of course," they said. They brought me to the owner of the club, a woman.

Later I learned her story. She had come to work in that club as a waitress, and the owner fell in love with her. They got married, had a child, and lived happily ever after. She ended up running the business.

The club occupied a three-story building. Downstairs, there were all kinds of sex devices on display, like whips and bathtubs. I don't think they were ever used: they just served as part of the decor. On the second floor were a bar and a stage. On the third floor were all kinds of nooks and crannies where the clients could sit with the girls one-on-one and drink champagne. Touching was not allowed, and there were video cameras everywhere to ensure that it wouldn't happen. Rules were very strict. The name of that club was Paradise. At first I felt very shy. Later I became more relaxed and began to enjoy it. After all, it was a chance for me to learn something new—and learn English as well.

After a few days, I met a lawyer in the club. He could speak Russian. "Come to my place tonight, and I'll give you some tips about life in New York," he said. He had a Park Avenue South address. I went to his place. He was a very well-mannered, mellow kind of guy. He treated me with respect, didn't make any passes. It turned out he had worked with Russian businesses for a long time, had a Russian wife, and he even knew my father. That lawyer promised to help me. First of all, he told me to return to Moscow right away—my visa had already expired. So I went back to Moscow, but left all my stuff in New York. I knew I would be back.

When I came back, I danced in one of the best clubs in Manhattan, the VIP Club, and I made between $500 and $1,000 a day. I stayed at the club for three months, and then I met a man, a banker from Chicago, who fell in love with me. His name was Richard. He came to the club one night, saw me dance, and we talked. He began to visit me on his trips from Chicago. After the third visit, he asked me to accompany him to Las Vegas. "Don't worry," he said. "You'll have your own private room, and I'll pay for your days off from work." I made it clear to him from the beginning that I worked for money only. Money and a green card were my first priorities. After that came owning my own house. I was very clear about what I wanted.

Richard began to support me financially. He helped me a great deal. I soon left the club. I studied at NYU and got a certificate as a real-estate agent. But I didn't really have a desire to work—I didn't have to. Richard rented me an apartment in Manhattan, and he was giving me enough money to live on. I didn't want to do anything. I was spending my time hanging out with friends, meeting a lot of people. I was having love affairs. For a year I lived absolutely carefree.

Richard wanted to divorce his wife because of me. But in the end, he didn't. Financial considerations prevailed: he didn't want to give his wife half of his money. Besides, he couldn't trust me completely. He wasn't sure I'd be with him tomorrow. I tried to behave myself, but I wasn't always able. I wasn't in love with him. That was the problem. I even hated him at times. We were very different people. I am a very emotional, hot-tempered person, and he's slow and fastidious. But I did feel warmth toward him, mostly because he taught me a lot. He could spend hours with me on my homework, explaining the meaning of new words and sentences. He was seventeen years older than I. In the end, I came to like him as a person, but not as a man. The very thought that this man was in my life became unbearable. I tend to have these fits of rage sometimes, when I have too much alcohol mixed with cigarettes mixed with resentment toward a particular person. At moments like that with Richard, I could break furniture, throw things at him. I used to run away from him, then come back. We stayed together for a couple of years. We had an arrangement: he paid my rent and gave me money, and we saw each other from time to time. He was a very wealthy man.

Being with Richard didn't satisfy me emotionally. I began an affair with another man, a Russian artist, very talented. For a while, I was going back and forth between these two men. I couldn't decide which one to stay with. One had money and power, the other was good at sex and love. Nobody was particularly happy with the situation. It all came to an end when I hit Richard. I beat him up. It happened in a hotel. He had promised to buy me a house. He had already written a check. But then he tore it up right in front of my eyes. "What will I get from this check?" he said. "I'll show you what you'll get," I replied. And I hit him in the eye and knocked him out. Then I broke the glass coffee table and turned the entire hotel room upside down. When the police arrived, I told them that he had started the fight and beaten me up. And he was taken to the police station in handcuffs. Since then, I have an order of protection against him. He's not allowed to come near me or even to call me.

After I split from Richard, I bought a house in New Jersey. I had saved enough money while living with him. I also had sold my apartment in Moscow and invested some money in stocks. So I was finally able to fulfill my dream and buy a house for myself and my daughter. But now I had to start making money. I had my real-estate certificate, but I never really liked the work. I decided to go back to dancing. I looked through the magazine that advertises topless clubs, and I chose a club in New Jersey. It turned out it wasn't really a topless club: the girls were dancing in swimsuits. I told the manager who was interviewing me: "I need to start working right away." I told him I was a professional. He told me to go onstage. I put on the red dress I had brought with me. "Hold up your skirt and show me your legs," he said. I did as he asked. "Fine, you can start tomorrow," he told me. So it wasn't hard to get the job.

There are all kinds of girls in the club—Americans, Hispanics, a few Russians. The girls always help each other. We have one goal: to get the client going and make him open his wallet. The best thing is to draw him into the champagne room, because that's what costs the most money: an hour alone with a girl costs $150, plus the bottle of champagne that costs between $120 and $200. Clients are not allowed to touch or kiss the girl, and these rules are strict. Every girl tries to build a roster of her own special clients, who come to the club to watch and spend time with her. In my first couple of weeks at this club I didn't make much money. I felt disappointed and angry, because in the past I had made a lot of money at this sort of job. But the clientele in New Jersey is different from the clientele in New York. Men who go to the clubs in New Jersey are not mature and sophisticated. Mostly, they're young guys, simpletons who sit and drink their beer and don't want to part with their money. They prefer younger girls who move quickly, who can spin around and do contortionist tricks.

I can't compete with those girls. They're in their twenties, and I am thirty-three. Besides, it is not my style. The way I work is to focus on a particular client, charm him, play with him, tell him stories. Eventually I found my personal clients, interesting people. One of them is in the car business. Another is a writer, a well-known person in New Jersey. They are in their fifties. They are my friends. They come to the club to watch me. They give me money. I dance for them, and then we sit and drink champagne. They have wives and they have families. But they come to the club, and they pay to see me. Maybe they want some excitement in their lives.

My daughter is thirteen. She doesn't know what I do for a living. I tell her I work as a waitress in a nightclub. I enjoy my work.

I enjoy going onstage every night. I have a nice wardrobe, and I like changing clothes, changing my hairdo every night. I feel like a woman when I'm onstage. I feel empowered.

Russian girls don't have a very good reputation. They are considered gold diggers. Recently, there was a series of articles in the *New York Times* about Russian models who were cheating men out of their money, suing their ex-lovers for millions of dollars. No wonder that wealthy, middle-aged men are often afraid of Russian women. As for me I like money, of course. But I would never sleep with a man just for his money. I'd rather dance in a club.

I am optimistic by nature. I felt comfortable in this country from my first moment here. I've had a lot of support. People have helped me, financially and morally. I never regret that I left Russia. I'm not a typical Russian anyway, since I grew up in France. So, I never felt like Russia was my home. When I travel—and I love to travel—I go to Europe: to Paris, which I love, and to Cyprus, where my parents now live. I went to Russia last year, and I didn't like it at all. Even young people, my age or younger, seem burdened. I could see the fear in people's eyes, fear for their future.

My parents don't know what I do for living. They know I dance in a club, but they don't know I take off my clothes. Maybe they guess, but we never talk about it. I do tell them about my relationships with men. My parents are good friends, my closest friends.

I have found in America what I couldn't find in Russia. I've met interesting men, men I could like. I like well-groomed, well-mannered men who know how to treat a woman properly, who treat her like a queen. I never felt comfortable with Russian men. I think of myself as an interesting person, but somehow in Moscow no one ever paid attention. I was treated no better than a horse with a beautiful exterior. Russia is a patriarchal type of society, and America is matriarchal. And I prefer the matriarchal society. It suits me better. In America, men appreciate my personality. They appreciate foreign women, cosmopolitan women. I have lived in Paris, in Brussels, and in Algeria. I've seen a lot in my life. I can tell many interesting stories. I have confidence in myself. And men like that. The fact that I am a dancer attracts them even more.

I don't like American women. They lack femininity. They are loud. They chomp when they eat. They pick their noses in public. And I don't find them smart or intelligent at all. American women have become like men because of their emancipation. Besides, they have repressed their poor men, driven them to a state of panic. As for myself, I play a kitten, a nice calm kitten. It's an act in a way, but at least I'm good at it. In the end, I always get my way. I get what I want without becoming like a man myself.

I like to be admired, to hear compliments when I walk down the street. It makes me smile. I plan to keep dancing for another two years. I would like to make some really good money, enough to open my own business. My dream is to open a big nightclub, with music and disk jockeys. But that would cost a lot of money. I'm not sure I could make that much. At the very least, I could open a boutique. I would also like to marry well. But right now I feel I'm not ready for marriage. I'm too used to having a free life. I am not sure I could live with anyone. Even seeing the same man every day would be too much for me, let alone living with him. Unless I fall in love. I need to be in love. I need to feel strong emotions. Otherwise, I don't feel alive. I would like to pay off the mortgage on my house, and then buy a new house. I want to keep moving forward, always forward.

I have to be tough. I cast aside people I have no use for. I play by my own rules. And I don't deal with men who don't want to play by those rules. My rules are courtship, flowers, and presents like diamonds and cars. Love and sex are also important. I have a shirt with this logo on it: "Love, sex, money." Those are my rules.

I am afraid to get old. That's my biggest fear: old age and poverty. But I believe that even if I didn't have to worry about money, my life would be the same. It's the way I want it to be. I'm pretty sure about that.

Julia
Dominatrix

Now thirty-nine, Julia lives in a loft in a big industrial warehouse in Jersey City. She arrived in New York from St.Petersburg in 1989 with a young daughter. After easily getting—and as easily losing—her job as a designer in the garment district, she decided to try her luck elsewhere. She found work as a dominatrix. After three months at the job, however, she was fired—"for being too kind to customers."

I came to America in 1989 at the age of twenty-eight. I left Russia because there was something in the air then, a sense that a civil war was about to break out. I had a ten-year-old daughter. So I took off because I feared for her life. I liked my life in Russia well enough. In fact I had a wonderful life there. But I simply believed that I had to flee Russia, in the same way that Jews ran away from Germany in 1933. I was prepared to clean floors in America.

In Russia, I was an artist. And I remained an artist in America and worked for a short time as a textile designer. But surviving in New York was hard. We settled in Queens. I was a single mother, with nobody to support me and my daughter. From the very beginning, I rejected the idea of going on welfare. I found it humiliating.

Then I heard about a Russian woman who made a living by working as a dominatrix. From what I heard about the job, it seemed artistic, sexy, and a little naughty—in other words, an ideal job for me. So, I went to the club where this woman worked as a manager. She introduced me to the owner. They both found me attractive enough and fit for the job. The name of the place was Pandora's Box. It was one of the two most expensive places of its kind in New York. You had to pay $30 just for admission. An hour with a girl cost $200.

The place looked like a cross between an expensive whorehouse and a fairy-tale movie. The visitors were greeted by the manager, who took them into a room furnished with velvet sofas and lamps in the Empire style. The visitors were then shown an album with the girls' photographs. Once a client expressed an interest in some of the girls, he was presented with their individual portfolios, which depicted a girl from different angles in various positions. Photographers who create such portfolios are usually very skillful. They know how to make a girl look seductive. After the client had picked a girl, he was brought a "menu" of services. Services on the menu included items such as humiliation (both public and private), strangulation, flogging, with a lash or a whip or something called a "czar's whip." The client had to choose the service as well as the level of pain he desired. The client also chose from a repertoire of scenarios that the participants would act out: abduction by Martians, a visit to a doctor's office, a pupil being punished by an angry teacher, a sailor and a prostitute, a sausage (in which a client was wrapped in cellophane). Most of the scenarios were modeled after popular TV shows—like *Xena, the Warrior Princess.*

Clients were also allowed to create their own scenarios. I once saw a young man who played the role of a partisan tortured by enemies. When he refused to give away his country's secret, the enemies began to torture his girlfriend (played by one of the "submissive" girls that the club provided). He cried, wept, and jerked off, begging the torturers not to "hurt my Mary but take my life instead!" The minute his time was up and the session was over, he got up and laughed. Men like him were actually nice to deal with. They were big children.

The girls who worked in the club fit into two categories. Some simply hated men. Perhaps they were abused as children, and they took revenge on men for the rest of their lives. These women were sick in the head, and I avoided them. The others were artists like me—actresses, directors, painters, or poets. For these women, the club was a way to make money by doing something relatively easy and harmless. Sex was not allowed in the club. Men were supposed to undress on their own. They were not allowed to touch a girl, except to lick her leather boots or the leather on her butt. Women, on the other hand, touched the men all over their bodies while tying them up, or attaching weights to their bodies, or applying condoms, or doing whatever the service required. But they never touched the men with bare hands; they wore rubber or leather gloves. So it was a very sterile procedure.

Most clients didn't want to experience real pain. Those who did were really sick. But most didn't care for it. Some men would bring prostitutes with them. A man would hire a woman from an escort service for a whole day and bring her to the club to play together—because the game would stimulate them sexually. Some men wanted to see their girls tortured or flogged in front of them, but not for real, of course. The girls definitely didn't want to feel any pain. So the dominatrix just pretended to hurt them. I remember a prostitute who once came to the club with a client. She was black, a fantastic beauty. I couldn't help but ask her why she was working for an escort service. It seemed to me that she could get a modeling job in an instant. Wouldn't she rather go into modeling? She replied calmly that she would be making much less money as a model, because of the competition, and she'd be hit on by photographers, producers, and others. In the end, she'd have to sleep with as many men as she does now—only for free. "So," she said, "What's the point?"

One of the most popular dominatrixes in the club was a film director from London. She was in constant demand; she was pretty, and she was a pro. She would usually work at Pandora's for six months and make enough money to shoot her movies in Canada for the rest of the year. She was one of the few stars in the club. As for me, I was not at all in demand. I was hardly making seventy dollars a shift, while others, like that film director, were making thousands. The truth is that I could never take my job too seriously. Instead of being angry and stern—as you'd expect from a dominatrix—I would giggle, or fondle and tickle the clients. I found the sight of a naked man so touching that my feelings would all get all mixed up, and I'd forget what to do next. And, instead of dominating a man, I behaved submissively. It's probably natural for me to be submissive when it comes to sex. I'd simply crack up when performing the role of dominatrix, which led, inevitably, to my downfall in this career. The other girls (never clients!) reported me to the manager. They wrote that although I was hired as a dominatrix, I was in fact acting submissive. The owner was nice enough to suggest that I switch roles, from dominatrix to submissive. But three months in the club was enough for me to realize that this was not exactly my calling. As I told my friends later, I was fired from sadomasochistic hell for being too kind and sweet.

I never liked the kind of relationship that clients have with the girls. The men allowed themselves to be rude because it's their call—no matter what. Even when tied up and seemingly helpless, even when flogged by a girl—the client is always a client. He's the one who pays. That's why there is no exchange of energy between the two people during a session: the client is simply sucking the energy out of you. I always felt exhausted after a session. I believe that's true of any sexual, or semisexual act performed for money. That's why hookers age so early; the job wears them out.

There aren't too many Russian girls in New York who work as a dominatrix. Unlike topless dancing, which is almost entirely taken over by Russians, this work is not so popular. There are a few reputable dominatrixes who are Russian immigrants, but, interestingly enough, they are Jewish, not Russian. Jewish women have it in them—they are domineering by nature. In fact, the most popular images of a dominatrix are of a German SS girl in a uniform or a Jewish witch with a crooked nose. But normally, Jewish women don't turn to the sex business. Normally, Jewish immigrant girls prefer to study and get a decent occupation—become an accountant, for instance.

I've been to topless clubs quite a few times as a guest. And I've noticed that women who work there often hate their job—unless they're Russian. I watched eight Americans girls go onstage one after another, and all I could see in their eyes was hatred and loathing for what they did and for the men who watched them. And then a girl goes onstage, and she's glowing. You can tell she enjoys every move, and you know right away that she's Russian. You can guess that she's probably supporting her entire family in Russia, that she lives with her boyfriend and is madly in love with him, that she doesn't sleep around, and that she's happy doing what she does. And she doesn't understand why anyone would suffer in such a fun job. But American women who have been raised to be feminists do suffer terribly.

Now I have a job that I really enjoy—taking care of children. This is not as a baby-sitter, but more like a governess. I stay with kids and I teach them Russian. In the future, I would like to open a day-care for children of my friends. They are beautiful, bright, and talented kids. I'd like to take care of five to six kids three times a week, and I could teach them Russian. That probably won't be a lucrative enterprise. But I'm not interested in money. As long as I have a roof over my head and enough money to buy a sack of brown rice, I am fine. Money is not my concern. I grew up in a family where nobody ever talked about money. My parents had a special talent for living poor: they knew how to turn that poor life into an interesting and exciting one. There wasn't a pair of matching chairs in the house, or two matching forks: every item in the household was bought in a secondhand store. And it's not as if we didn't have money. My father was a well-known artist in St. Petersburg, an illustrator of children's books. My mother was a writer. Together, they made decent money. But my parents considered it bad taste to spend money on clothes or other material things. In my family, the money was spent on partying, on food and drinks. My parents' house in St. Petersburg was always filled with "starving" artists. There were always parties in our home. I believe I inherited this talent of being poor from my parents. Money is not important to me.

After I left Pandora's Box I began to shoplift. I couldn't find a way to make money and buy things. So I decided I would simply take things that I need. I was very modest. I was only taking what was necessary—like a few tomatoes and a piece of cheese for dinner. Or, when I needed new shoes, I would go to a store and steal a pair of shoes. I never felt shoplifting was a big sin. I still don't believe that. But in the end, I realized that the real reason I did this was not the lack of money. I did it out of spite. Pride was the real reason. Finally, I decided I would never steal again. Even if I had nothing to eat. I'd rather ask people on the streets for money. It's only money after all.

Another thing that's not important to me is sex. I was never a physical type. When I was young, I was very promiscuous; I slept with a lot of men. But even then—it wasn't sex that mattered. I like being in love. I like romances: I create them for myself all the time. I like receiving letters and gifts in the mail. I am more of a medieval person. The Renaissance (with its cult of the body) is not for me. Maybe that's why I don't fit in with Americans. They are a very physical people.

I am grateful for the experiences I have had in America. Even though it has been a harsh experience. America has been my Gulag in a way. My life in Russia was easy. I knew how to be the daughter of my interesting and famous parents and be part of the cultural elite in a big city. That was all I knew. In America, I learned what it's like to be an Eskimo who has come to conquer a big city . . . a city where nobody really needs him. America taught me not to whine, not to burden others with my misfortunes. It taught me to be alone.

IT'S A NEW OLD WORLD

Nikolai Stepanov
Night Driver

He has spent his life driving—cars, cabs, and trucks—all over Russia and even outside its borders. He delivers cars from buyers to customers, driving alone for long distances on deserted and unsafe roads. He has thought about emigration; he would like his daughter to have a different life in a different country, but he believes that starting a new life would be too much of a challenge.

Roots are important. That's why I can't leave this country. My roots are here.

Between 1985 and 1990, when everybody around me was talking about emigration, I began to think about it, too. Maybe my life was easier than that of other people, because there were lots of things I wasn't aware of. I come from a working-class family. We always worked hard, never expecting much. My life was never particularly exciting or beautiful. So my approach to life was more or less calm, passive. But when people around me began to leave the country—one after another—and I had talked to some people who had been abroad, I began to compare life there with life here, in Russia.

I was still young, healthy, full of energy. Why should I be stuck in my life when I could be doing the same things yet living much better? I don't mean becoming a millionaire. I mean, just having a decent life. Having my own apartment, my own car, good clothes—all these things started to matter at that time. People were looking at you, judging the way you dressed. And I often felt that something was wrong with me. I felt inferior. That's how it all started. Because, you see, I didn't have a degree. But I was in good health, and I knew I could do my work. I'm a dependable person. I can perform the same job for a long period of time, stay in one place, and do high-quality work. But I also want to be paid for the work I do. I want to be able to support myself and my family, and to provide them with a certain quality of life. I don't want to wake up every morning worrying about my daughter, about her future.

But I didn't leave the country. Why not? I remembered once living for six months in Poland. It was a socialistic country, a Slavic country, and life was pretty much the same there as in Russia. I didn't have problems with the language. And, still, I was tortured by nostalgia. Things I hadn't paid much attention to before suddenly grew enormously important. I would watch something on TV, notice a familiar place—a house, a street corner in some city—or I'd hear Russian speech, and that was it: I was ready to cry. And the food was good there, but not the same. It didn't taste right: the salt didn't taste right, the mustard, the butter. Nothing was right. I never felt at home there. Yes, I was working. I knew everybody and everybody knew me. But still, I felt like a visitor. I could never accept the idea that Poland was a place where I could live.

I tried to shut this feeling down—by drinking vodka, reading books—but nothing helped. I was never in the right mood. I couldn't stay there. It's so much easier for me here. Everything is familiar.

But at the same time, life is becoming unfamiliar here, too. Things are changing. For a long time, I couldn't comprehend the fact that I didn't have to have an official job, didn't have to be registered at any particular enterprise. All my life I've worked as a driver—driving cabs, trucks. I didn't make a fortune, but I always had a stable income. It was enough to feed my family and me.

Since all these changes took place in Russia, my mentality has changed, of course. The boundaries have been extended. What used to be a problem isn't a problem anymore. Like all this stuff about official jobs, or hard-currency transactions, which used to be illegal, but not anymore. I don't know if I can adjust to a completely new life. It's all hard for me. I wouldn't want to have my own business. Maybe I'm not smart enough. Or maybe, I don't like taking a big risk. I prefer to work for somebody. My job now is delivering cars from suppliers to customers. I drive the cars from one place to another, and I drive everywhere. I make good money.

I'm paid somewhere between $150 and $900 for a trip. Sometimes, it takes days. It can be dangerous, too. The roads are deserted and unsafe. I drive alone all night. And there are people out there who can shoot you, take away your car, tie you up to a tree and strip you. Anything can happen. But at least I know it can happen; I know what to expect. It all depends on me. I rely entirely on myself. And I like that. I don't like to depend on other people, like a partner or a shareholder. In business you have to deal with other people, to depend on them. But on the road, I am on my own, depending only on myself. I try to be careful, to look at the road. I take note of everything, every small detail—a car behind me, an accident at a gas station, people who stop their car in the middle of the road. I take in all these signs, and I don't even have to think about them, to analyze them. My body reacts immediately. It happens almost automatically.

Maybe my experience as a cab driver taught me to be attentive, to take in both the big picture and the details. I know I can find a solution to any situation, not only in Russia, but also out of the country. Without even knowing the language. Maybe it would take a little longer abroad, but I could work my way out of any situation, eventually. I'm pretty sure of that.

It's too late for me to emigrate now. I'm forty-two. The thing is that I don't want my daughter to live here. I would love her to grow up somewhere else, or have a family somewhere else. She's six now. I want her to have a different life. I don't want her to live here. I'll try to do everything I can to make it possible. I'm doing something already, by paying for her English classes. I'm trying to give her a good upbringing. We'll see. I'm too old to leave, too old to adapt to another life. If I were thirty or thirty-five now, if I didn't have a disabled mother, if my entire life experience were different, I would definitely emigrate, because life is too hard here. Too heavy. It takes too much of an effort just to survive—to get good food, buy a TV, go to a resort by the sea for a month. That's all, nothing else. And I'm working so hard for that. I don't have time to see a play, to go to a museum. The last time I was in a museum I was fifteen. I couldn't even think of doing something like that now. There is just no time. And there is no feeling of stability. I feel fear sometimes—not for myself, but for my child and my parents. If something happens to me, who will support them? I can't rely on the state. I can't rely on any organization or charities. I can rely only on myself.

Once I was asked to transport drugs. It was going to be a high-paying job, good money. Of course, there was a reason why they asked me. I know the roads. I know the ins and outs of crossing borders; I know how to deal with customs officers. I have a good reputation.

Frankly, I gave this offer some thought. But in the end, I declined. If I'm gone, who will be there to help my family? I have no relatives, no brothers. But I thought about it. And not because I'm greedy. It's because I want my family to live well. That's the only reason. That's what makes you consider such "offers." So you try to figure it out: Can you cross this line or not?

Alexander Sinitsin
Dreaming of Past Glories

> RAISED *in a poor family, he took advantage of the business boom with the advent of perestroika. He bought, sold, and manufactured garments, and later chandeliers. As a child he dreamed of moving to America and starting a new life there. In 1993, when he was twenty-five, he visited the United States, but he didn't like what he saw. His passion is collecting and restoring antiques. An admirer of the golden age of great nineteenth-century salons of old St. Petersburg, he dreams of re-creating that lifestyle.*

I was raised in a very poor family. So early in my life I faced the issues of either emigrating or trying to achieve some success in my own country. The end of my military service coincided with the beginning of perestroika. It seemed like the time had come to do something to make money. I had a friend, Sergey, who lived in the same building. He had something like a club in his apartment. A lot of young people—people my age—would go there. They all had different interests and occupations. Many of these people were involved in some kind of business. At that time, in 1988, private business was still illegal, but a lot of people made good money selling or speculating on vodka. Later, they invested money in production industries, such as manufacturing footwear. I was amazed that young people like me could make such good money. My eyes opened: I realized there were ways to make money that I hadn't even been aware of.

I got involved in a retail garment business. At the time, Sergey and his friends were selling jersey fabric from Finland; they sold it illegally and made big money on bulk sales. But when I tried to sell it, nobody would buy from me. So, rather than selling the fabric, I decided to make something out of it, like women's clothes. I had a friend who was a professional tailor, and we started a business together. I invested money, did the marketing and managed the whole thing. That was my first business deal. Later I worked with other companies involved in selling garments. I was buying and selling clothing, and making sales trips to other cities. Then I came across a company that was producing chandeliers. It was like finding a gold mine. The chandeliers were selling really well, and I was making good money. It was a constant, steady income.

My passion, though, has always been to collect and restore antiques. I grew up in Leningrad.* I have always adored the city. My fantasy as a child was to have lived in this city during its golden age, in the nineteenth century. It was an era of superb culture, of literary and artistic salons. I always wanted to re-create that environment.

For a while, I pursued a single idea: to create a real salon in St. Petersburg, where all variety of creative people could gather and talk. I wanted to buy an apartment and furnish it in the nineteenth century style, to create beautiful interiors that would inspire people, console them, and encourage calm, intelligent conversation. I even began collecting business cards from artists I met on my trips, on planes and in the trains. I purchased furniture for the salon. But then, I wasn't able to find an apartment I could afford.

I visited Washington, D.C., because I had been told that it was similar to St. Petersburg; and I did find some similarities, actually. All these neoclassical gardens and plazas filled with sculptures, busts of the famous poets and philosophers—Goethe, Dante. But the people there are different. People were selling drugs in those plazas, and I saw provocative advertisements. I couldn't find a place to be alone for a while, to contemplate. One needs some tranquillity to be creative.

The classical America that appeals to me cannot be found on the streets today. With my interest in antiques, I would have to gain entry to the elite circles. Only the American upper class can afford to buy antiques. They can enjoy them like they enjoy the taste of a good wine.

---

* Leningrad once again was named St. Petersburg in 1991.

Russia is different. We all came out of the same cocoon, so to speak. There is no class division, no snobbery, no feelings of inequality. Consider one fact: the new Russian millionaires now buy and restore enormous apartments that occupy an entire floor of a building. Next to them live the poorest people, often still in communal apartments. In practically any other country, it would be impossible for a millionaire and a poor person to live in the same building, to constantly run into each other.

In 1991, the insane years took off. Liberalization of prices allowed some people to make fantastic profits due to the discrepancies between salaries, the cost of products and what they could charge for those products. Everybody was enjoying large profits, including me. People were making good money, mostly in secret. Since nobody publicized profits, we never knew exactly how much the other person was earning. One could live on $5 a month. Rent, utilities—these cost nothing. So, people who were making $500 a month could live a luxurious life. They were spending money, making trips abroad, buying cars and apartments. Nobody wanted to invest money in production, partly because people were afraid that things would reverse, that the Communists would come back. I myself believed that until the elections of 1996.

The year 1993, when I came to the United States, was the peak of my career. A couple of people were working for me. I was an "exploiter." I had been thinking about America since I was a child walking around with holes in my boots. I grew up in a poor family. My mother was a doctor but she didn't earn much. America seemed like a different galaxy to me: I had a romantic image of the country. All my life I nurtured this dream: when I turn twenty-five, I will go to America and begin life anew there. In 1993, when I turned twenty-five, I told myself, "Time to go."

It was easy to get a visa, and I had an invitation from people I hardly knew. From my first moment in America, I felt intimidated by its size, its complexity, its diversity. There were too many different kinds of people, different faiths, different faces and skin colors. The only thing that united these people was the green dollar and the stars-and-stripes flag swaying above them. I felt very confused from the first moment I arrived. I couldn't even use a pay phone in the airport to call my friend, the only person I knew in New York. I didn't know how to dial the number, how to start and how to end the call. Luckily for me, there were Russian immigrants on the plane with me, returning to New York. So, I asked them for help. They dialed the number for me, and at last I reached my friend. If I hadn't gotten in touch with him, I would have been lost. From my first step, I realized it was a difficult country.

I took a cab. It was an old Cadillac with a door that wouldn't lock, so the driver used a piece of rope to keep it closed. When we were driving from the airport, I was surprised by the amount of trash on the road. Once again it reminded me of Russia. Later I saw a teenager at the bus terminal in New York. He was absolutely stoned, singing and dancing, waving his hands, almost slamming into the old fat guy standing next to him.

Many young Russians whom I met in America had problems assimilating. Of course, it's a lifetime task. I had to choose: stay in America or go back to Russia. I liked a lot of things about America. I liked the feeling of political stability you have there. In Russia, at that time, it seemed that an explosion was inevitable. People expected a new revolution. In America, nobody wanted revolutions. They solved their problems once—during the Civil War—and forever. Now they were living their lives.

But I didn't stay in America. What prevented me from staying was, foremost, my ambition. I had been making good money in Russia, and I couldn't hope for anything as good in America. Also, in America, I realized what it means to work really hard, not the way I had in Russia. In Russia I had time to go to museums, to travel, to have my hobbies. I could wake up at any time in the morning and go to sleep at any time of the night. I could control my workday and plan it as I liked. Maybe, if I had put a long-term stake in the United States, I would have succeeded. But it would have taken a lot of energy. Competition is so intense there. There are so many talented, educated, healthy young people in the country, and each one of them wants to be first. In a way, I felt I was too weak for the country.

Many of the Russians whom I met in the United States were nice people, but they lacked a quality that I consider to be very important: honesty. They thought they could push their way into American life and succeed by being aggressive and dishonest. They took pride in taking advantage of "trusting Americans." A lot of people in Russia have this attitude. There are many jokes that make fun of Europeans and Americans. For instance, look what fools they are: they have these self-service stores where our people can shoplift. But I don't think it shows that Europeans are silly; it shows how inferior we are. That's why they live well in Europe, because they don't steal and they don't break things. And our so-called slyness has brought us nothing but chaos, a big mess.

When I returned to Russia from my trip to America, it was one of the happiest moments in my life. I wanted to kneel and kiss the ground. It felt like I had been away for at least a year, though it was only one month. There was a terrible mess at the airport, and the cab to the city cost a fortune. But I was happy all the same. I was home where I had friends, connections, money, and where everything was familiar. I picked a new business route for myself along the Black Sea. I wasn't making big money, but it felt like I was on vacation. I would bring along goods to sell and stay for a couple of days. I rented a room in a house just fifty feet away from the sea. I could spend all day on the beach. I could eat fruit, meat, and drink good wine. It was like being in heaven. And that was my job. Often, lying in the sun, I recalled my friends in America. They eat junk food just to save some money; they live on illusions. I was living in the present. I was living a real life. And here, in Russia, I felt that I was worth something. I was above average. But I don't have these feelings anymore.

Things began to change after I returned. People were allowed to legalize their income. So, for the first time, there were people who were rich, truly rich. I saw people who were buying very expensive cars and new apartments. I never dreamed of such a life, even in my best years. The funny thing is that, after the question of income stopped being a secret, I suddenly realized that the business I was doing was actually a small business.

I should have operated on a much bigger scale. That was my first disappointment. And, then, it was becoming clear to me that the time of easy profits was coming to an end. That time when legends were born about Russia—for instance, if you put a stick in the ground in Russia, it soon would be covered with golden coins. That time was over. Making money was becoming more and more difficult. We were approaching the West's way of doing business. You need to be really good at what you're doing. You have to know the market, and you have to work really hard to get good results. Thank God, I have some experience and good connections to help me keep my head above water. But I can't say I'm happy with my profits. It's hardly enough.

More and more I think that maybe we didn't take the right course after all, that maybe this course leads to a dead end. No country in the world can live merely as a parasite, the way Russia does now. Here, in Russia, we seem to have lost our sense of shame, conscience and true creativity. With privatization, many people were given control over large enterprises, entire industries literally for free, as a gift from the state. Most of these enterprises were sold, and the funds went down the drain. They were spent, wasted, so that a few people could make big, quick profits. Nothing was used for modernization, to enable our industry to compete on the world market. So we spent the funds, and, now, what's next?

It's too hard for a person to survive here. Many people cannot. A lot of people, professional people, used to rely on the state. They didn't want to change occupations, to go into business. They believed the state would always need engineers, scientists, production workers for its plants and factories. Nobody needs their plants anymore. Entire cities that were built around those plants—like CAMAS, a famous automobile plant—are useless. Nobody needs those people. They don't have a chance. There is a new official term in use now, "depressed city." The country is full of "depressed areas" and "depressed cities." When I plan a sales trip, I carefully decide where to go. I won't go to just any city. There are big cities with huge populations, but without a single penny in circulation.

I miss the nobility in people's behavior, in personal relationships. We lack it in our present life. I have nothing against the new Russians. The more rich people we have in the country, the better. I believe culture is closely connected to wealth. Like it or not, a rich person has to be educated, cultured. It's not as funny as it may sound. If you're rich, you deal with sophisticated people, European businessmen for example. You have to win their trust. Culture and business go hand in hand.

I don't like doing business. I'm not doing it because I like it. It's how I make my living. It makes it possible for me to have the life I want and to collect things that I like: antiques and works of art. Once, I had a crazy idea: I thought of offering my services as a consultant to the rich friends who had money, advising them on what to buy. You can buy some incredible things here for very little money, two to four times below their real value. But nobody seems to care about what they're buying. Unfortunately, despite the fact that the Soviet regime encouraged education, that education was often technical and superficial, not deep. People don't understand with their hearts anymore, whether it's a book, a film, a sculpture. An ancient statue is just a piece of marble to them. They don't feel its warmth. I feel the warmth of old things.

Alexander Obraztsov
Fighting Oblivion

ALEXANDER *is in his fifties. He writes plays, short stories, and poetry. He had to wait many years for his first book to be published; it happened just as perestroika arrived. The book wasn't given the attention it deserved. He thinks Russia has a lot to offer to the world, but the world may not notice. "The only thing we've always had in abundance," he observes, "the only thing we're capable of producing, are high-quality spiritual values. And suddenly, nobody needs them. Nobody needs them because they're not packaged properly."*

I have never thought of emigrating, never considered it seriously. An ideal situation for me would be to buy a small cottage—well-heated, somewhere in Finland—where I could sometimes escape, hide for a while, catch my breath—and then dive back into the world. Life is difficult here, financially and creatively. Creatively, because it's hard to get work published or produced. Still, you can find your own niche. I'm getting more and more involved in journalism, a new medium for me. You have to convince people from the press that they need high-quality literary works. If they believe in you, then they'll publish you. Things happen in the theater once in a while, too. So, actually, it's possible for a writer in Russia to make a living in literature; he doesn't have to become a *kommercant,* a businessman, or unload cargo at train stations.

You need to hustle and not let people forget about you. You can't make a lot in journalism. Average rates are approximately 25,000 rubles, about five dollars for one typed page. I can easily write five, six, ten pages. The problem is that there's usually a delay in payment; they pay you sometimes a month after the text is published. But that's fine. Then there are always other opportunities, which you sometimes forget about. For instance, you submit something someplace at some time, and suddenly they call you. Or some of your work is performed without your even knowing it. Recently, I found out that one of my plays was being put on at Dodin's theater—the play I cowrote with Ludmila Razumovskaya. You forget those things, because so much is happening.

You kind of leave your mark everywhere, a little something here and there, and eventually it pays off. Last year, an amazing thing happened to me: I was granted a stipend for my writing by one of the Moscow writers' unions. I even forgot which one. I filled out a few applications, and I was given the stipend. The good thing is that they keep supporting us writers; they throw us a bone from time to time to keep us from dying out. Some old writers receive lifetime stipends, a million rubles, about 200 dollars a month. That's a lot by our standards. So I got this stipend, and when I came to the Theater Union here in St. Petersburg, they gave me another stipend. I was shocked. In my entire life I never found money on the street, and suddenly I felt like I had, and big money—500,000 rubles a month. So, in one year I made six to seven million. That's more than a thousand dollars a year—fantastic!

Even in America it's a big deal to find a thousand dollars. So, during these last few months, I lived with the shock of my sudden luck. The point is that you can always make some money, but only if you participate in life. Once you give up—like the frog in the milk jar—you go down to the bottom in an instant. I remember an old woman who worked in the Theater Union for many years. A marvelous person, knowledgeable, understanding—she knew all the playwrights, she knew who was worth what. Then she retired one day and simply died of hunger. People forgot about her. She was starving; one day she fainted on the staircase and died. There are many cases like that.

A friend of mine, also a playwright—a published playwright—works as a janitor. He has four zones to sweep. He's paid 60,000 rubles for each section. He works like crazy clearing off all the dirt and snow. And he makes only 200,000 rubles a month. It's very little.

When I meet him he's always complaining. A lot of people still think it's a good thing to complain. People feel sorry for you, they comfort you. That's the way it used to be. But times have changed. Complaining doesn't work now. People don't feel sorry for you if you complain. They despise you. I guess it's because there are too many reasons to complain now, and too many people who have a right to complain—all these old women begging on the streets, homeless people.

So, when a relatively young and healthy man begins to complain about how his life is hard, it doesn't sound too compelling. Before, everybody felt the oppression. Even though you didn't see the KGB out on the streets, you could feel their presence. People had a right to complain. Now they don't. I guess that's the main difference.

Now I have to create an audience for my work. My first book was published just as perestroika arrived. The book went unnoticed. Nobody at that time cared much about fiction—even though the book received good reviews. One of the most exacting literary critics in St. Petersburg—Toporov is his name—gave it a great review. But it went unnoticed. I have a lot of material—short stories and poetry—accumulated in my desk, but none of it is published. I suspect it's because I'm a free person, too free for this country. When a person here shows no sign of slavery, it irritates people. He becomes a stranger, alienated from the rest.

I'm trying to create a community of writers. I've completely stopped any communication with fat literary magazines. I think they brought more harm to our culture than anything else: they and the state theaters, the last bulwarks of bolshevism.

If theater is the last, but still living, bastion of fundamental bolshevism, the Union of Writers is a refuge for the ailing and insane old men. When you come to a writers' meeting and see all these bald, lame, crooked, hunchbacked people, it looks like a freak show. And they still think of themselves as pillars of Russian culture, though nobody in the new generation knows their names. They're outdated. They've broken up into five small unions that fight among themselves for the old writers' union building, which burned down long ago. It's a metaphor for their existence: fighting for a building that's burned down. You can still see its frame, whatever is left of the building, standing across the street from the Big House, former KGB headquarters.

The other thing I can say about my current literary work is that my productivity now depends on the market, on the possibility of publishing or producing my work. In other words, I can no longer write stories that I know won't find a reader or plays that no audience will see. For instance, I know I can easily publish short stories in the newspapers, so I write short stories. I can't find a theater to produce my full-length plays, so I write short plays with small casts, or stage adaptations of novels, such as Gogol's. It wasn't like this in the past.

Before perestroika, I used to write without having any hope of being published. It never prevented me from writing. I used to think that you wrote because it came directly from your heart. Now, writing must be more pragmatic. Maybe it's the age. I'm at a certain stage in my life where I can write as easily as I breathe. I'm not tortured by questions of how to begin the story or how to end it. I can start with anything, with a simple sigh, and keep on going.

I notice the same thing happening with other writers. So, it's not just me. I probably take it easier than others, though. Maybe it's because I've survived a terminal illness. It's like coming back from the dead. I'm living a new life. One of my friends, Sasha Popov, hanged himself. He couldn't take it. He died merrily—died like a hero, I think. He called me a few hours before he did it. He sounded very excited and happy. Partly it was madness, of course. Laughing, he told me that there would soon be a carnival, people would come out into the streets, our children, something like that. He knew that he was going to hang himself in about an hour or so. It was different from any description of suicide that I've ever read.

Sasha's case is still a mystery to me. Before he did it, he sorted through his writing and put everything into folders with great care: he was a meticulous person. He had built a shelf that matched the size of the folders exactly and accommodated them all. He had calculated everything so precisely, including the fact that he would become famous after his death. That was his only mistake—a terrible miscalculation. I think he was imagining himself after death—kind of like a spirit flying above us, observing his own fame—laughing at his enemies. He was a strong person. He had always thought of himself as a fighter, but when the time came for a real fight, he just couldn't do it. Because, I think, now is the time for real struggle—struggle in its pure form. What we had before was a dirty struggle, a criminal struggle, with no rules. It was a struggle against ideology, against the Communists. Now it's a struggle against oblivion, the force of forgetting. It keeps crashing into you, like a gigantic wave.

One of the things that changed with perestroika was our approach to the West. We were finally allowed to travel, to see the world. And we realized that we were romanticizing the West in many ways. We used to think, "The West knows and understands everything, it will help us, make its fair judgment, put things in order." It was a "Europe will help us" kind of approach. In fact, we've already found out that Europe doesn't care about us at all. All they care about is preventing us from being a danger to them. It's become clear that neither Europe nor America needs our spiritual values. They think they have enough—more than enough—of their own. But they're mistaken.

Because real spiritual values are rare. The fact is, the only thing we've always had in abundance, the only thing we're capable of producing, are high-quality spiritual values. And suddenly, nobody needs them. Nobody needs them because they're not packaged properly. By packaging, I mean form. Russia was always famous for producing spiritual values and not for packaging them. At the end of the nineteenth century, Russia suddenly learned how to package, and the world realized that Russia can, in fact, produce. When Dostoevsky gave his insights the form of an urban criminal romance, it suddenly made those insights universal and accessible. That is what I mean by proper packaging. It's true of industry, too. In Russia we have good butter, good meat, good milk. Good quality fabric, stockings. Nobody buys these products, just because of the packaging. People prefer things from the West.

Russia has had a unique experience: for the first time in history, God allowed an entire huge nation to go out on a limb. Common sense tells us that under such circumstances a nation should simply obliterate itself: people would devour each other—and, in fact, that's what was happening here in the 1920s and '30s. But, somehow, they didn't eat each other up completely; in the end, they managed to create a reality of their own, an odd reality, where it's still possible to live. In fact, the reason why the West doesn't want to have our "packaging" now, doesn't want to recognize our art, literature, or music, is that they don't want to admit that something worthwhile, something good, can be nurtured in a totalitarian society. They can't believe that values created by artists within a totalitarian society can be of any use to them. They think they know all about totalitarian regimes. But there are niches and caverns dug out by people living with totalitarianism that ought to be explored. Knowing what they are may be crucial for the survival of mankind.

Snapshots

Yelena Kiyko, Taboos

Yelena is twenty and a straight-A student who also works as a programmer for an investment bank where she puts in forty hours a week. She looks very tired. "It's a pity that you work so hard that you are always tired," I say.

"That's America," she says with her easy laugh.

"What do you mean?"

"America is so much more stressful than Russia and most other countries."

"I'm writing a book about the last wave of Russian immigrants," I tell her.

"Why?"

"Because I'm interested in why people move."

"Nobody knows," she laughs.

"Really?"

"The first year that you're here, everyone asks you. By the third year, it's a taboo subject."

Gennady Katsov, Poet and Café Owner

What I like most about America is that it has everything—including problems. All kinds of problems. And Americans are the first to admit it. And that's what makes them a strong nation. I believe there are strong nations as well as strong people. Strong people are not afraid to talk about their problems. They try to overcome them. Weak people act out the old joke about the Brezhnev days: the train is stranded on the track, and the train operator says, "Let's make a u-u-u-u sound and pretend we are moving."

Infantilism is so characteristic of Soviet people because we were never responsible for anything. We could vote for only one person, buy the only brand of vodka available in the stores, share the same sausage, and discuss the same article in the newspaper. Russia is still juvenile. That's why it thrashes around from one extreme to another. It's scary what's happening in Russia. Shukshin, a Russian writer, once said, "We never knew what it is like to live well. Why should we start now?" I wanted to know. That's why I left Russia.

Sophia Gruzdeva, Milk

Sophia, an engineer in her fifties: "I realized I was dealing with an unpredictable system, which gains strength by abusing people. In a way, I'm living a second life now, different from the first. The principal difference is that an educated person in this country can live with style, modesty, and decency. And that was impossible in Russia, on a practical level. You had to bend down in order to get certain things, to be humiliated just to have a piece of bread and a glass of milk."

Andrey Gritsman, the Importance of Medical School

Andrey Gritsman, a pathologist and poet, lives in New Jersey. "My father was a soldier in World War II. His generation was interesting because, on the one hand they said that everything would be all right if you worked hard, tried to achieve your goals, and didn't make too many waves. On the other hand, my father told me: 'You must be a physician, you must go to medical school, because one day you could be imprisoned and sent to a concentration camp. So you need to be able to survive, and you have a better chance to survive if you're a physician.'

Now, in America, I work in a very closed system, an exclusive, wealthy medical community serving old money. I'm good, so I was accepted into this community. I realize now that, regardless of how important it is for these people to belong to the local Jewish Federation, or the Greek Orthodox church, or the Lutheran church, what they really care about is how to make money as smoothly, expeditiously, and relentlessly as possible. So, you have to play by certain rules. If you're good at what you do and if you understand these rules then you're okay. This may sound bad, but it's also an interesting perspective, because it is entirely non-ideological. The things that I like about this system, I also hate—this flatness and relentlessness. Basically, I'm an alien. I don't belong anywhere."

Victor Boyko, Prodigy

Victor, a thirteen-year-old freshman who had emigrated from Russia six months earlier, and his professor meet with the director of undergraduate studies for computer science.

It seems Victor is too good a student.

Director: What do you know about computer science?
Victor: C, C++, Pascal, Prolog, Fortran [various computer languages]
Director (a little skeptical): What was the most sophisticated project you did in any of those languages?
Victor: Nothing too sophisticated.
Director: Try to give me an example.
Victor: Well, I wrote a package to simulate particle flow in high-temperature superconductors.
The professor and Victor then have a conversation about the differential equations Victor used. Victor clearly understands the material.
Director: What do you know about "data structures?"
Victor: I don't know. What do you mean?
Director: Well, if I insert a sorted list into a binary tree, what shape does the tree take?
Victor (after 5 seconds): Well, it looks like this, I guess. (He draws a sloping line to the right, the correct answer.)

The director leaves for a while. Victor and his professor are talking about graph algorithms.

When the director returns, he and the professor ask Victor to write a high-level algorithm to count the number of connected components, a fundamental method of computer graphics.

Victor writes an algorithm in set notation. One of the stopping conditions requires comparing two sets. The professor asks him how to do this efficiently. Victor responds that he would use a data structure called "bit vectors."

The professor says it would be better to establish a "flag" to indicate that something has changed. Victor stares at the professor for a few seconds. He says, "Yes, I see, but then it wouldn't be so pretty."

Epilogue: The Open Question

LIVING IN A BLUE WORLD, a person may not notice that the background color everywhere is blue. The eyes find the color natural. It takes someone from a different world, say a Red world, to understand what is so special about the Blue world. The comparison brings clarity to both.

Reading these oral histories, one notices several things about the Red world from which the immigrants come. First, one notices how pervasively the Soviet system affected the lives of its citizens. The system determined where one could live (for "troublemakers," anywhere but Leningrad or Moscow), what one could study (philosophy meant Marxism-Leninism), where one worked (graduates of particular institutions were assigned to specific jobs), and what would lead to prison (plays about the rise to power of a fictional character). Our Blue world has certainly seen arbitrary and excessive government power wielded against "troublemakers," often for racial reasons. The government can also threaten to stop funding "obscene" art in various cities. Racism, sexism, and favoratism play a role in hiring and firing. Every society imposes its malicious effects on people.

Still, the differences in degree create a difference in kind. Radical theater productions in the Blue world have more to fear from an indifferent public than from an oppressive government. The government is not a force to be reckoned with in the daily lives of most Blue citizens.

Second, one notices the creativity and courage with which people resist the system in the Red World, regularly defying authority through satire, semiclandestine meetings, or a show of solidarity against the police.

Third, one notices the stability that a system of five-year plans provided for people, who, if they were lucky enough to practice professions they loved, knew they could practice them for a long time. This applied to everything from manufacturing to tank design to classical music. Such stability enabled the Russian space program to give great responsibility to individuals in the knowledge that they would stay with a project from beginning to end, a chance no American high-technology company, let alone NASA, would take today. (France, widely characterized by some of its own political class as "a Soviet Union that works," also promotes job stability, and its companies and government expect and receive long-term loyalty.)

The desire for stability and law and order plays a role in the politics of all countries. In the mid-1980s, before perestroika, young Soviet immigrants used to say that Americans didn't really understand what freedom meant. Freedom from street violence was as important, they said, as political freedom.

With stability and government regulations comes the almost total unimportance of money in the Red world. Getting food was a matter of standing in line, getting an apartment was a matter of influence, and getting ahead often entailed moral compromise. This led to a certain indifference toward one's job and a greater reliance on the pursuit of dreams, creativity, and conversation. There is freedom in that.

The Soviet system is dead, but in Russia it has been replaced by a system that has yet to find a balance between anarchy and autocracy. For many citizens, the improvement is still theoretical at best.

We in our Blue world go on with our lives in the belief that liberal democracy is the natural state of men and women. But is it? Is it natural for people to enjoy liberty of movement, work relentlessly in pursuit of sometimes unnecessary material possessions, and face an insecure, unstable future? Or is it natural for them to be controlled, threatened, guided, given a role, and offered a certain stability?

The many stories told in this book capture all sides of the issues: the good, the bad, the exciting, and the absurd. The answers are far from clear.

Chronology:
Highlights of Twentieth-Century Russian and Soviet History

August 1, 1914
Russia under Czar Nicholas II enters World War I on the side of the Allies (France, England, and Italy) in opposition to the Axis powers (Turkey, the Austro-Hungarian Empire, and Germany).

February 1917
February Revolution. A provisional government is created, but then is followed by a split between the two left wing groups: Bolsheviks and Mensheviks.

March 1917
Czar Nicholas abdicates.

April 1917
With the help of the Germans, Vladimir Lenin returns to Russia from exile in Switzerland on a sealed train that arrives at the Finland Station in St. Petersburg on April 13, 1917, one month after the fall of the monarchy.

May 1917
Russian Council of Workers demands peace conference.

July 1917
Menshevik Alexander Kerensky takes over government. The war with the Germans continues.

October 24–25, 1917
Bolsheviks seize power, replacing the provisional government. Kerensky is deposed. Lenin becomes premier of Russia. Aristocrats emigrate, expecting to be gone for only a short while.

December 1917–March 1918
The Soviet Union and Germany sign an armistice and then a treaty known as the Brest Treaty, granting Germany and Turkey large parts of Russia as well as Estonia, Lithuania, and Latvia. Russia also agrees to grant independence to the Ukraine. This treaty is repudiated by the Soviets after Germany loses.

July 1918
Czar Nicholas II and his family are executed.

August–December, 1918
British, French, and Americans land in various parts of Russia to help the Whites (the czarists) fight the Reds. The intervention fails, and the Western allies leave the Soviet Union by January 1920. The Whites fight on until November 1920.

January 1924
Lenin dies, succeeded by Leon Trotsky and Joseph Stalin in an uneasy partnership. Trotsky loses power rapidly.

1926
Stalin takes control.

1927
Trotsky ousted from party. He was deported in 1929 and assassinated in Mexico in 1940.

1934
Stalin begins purges in an attempt to replace Soviet leadership with people loyal to him. In 1937, all major party leaders, such as Grigory Zinoviev, Lev Kamenev, Nikolay Bukharin, as well as most of the army high command are tried and executed. Those who are not executed are sent to the prison complex known as the Gulag.

1939
Soviet Union allies itself with Germany to divide Poland. Lithuania, Estonia, and Latvia are annexed by the Soviet Union.

June 22, 1941
Germany invades the Soviet Union.

September 1941
Soviets of German nationality are sent east; most die of exposure because they are given no shelter.

1941–1945
Ukrainians and others collaborate with the Germans in their fight against the Soviet Union. Many flee to the United States during the "second wave" of immigration (1945–1947).

1943
German army surrenders at Stalingrad, signaling the end of the German advance and the turning point of World War II.

1944
Crimean Tartars are sent to Siberia.

1945
End of World War II finds the Soviet Union greatly expanded.

Chronology

1946
Cold War begins. Gulag prison camps in eastern Siberia fill up with ex-soldiers who had been prisoners of the Germans.

1948
Soviet Union supports Israel with planes in its war for independence, but Israel soon allies itself with the West. Solomon Mikhoels and other leaders of the Jewish Anti-Fascist Committee are executed, and a campaign of anti-Semitism is encouraged.

1951
Doctors' Plot: A group of Jewish doctors are falsely accused of trying to kill Kremlin leaders and are put on trial, leading to a systematic campaign of anti-Semitism.

1953
Stalin dies. Nikita Khrushchev becomes Party Leader and denounces Stalin's purges, including the Doctors' Plot.

1957
Soviet Union is first to launch a rocket to outer space.

October 1961
Berlin Wall is built to prevent East Germans from fleeing to the West.

1964
Khrushchev ousted and replaced by Leonid Brezhnev. Soviet Union becomes a superpower. A strong military-industrial complex is built. Economy is behind in consumer industries and electronics.

December 1979
Soviet Union invades Afghanistan, starts a war that eventually displaces five million people in that country, depletes the Soviets' treasury, and becomes wildly unpopular in the Soviet Union. The U.S. CIA helps Afghan guerillas with arms and logistics.

Late 1970s
Limited Jewish emigration is allowed, thus starting the third wave.

1982
Brezhnev dies and Yuri Andropov takes control.

1984
Andropov dies and Konstantin Chernenko becomes leader.

1985
Chernenko dies and Mikhail Gorbachev becomes general secretary. Calls for economic reforms (perestroika).

1986
Chernobyl nuclear reactor catches fire and releases radiation.

1988
Gorbachev announces significant reductions in Soviet military strength, also leading to far reduced demand for scientists and engineers.

November 1989
Berlin Wall comes down.

February 1989
Gorbachev pulls the Soviet Union out of Afghanistan.

June 1990
Boris Yeltsin resigns from Communist Party.

November 1990
Private ownership of farms and small businesses becomes legal.

June 1991
Yeltsin wins the election for president of the Russian Republic, the first election for a country leader in the history of Russia.

August 1991
A Communist coup: Gorbachev is briefly arrested and Yeltsin speaks to crowds from a tank in front of the parliament building in Moscow. Gorbachev is released but then resigns in favor of Yeltsin.

November 1991
Import/export restrictions are eliminated, thus allowing foreign goods to replace domestic ones.

1991
Soviet Union dissolves and becomes 15 different countries including the Russian Federation. Many of the other 14 remain militarily and economically dependent on Russia. Three-year war between Armenia and Azerbaijan for control of the enclave of Nagorno-Karabakh.

1992
Yeltsin stops controlling the value of the ruble and ends government subsidies of food. Imports are allowed. Ruble plummets and inflation begins. Four-year civil war in Tajikistan begins.

September 1993
Yeltsin unconstitutionally dissolves the parliament and calls for new elections. New elections in December with a new constitution based on the French model, giving broad powers to the president.

1994–1996
Russians attack and then withdraw from Chechnya after bloody defeat.

August 1999
Vladimir Putin becomes prime minister.

March 2000
Amidst another war with Chechnya, Putin is elected president.

October 2001
Russia joins the United States in military action against the Taliban.